D1001993

NOSTALGIA AFTER APARTHEID

RECENT TITLES FROM THE HELEN KELLOGG INSTITUTE SERIES
ON DEMOCRACY AND DEVELOPMENT

Paolo G. Carozza and Aníbal Pérez-Liñan, series editors

The University of Notre Dame Press gratefully thanks the Helen Kellogg Institute for International Studies for its support in the publication of titles in this series.

Erik Ching
Authoritarian el Salvador: Politics and the Origins of the Military Regimes, 1880–1940 (2014)

Brian Wampler
Activating Democracy in Brazil: Popular Participation, Social Justice, and Interlocking Institutions (2015)

J. Ricardo Tranjan
Participatory Democracy in Brazil: Socioeconomic and Political Origins (2016)

Tracy Beck Fenwick
Avoiding Governors: Federalism, Democracy, and Poverty Alleviation in Brazil and Argentina (2016)

Alexander Wilde
Religious Responses to Violence: Human Rights in Latin America Past and Present (2016)

Pedro Meira Monteiro
The Other Roots: Wandering Origins in Roots of Brazil *and the Impasses of Modernity in Ibero-America* (2017)

John Aerni-Flessner
Dreams for Lesotho: Independence, Foreign Assistance, and Development (2018)

Roxana Barbulescu
Migrant Integration in a Changing Europe: Migrants, European Citizens, and Co-ethnics in Italy and Spain (2019)

Matthew C. Ingram and Diana Kapiszewski, eds.
Beyond High Courts: The Justice Complex in Latin America (2019)

Kenneth P. Serbin
From Revolution to Power in Brazil: How Radical Leftists Embraced Capitalism and Struggled with Leadership (2019)

Manuel Balán and Françoise Montambeault, eds.
Legacies of the Left Turn in Latin America: The Promise of Inclusive Citizenship (2020)

Ligia De Jesús Castaldi
Abortion in Latin America and the Caribbean: The Legal Impact of the American Convention on Human Rights (2020)

For a complete list of titles from the Helen Kellogg Institute for International Studies, see http://www.undpress.nd.edu.

NOSTALGIA AFTER APARTHEID

Disillusionment, Youth, and
Democracy in South Africa

AMBER R. REED

University of Notre Dame Press
Notre Dame, Indiana

University of Notre Dame Press
Notre Dame, Indiana 46556
undpress.nd.edu

All Rights Reserved

Copyright © 2020 by University of Notre Dame

Published in the United States of America

Library of Congress Control Number: 2020946988

ISBN: 978-0-268-10877-9 (Hardback)
ISBN: 978-0-268-10880-9 (WebPDF)
ISBN: 978-0-268-10879-3 (Epub)

To Aphiwe

CONTENTS

ILLUSTRATIONS

PREFACE

For a month or so in 2012, it seemed everyone in the rural Eastern Cape where I was conducting ethnographic research was talking about Jacob Zuma's genitals. In May, two men had sneaked into a Johannesburg art gallery and used a red cross and black paint to deface Brett Murray's provocative painting of President Zuma, *The Spear*. The large canvas depicted the president in a style reminiscent of Lenin-era Soviet propaganda, only with his genitals fully exposed. Nationwide calls for the painting's removal (including from Zuma himself) and the subsequent act of vandalism were premised on the notion that this painting went too far, that it was an abuse of the constitutional right to artistic expression and free speech in its overt sexuality and visible disparaging of the nation's president. Protests erupted throughout the country on both sides of the issue. A complicated series of court cases and appeals followed in the subsequent months, ultimately upholding the gallery's right to continue to display the painting (Laing 2012). During the time of this controversy, I was living with a Xhosa family in a small hilltop village just outside of the rural Eastern Cape town of Kamva.[1] People in the area were almost unanimous in their anger over the painting's creation and display. They kept repeating the same sentiment to me: Human rights are important, but they must not be abused to the point of insulting someone's dignity. In other words, they felt that there is a limit to individual rights and that their fellow citizens had crossed the line by supporting the painting.

This incident, and the reactions of Kamva residents to it, encapsulated much of the broader issues I was investigating in rural South Africa. On the one hand, the country's recent overthrow of the apartheid state and embrace of liberal human rights saw freedom of expression as central to a healthy democracy. After decades of government censorship along racial lines, the ability to criticize even the highest office was essential. On the other hand, many South Africans found these liberal messages at odds with local value systems. People in Kamva said it was against their culture to so greatly insult a figure of authority like the president. What we see in twenty-first-century South Africa, then, is a country where national values of liberal democracy are often resisted on the grounds of culture in local settings. So, I wondered, what happens when local residents, often deeply invested in these acts of cultural resistance, are the ones tasked with teaching democracy to young people?

I did not set out to write a book about democracy, and I certainly did not expect to be writing about nostalgia for one of history's most reviled, racist systems of governance expressed by those who arguably suffered most at its hands. When I began ethnographic research in rural South Africa's Eastern Cape Province, I was interested in the ways that young people both were affected by and contributed to the agendas of nongovernmental organizations (NGOs), particularly those seeking to promote ideological and cultural change in rural areas far removed from the centers of government (Reed 2011; Reed and Hill 2010). I wanted to understand the role of NGOs in constructing or inhibiting youth agency and activism, but it very quickly became apparent that this focus was far too narrow to capture the lives of young rural South Africans. During the many conversations I had with activists, parents, teachers, and young people in the Eastern Cape, I kept getting steered toward the perceived cultural intrusions of Western-influenced democracy as it played out in local contexts and the resulting nostalgia for apartheid as a time of security, social control, and greater cultural freedom. For my research participants, NGOs seeking to enact ideological change became a conversational entry point into larger expressions of immense frustration with the status quo and anger over the push for an unpalatable version of democracy. "Freedom," it turned out, did not feel so free; instead, it rested on Western ideas of personhood and subjectivity that felt confining, imposing, and alien. To make matters worse, these political changes were paired with dashed hopes for socialist economic policies and increased wealth inequalities via neoliberal channels of governance. As many anthropologists have done before me, I adjusted my focus to what people wanted me to talk about rather than the other way around. Conversations about the future were sidelined in order to make way for stories about the past.

Since the early 1960s, African states have thrown off the official yoke of colonialism in relatively quick succession, rapidly and drastically changing the political landscape of the continent. Many of these revolutionary movements became pawns in the Cold War scramble for influence on the African continent, and thus governmental aspirations often took on socialist or communist angles. With the fall of the Soviet Union, however, much of Africa was swept up into the dual global trends of liberal representative democracy and neoliberal economics, two sets of ideas that have become naturalized and seemingly inextricable in the view of many people in the twenty-first century. Despite the fervent hope and excitement imbued in postcolonial democratic movements and Pan-African alliances across the continent, both news reports and scholarly analyses have shown us the myriad problems with trying to adapt Western systems of governance, morality, and justice to diverse African contexts with complex racial, cultural, and political histories—not to mention the challenge of deepening inequalities wrought by the new economic order and sustained by the legacies of colonialism.

In South Africa, these problematic realities are demonstrated over and over again in the "corrective" rape of lesbians (Brown 2012), controversial medical treatments for HIV/AIDS, legal ambivalence about the spread and consequences of witchcraft, frequent service delivery protests, and allegations of widespread government corruption and political cronyism that keep poverty, crime, and unemployment rates high. This book explores the ways in which people encounter and resist discourses of liberal democracy in South Africa through the lens of rural youth in a small town in the Eastern Cape. More specifically, I examine how these issues play out in both NGO interventions and public school teaching on democracy and human rights. In the process, I illuminate a serious political, ideological, and theoretical challenge for both the nascent state and the discipline of anthropology itself: nostalgia for apartheid.

ACKNOWLEDGMENTS

I am greatly indebted to the generous funders who made this research and the resulting publications possible: the University of California, Los Angeles (UCLA) anthropology department; the UCLA International Institute; the University of Pennsylvania anthropology and Africana Studies departments; the Drexel University anthropology department; the Southern Oregon University sociology and anthropology department; and the American Philosophical Society. These institutions provided much-appreciated support for the completion of this work over the past several years.

I owe a huge debt of gratitude to and am immensely appreciative of the Sonke Gender Justice Network, both for allowing me access to their Cape Town offices, staff, and community programs and for encouraging the internal critique that made this research possible. While I have highlighted organizational shortcomings and program limitations in some of the pages that follow, I hope it is apparent that I mean to situate these issues within larger nationwide and international structural inequalities and ideological discourses that are beyond Sonke's control. It is always far easier to critique than it is to offer solutions to human suffering and injustice, and because of this I admit the limitations of my own work as well as commend Sonke's tireless attempts to improve the state of South African society for all of its diverse citizens as well as the foreigners living within South Africa's borders. I am especially grateful to Dean Peacock, who has been a tremendous source of support throughout my work in the country and a highly knowledgeable interlocutor. As an academic, it is refreshing to find an organization so open to external analysis and committed to the value of social science research. Sonke, thank you for opening your doors to me, and I hope you find the pages that follow informative and useful.

The residents of Kamva in the Eastern Cape are not only the protagonists of this book, but the reason it has come to fruition at all. There

are no words sufficient (in English or isiXhosa) to express the tremendous
gratitude and love I have for all the individuals who welcomed me into
their community, despite their rightful apprehension of outsiders and especially, given their history, of white people. They did not just allow me
access to their community, but consistently went out of their way to help
me get the information I needed and make me feel at home. I could not
have hoped for a more welcoming and friendlier field site, and I am eter-
nally grateful for everything the experience has taught me not just about
Xhosa life and South Africa but also about myself and the larger world.
It is my sincere hope that I have represented the Kamva community in
a way that residents find truthful, honest, and fair. Beyond this, I hope
that they find this book a useful tool for communicating to the larger
public, NGOs, and government institutions their grievances with an intensely unequal system that privileges Western epistemologies at the cost
of alienating large swaths of the South African population and maintaining historical inequalities along racial, cultural, and geographic lines. In
particular, I wish for the young people in Kamva to find this an accurate
representation of their diverse voices—ones that consistently remain un-
heard by the public at large because of highly unequal access to educational, political, and economic institutions in South Africa, yet deserve
to be heard. An especially large thank you goes to the Makaula family,
who have made this work possible and expanded my world for the better.
Enkosi kakhulu, ndiyanithanda nonke.

A sincere thank you to the many academic mentors without which
this work would not have been possible: Sondra Hale, for her faith in my
abilities through the years and her inspiring commitment to activism and
fighting injustice both in Africa and beyond; Andrew Apter, for his introduction to seminal Africanist texts that have forever changed my thinking
and also for his support of my work; Marjorie Goodwin, for helping me
understand and articulate the voices of youth and realize the importance
of language ideologies for understanding the world more broadly; Ned
Alpers, for providing me with a much-needed historical perspective not
only on South Africa but also its place in the larger region, about which I
previously knew relatively little; Steven Robins, for facilitating research in
South Africa and providing essential academic support from Cape Town;
and Deborah Thomas and John Jackson, for giving me invaluable guidance on the writing and publication of this book as well as a wonderful
academic home from which to write the majority of it. And thank you

to the many others who read this work in some form and offered feed-back: Nikhil Anand, Dhanveer Brar, Jean Comaroff, Hubert Cook, Kelly Gillespie, Casey Golomski, Clemmie L. Harris, Kevin Ahmaad Jenkins, Sean McEnroe, Margaret Perrow, Jessica Piekelek, Lisa Poggiali, Kaushik Sunder Rajan, Dominick Rolle, Oliver Rollins, Grace Sanders, Noah Tamarkin, Eve Tulbert, Keren Weitzberg, and Alden Young.

Last, but certainly not least, I want to thank the many family mem-bers and friends who supported me emotionally on this journey and of-fered their proofreading skills as I approached the final product. Mom, Dad, and Janna, your unwavering faith in me since the beginning has made this possible. I am so lucky to have a family who supports me in following my own path even if it differs substantially from their own. Annice Ormiston, you are a voice of sanity amid the craziness of life, and I am so grateful for our regular chats. Stacy Rosenbaum, Michelle Kline, and Anne Austin, thank you for reading countless grant proposals, ar-ticles, and drafts—and for providing much-needed perspective (and pho-tographs of adorable animals) along the way. Isaac, thank you for listening to me repeat my research summary a thousand times, enduring my ab-sences, and providing a constant reminder of the need to take seriously the voices of young people. It has been so wonderful to have you in my life throughout this process, keeping me honest and providing comic re-lief. Noah, you are the most supportive partner for which an academic (or anyone, for that matter) could ask. Thank you for always listening when I had a dilemma in the midst of research, for unselfishly supporting me during my fieldwork sojourns despite the long absences they necessitated, and for forcing me to constantly reevaluate and critique in ways that may have been painful in the moment but have no doubt vastly improved the work presented here. And thanks for that car rental, too.

GLOSSARY OF ISIXHOSA WORDS

Note: In isiXhosa, the X, C, and Q are pronounced as distinct guttural clicks.

Bhuti: brother

Hlonipha: respect, both in actions, demeanor, grammatical construction and specific vocabulary

Inkosi: chief

Inkululeko: democracy, freedom

Inkwenkwe: boy

Intonjane: the female puberty ritual

Isidudu: a porridge made with ground maize

Kombi: minivan

Lobola: bride-price

Magoti: daughter-in-law

Sisi: sister

Tsotsi: gangster, criminal

Ubuntu: humanity

Umgidi: celebration following a Xhosa male circumcision ceremony

Umzi: household

Map of South Africa. Wikimedia Commons, 2009

Introduction

On a warm spring day in 2012, I squeezed in among the young children squirming in their school auditorium seats as they waited for the Heritage Day assembly to begin at Cedarwood Primary,[1] a rural school in the Eastern Cape. The bright colors of traditional Xhosa costumes decorated the audience members and performers alike: intricate beaded necklaces, white dots of face paint, and long colorful skirts. The smell of food being cooked outside in large cast-iron pots wafted into the room, promising a feast after the day's activities were over. Music blared over the hired deejay's loudspeaker, and children danced along in their seats and in the aisles as they waited for the event to get under way.

The holiday, celebrated every September 24 since 1995, honors the diversity and richness of South African cultures. Like much of South African postapartheid legislation, Heritage Day is billed as a way to make good on the promises of the antiapartheid movement. It signals the end of a cultural hierarchy based on white supremacy and helps usher in an era of equality and inclusivity. As Nelson Mandela stated in his 1996 speech at the first celebration of the holiday, "We knew that, if indeed our nation has to rise like the proverbial phoenix from the ashes of division and conflict, we had to acknowledge those whose selfless efforts and talents were dedicated to this goal of non-racial democracy."[2]

FIGURE I.I   Children in costumes wait for the Heritage Day celebration to start. Photo by author, 2012

Cedarwood's celebration that year began with an elderly female teacher taking the stage to introduce the day's events. She started by telling the audience of several hundred attentive students about their responsibilities as African children: "Today we are half African and half Western. But you must be one. You must know where you belong. You belong to the era of asking why, but don't ask why. . . . And remember that a girl does not move around. She is the flower of the home. A girl that does not wish to get married is not speaking the honest truth. She must get married to belong somewhere." This part of her impassioned speech surprised me. Heritage Day was started as a way to embrace a new era of multiculturalism and acceptance, but here was someone using it as a platform to resist the incursion of foreign ideas. The democratic revolution that swept South Africa after the fall of apartheid ushered in an era of attention to cultural pluralism and ethnic diversity, and Heritage Day was a holiday meant to help further this goal of national unity. In a country with eleven official languages, such events held the promise of cross-cultural communication in the service of democracy building. And yet this very same ideology of multiculturalism was now clearly seen by people like the elderly teacher as threatening to erode cherished and timeless cultural values. Ideas from the "West" encourage young people to ask their elders why, to push back against traditional African gender roles of female propriety, to subvert ostensibly quintessential elements of Xhosa culture, and to turn their backs on what it means to be African. In retrospect, however, I should not have been surprised by the introduction to Heritage Day on that warm spring day: this teacher is but one of many people expressing deep ambivalence to the ideals of democratic liberalism in rural South Africa today.

By that September, I had already listened to countless diatribes on the evils of democracy and universal human rights from teachers, parents, and students alike. Noluvo,[3] a young girl who had gone through the local school system and was born at the end of apartheid, expressed impassioned views on how democracy was ruining Xhosa culture by introducing outside values. She, along with many other community members, insisted that apartheid may have been deeply racist and unfair but that it had been preferable to the cultural incursions and crippling disappointments of the postapartheid government. Even Ndiliswa, a neighbor in Kamva who is a successful doctor and has benefited immensely from the opportunities afforded nonwhites after apartheid, had told me that in many ways life was better during apartheid. And I had not just heard but also seen this ambivalence to liberal ideals as well. One school principal told me that he supported the law against corporal punishment on the grounds of children's rights, only to hit an allegedly misbehaving student in front of me shortly thereafter. Classroom lessons officially intended to stimulate critical thinking and discussion were presented by means of rote teaching methods during which students were expected to align with the teacher's views and demonstrate obedience to authority rather than freedom of thought.

Despite all this resistance to national rhetoric on the local level, democracy and human rights education abound in South Africa. Schools play a large role in working to produce democratic, rights-bearing citizens not just in assemblies but also in classes like Life Orientation, Social Sciences, and Arts and Culture. Beyond school walls, nongovernmental organizations (NGOs) play a prominent role in efforts to teach democracy to youth as well, in the form of extracurricular programs, community training, and teacher education. Schools and NGOs frequently work in tandem to create young citizens who know their rights and will exercise them and who will resist practices seen as antidemocratic such as gender inequality and corporal punishment. One prominent NGO, the Sonke Gender Justice Network, is an organization that started in urban South

Africa but now works across the continent and encourages the very "asking why" that the elderly teacher adamantly warned students against. The organization had operated programs at Cedarwood just a few years before the Heritage Day assembly. Sonke was in Kamva from approximately 2008 to 2011. It trained students to make digital stories that highlight domestic violence and champion gender equality. It empowered young peer educators to report instances of abuse and challenge elders' authority. It ran community workshops advocating responsible fatherhood and safe sex. Today in South Africa, Sonke is far from an anomaly; an abundance of NGOs work both to fill in the gaps left by government education and to oppose any teaching seen as antidemocratic. Organizations like Sonke see youth education as a critical part of their mission, even though they frequently come up against resistance on grounds of culture. Sonke staff, alongside trained community facilitators, encourage girls to be independent, boys to take up traditionally female tasks in the home, and children to speak out against actions that violate their basic human rights, even if these actions are considered important to notions of cultural identity. These are highly controversial lessons in places like the rural Eastern Cape, and when filtered through local facilitators, there is no guarantee they will be translated to youth intact.

In this book, I present what at first glance appears to be a paradox: young people are learning about democracy and human rights from educators and elders who are increasingly disappointed with these institutions. In the pages that follow, I examine the contours and scope of democratic education in the postapartheid nation: What might it mean to have a generation of rural youth taught about democracy by those who are most dissatisfied with it as a political and ideological system? How do youth navigate the deep ambivalence of their elders regarding South African democracy? Through this local case study, I show how close ethnographic engagement with political education can offer a new way to wrestle with global ambivalence toward democracy and the recent upticks in authoritarianism seen in a variety of settings around the world today. Are we entering some sort of *post*democratic future, and if so, what role does education play in this shift? Educational spaces such as schools and NGOs are primary battlegrounds for the production of democracy, and in order to understand the widespread backlash to liberal, rights-based politics and the seemingly ubiquitous nostalgia for more authoritarian regimes, we have to place these spaces front and center in our examination.

DEMOCRACY AND ANTHROPOLOGY

When we use the word *democracy* in South Africa, not to mention elsewhere, to what exactly are we referring? While popular culture and the media may use the term as though it is transparent, social scientists have shed light on the various local contexts in which democracy is negotiated and produced, to drastically different ends (Paley 2002, 2008). In this book, I align with theorists who ascribe to the idea of *democracies*, a multivalent and dynamic term for a shifting set of political and ideological practices (Owusu 1997). Democracy is not an end product but instead a process that people negotiate on local levels and that depends on cultural, economic, geographic, and historical variables. This is especially apt to educational settings, where different teachers understand, and therefore present, democratic ideals in drastically different ways. The methods of ethnography are uniquely suited to uncovering this process of democracy building, as they are able to ask how political systems are crafted from the ground up rather than the top down. An emphasis on long-term participant observation necessitates looking at alternative worldviews and the discrepancies between official political discourse and people's everyday relationships with institutions of governance. While the South African national curriculum tells one story about democratic education, actual rural classrooms tell a very different one.

Cultural anthropology's fundamental doctrine of cultural relativism has been rightly challenged for its moral and ethical limitations (Abu-Lughod 2002; Hale 2013; Ortner 2006), yet it allows for an examination of alternative perspectives on issues of freedom and human rights germane to this discussion. For example, the elderly teacher at Heritage Day has a very different idea of what "freedom" should look like, especially when it comes to women and girls. When projected through the lens of contemporary cultural anthropology and its emphasis on exposing unequal relations of power, then, official rhetoric on democracy breaks down and changes shape in local contexts. Democratic liberalism's origins as a product of exploitative Western power relations with the periphery become impossible to ignore. Because of this complex history, anthropological methods offer the ability to expose the master narrative of democracy as a kind of false consciousness that is misaligned with many people's cultural realities. In this book, I apply this framework to the complexities of South African democracy, examining how people reconstitute official and unofficial discourses on democratic values and human rights once enacted in rural contexts far from the seats of legislative and juridical power. Democracy is not the idealistic social and political equalizer many people imagine it to be but rather is constrained within structural power relations and enacted within and through long-standing historical inequities. Consequently, I agree with other scholars who argue that there is no definitive and unambiguous definition of democracy, because it is an ever-shifting signifier that is inextricably tied to culture and history. As Mukulika Banerjee has succinctly pointed out, "*Democracy* is one of those big words, like *freedom* and *terrorism*, that in common currency is more often used than analyzed" (quoted in Paley 2008, 92). I am less interested in defining democracy's parameters than I am in illuminating how South Africans attempt to do this work for themselves and what the process reveals about their worldviews and socioeconomic realities. Westerners often define democracy as "rule of, by, and for the people," but this falls short of capturing the many different ways political systems are implemented in local situations. For example, South Africa is a parliamentary representative democracy in which citizens elect representatives to serve in their best interests rather than play a direct role in everyday political decision making.

Furthermore, democracy should not be taken as synonymous with liberalism, a term that is extremely broad and highly contested. In this book, I use liberalism in the tradition of philosophers like Locke and Rousseau and as furthered by thinkers like Feinberg and Rawls in more contemporary discussions. These writers generally see individual freedoms as an a priori assumption and consider any attempts to limit freedom on the part of government as bearing the burden of justification (Feinberg 1980; Locke [1689] 1960; Rawls 1996; Rousseau [1762] 1973). It should be noted that these are not necessarily principles to which my research participants adhere (as we shall see, they quite often oppose them, to varying degrees) but rather ones that are in line with the kinds of global human rights laws that influence South African legal and judicial policies: individual personhood, children's rights, gender equality, and religious freedoms, to name a few.

Debates on the universal applicability of democracy and the resistance to Western liberalism are certainly not new in anthropology and the social sciences generally. In the past couple of decades, scholars across the globe have become interested in the ways that democratic governance, in all its varying forms and levels of scale, affects the everyday lives of citizens as well as contributes to larger international discourses (Brown 1998; Geschiere and Jackson 2006; Paley 2002). Far from transparent and equal, Western-based democracy is often a hegemonic and oppressive institution for many people in the Global South, in Africa and elsewhere. Furthermore, the political transitions on the African continent since the 1960s have made it abundantly clear that there is no "one size fits all" model for democracy. Instead, democracy by necessity must be "domesticated" to African realities (Owusu 1997). In fact, for many Africans, Western-based democracy has meant a dangerous unraveling of moral and social life. Anthropologists have shown that democracy's push for equality has, for some, meant encouraging dark forces—whether it is sorcerers-cum-lions in Mozambique's rural Muedan plateau (West 2005) or witches next door in urban Soweto (Ashforth 2005)—to multiply and escape punishment under the guise of "multiculturalism" and "tolerance for diversity." In addition, the decentralized nature of many African democracies, with systems of elected or appointed representatives far removed from the lives of most rural people, has meant that many Africans feel a lack of representation as compared to so-called traditional forms of authority, such as chiefs or tribal councils. This, along with the role of colonial governments in maintaining such institutions, helps explain the persistence of traditional authority in the face of massive political change (Comaroff and Comaroff 2018). And traditional authority is not necessarily at odds with the concept of democracy, as many precolonial societies actually retained spaces for direct political participation through local institutions (van Allen 1972). In other words, the common perception of Africa "failing" at democracy should be recognized as a misinterpretation. In fact, many Africans feel exactly the opposite is true: current versions of democracy, largely borrowed from the West, are failing *them*.

South Africa's democracy after apartheid is commonly portrayed with a cliché: the Rainbow Nation. The phrase alludes to the cultural, linguistic, ethnic, and racial diversity that makes up a politically unified country, represented in its iconic multicolored flag. Meant to be more than just a superficial metaphor, this national ideal of diversity tolerance undergirds much of South Africa's ideological commitment to democracy—not just as a political system, but also as a social worldview and moral philosophy meant to heal the wounds of a deeply unequal past. While the international news media has largely praised the transition to democracy after

the atrocities of apartheid as peaceful, closer analysis of quotidian practices reveals the difficulty of juridical and legislative decisions in such a
diverse context. Importantly, these rosy pictures of the past render less
visible the immense violence and loss of Black lives that accompanied
both the fight for freedom and the reconstruction period that followed.
Rather than an easy transition, liberal democracy and universal human
rights are often hard pills to swallow for many South Africans. Ostensibly
meant to be a great equalizer, democracy can be threatening and divisive,
particularly for historically oppressed communities.

In rural South Africa, democracy is seen as failing people in two main
ways. First, it has not ushered in the age of economic freedom that the
antiapartheid movement championed. While the apartheid-era African
National Congress (ANC) had close ties to the South African Communist Party and upheld ideals of socialist wealth redistribution, Mandela's
transition to power included a further alignment with global neoliberal
capitalism. This has meant that Black communities maintain much of the
same structural inequalities that epitomized apartheid: food insecurity,
inadequate health care, crumbling schools. Today South Africa holds
the notorious distinction of being the most unequal society in the world
(Beaubien 2018), and this inequality still exists mostly along racial lines.

South Africa's persistent inequality demonstrates how the naturalization of a connection between democracy and capitalism undergirds many
people's disappointments with the current state of affairs. As the anthropologists Jean and John Comaroff explain:

> The reason that world politics is presently so fixated on democratiza-
> tion follows directly from this. It lies precisely in the hegemonic, in-
> deed ontological, association in the West of freedom and self-expression
> with choice. Democracy has become to Homo politicus what shopping
> has long been to Homo economicus: a sacred, cosmic fusion of free will
> and righteous human satisfaction. They are, so to speak, two sides of
> the same coin, two regimes of consumption underpinned by the same
> mode of ideological and material production. (1997, 125–26)

Thus democracy and capitalism are inextricably linked with and constitutive of one another in that the freedom to consume is conflated with—
some may even argue has replaced—political freedoms. The ethnographic
work that comprises this book illustrates how current conflations of

democracy and capitalism in the contemporary South African state are part of a larger narrative of dominant Western liberal political and economic values. This linking of neoliberal economics with democracy has serious ramifications for young people's political subjectivity.

Second, democracy is failing ordinary South Africans in its perceived attack on so-called traditional culture. On the surface, respect for cultural and racial diversity is enshrined in the postapartheid South African Constitution (see the appendix). This oft-praised document upholds and protects many traditional institutions such as customary courts and chiefdoms as a way to make good on the promise to recognize cultural plurality in the wake of a white supremacist state that devastated non-European cultures. For example, local chiefs in South Africa are supported both financially and politically, and their right to exist is written into law. In practice, however, this constitutional celebration of cultural, linguistic, and social diversity only goes so far. Instead, hegemonic ideologies of Western liberalism underwrite South African law: the South African Constitution Act of 1993 drew heavily on ideas from Canadian, American, and German documents (Davis 2003). This has resulted in the widespread perception that the state is unwilling to address serious social ills because liberal democracy offers them no recognition or resolution that fits African realities. We see this in the proliferation of incidents of the occult: those who press the state to apprehend malicious witches are treated as irrational rather than operating under a different but equal epistemological worldview (Comaroff and Comaroff 2004a). While South Africa claims to celebrate indigenous and African beliefs as equally valid to Western, Eurocentric ones, this is far more controversial when it comes to practices that are at odds with the constitution and the legal system. European Enlightenment values of scientific rationality and the observable world structure South African law, undercutting any genuine attempt at recognizing and treating different cultures as equal. This bias creates a hierarchy of epistemologies within the Rainbow Nation such that Western-based liberal values are given precedence over other systems of knowledge and justice. Consequently, this leaves teachers like the elderly woman at Heritage Day feeling marginalized and sidelined for what they identify as their traditional beliefs.

Such murky waters of governance and legality in the South African state make the teaching of democracy to youth highly context-dependent and controversial. As one might imagine, young people absorb very different perspectives on issues such as witchcraft, justice, and human rights depending on their particular positioning. Geography, race, gender, culture, and class are all factors that influence the type of political education one receives and the ways in which this education is filtered and presented (Harley et al. 2000). The presence of such disparate lessons on politics and culture undoubtedly has an impact on the production of a future generation of citizens in significant ways. Thus people's rejection of liberal democracy has critical ramifications for projects of youth socialization and identity production along cultural, ethnic, racial, and gendered lines. It also reminds us of the crucial and complicated role of education in building democracy long before citizens start casting their votes or running for elected offices.

South Africa's democratic transition and the ways in which it has failed ordinary citizens are well documented in the social science literature (e.g., Ashforth 2005; Besteman 2008; Hickel 2015). However, this book's focus specifically on young people's political education offers a fresh perspective on the issues of South African liberalism and democracy. Rural educators in the Eastern Cape both consciously and unconsciously construct views of democracy through resistance to Western liberal ideals. This is a reminder that democracy is not solely imposed from above, and here is where the real strength of ethnographic analysis lies. Scholarship must pay attention not just to national legislation and prominent political actors but also to local communities that resist and renegotiate new values and realities in context-specific and culturally informed ways. Ethnographic methods offer the ability to subvert traditional top-down approaches from other disciplines and media reports and examine how individual agency, including that of children and youth, plays a role in citizenship construction and democratic state building. Resistance to democracy via educational institutions illustrates how local value systems often contradict and challenge national political projects in highly consequential ways.

The connections between capitalism and democracy in South Africa are predicated on the increasing globalization of the African continent and the larger world. Of late, social scientists have focused on the nature of the state vis-à-vis transnational flows of both ideas and capital as well as decentralization of government in the twenty-first century. While early studies of globalization suggested a potential for homogeneity as a result of rapid flows of capital, ideas, goods, and people, more recent contributions have questioned this supposed dilution of state power and borders in favor of more nuanced models of state-nonstate alliances. Rather than presume a dying nationalist sentiment and erosion of borders around the globe, anthropologists have demonstrated the resiliency (albeit changing nature) of state power and the tenacity of nationalism and local identity in the face of a globalized world (Chalfin 2010; Piot 1999; Roitman 2005), something that is obvious in light of recent pro-isolationist votes for Brexit and Trump (Reed 2017). In light of theorists who argue for the continued relevance of the nation-state as a guiding concept of governance and identity politics, this book highlights the importance of South African ideals of nationhood and democratic belonging, as well as their intersection with the politics of ethnicity, racialization, and culture in the postcolonial state. While citizenship construction and the political socialization of youth are based on national belonging to a specific ideological perspective, diverse cultural and racial politics create feelings of alienation from the state and alignment with conservative traditionalism that stand in marked contrast to nationalist sentiments. The nation-state remains a critical concept in my analysis both for its continued centrality in political identity and for its role as an object of local resistance.

THE CRISIS OF CULTURE

Political backlash on the grounds of culture is a problem that extends far beyond the borders of South Africa or anthropology. Scholarship and the popular media have been increasingly preoccupied with the problem of antidemocratic sentiments and the resurgence of "tradition." Why do people the world over appear to be rejecting discourses of equal and inalienable rights? Why is the notion of freedom threatening to so many people? Why are authoritarian-style politics seemingly on the rise, and what is their connection to culture?

Take this story from South Africa in 2018. A video went viral on YouTube after a choirmaster at an Eastern Cape school had girls dress in "traditional" Xhosa costumes for a performance, which meant being virtually naked. He defended his decision on the grounds of culture but was met with widespread backlash that argued he had exploited the girls and should be fired (Cowell 2018). The ensuing conversations that this event triggered had people defending culture against the onslaught of liberal human rights and also castigating those who use culture as an alleged scapegoat to violate the rights of women and girls. Was the choirmaster an honest adherent of Xhosa tradition or a dangerous pedophile? This ongoing debate on the role tradition should play in modern South African society and its intersection with liberal human rights is a constant battle for the young democracy. Scholars have offered various explanations for the recent rise in what we might call traditionalism, in South Africa and elsewhere. For example, the anthropologist Jason Hickel (2015) shows how migrant workers in Kwa-Zulu Natal Province reject liberal democracy because it challenges traditional hierarchies of the home and thus becomes equated with chaos, societal disintegration, and even death. In a recent edited volume, John and Jean Comaroff (2018) show how traditional authority figures across Africa have always been a prominent part of social life, albeit in ever-evolving forms that challenge Western liberal politics.

Because of the tenacious hold apartheid had on the country for decades, South Africa is a relatively young democracy vis-à-vis the rest of the African continent and the postcolonial world. In the realm of democratic state building, South Africa is still in its infancy. While most other African countries shed the yoke of colonial powers during the height of the Cold War scramble for power on the continent (Piot 2010), South Africa has confronted a later version of independence that has become tethered to the logics of free market capitalism such that democratic freedom is often equated with consumer freedom (Szeftel 2004). While previous fights over spheres of influence in Africa pitted the socialist agenda against the democratic one, the key players in today's battle appear to be the logics of neoliberal "rationality" versus hierarchical and "oppressive" traditionalism as viewed from the West. These false binaries have become entrenched and naturalized, despite the fact that they are products of particular histories and global economic structures. Tradition is often not so traditional; rationalism, not all that rational. Much of the ethnic consciousness and multiculturalism at the forefront of South African democracy that is attributed to precolonial times may actually be only as old as the colonial state itself. For instance, as demonstrated in the case of Rwanda (Mamdani 2001), assumed ties between ethnic groups and the nation-state are actually the product of European imperialism and its racial "civilizing" projects (Bayart 1989; Pierre 2013). Here what is relevant is not necessarily the actual origins of practices labeled as traditional but rather how they have become cemented in the public imagination and pitted against liberalism as a political tool.

Along these lines, it is important to recognize that religious missionary activity played a prominent role in producing what we now think of as traditional culture in South Africa, and religion remains a guiding framework for many people's understandings of contemporary politics and cultural identities. Xhosa residents in the Eastern Cape often justify antidemocratic sentiments on the grounds of culture, despite the fact that many practices lack evidence of precolonial roots. For instance, claims that Xhosa elders ought to beat their children as a form of discipline based on the idea that "to spare the rod is to spoil the child" has been deeply influenced by Christian theology introduced by European missionaries in the nineteenth century. Because of the ways in which tradition gets obscured over time, this book also aims to illustrate the complex intersections of colonialism, democracy, apartheid, and local cultural processes rather than reduce acts of resistance to essentializing concepts such as culture (Hobsbawm and Ranger 1983).

Anthropologists—among others—have long struggled to define the parameters of exactly what constitutes culture (Ortner 1984). Without reiterating this debate in full here, some common links in the definition are culture as inherently social, learned, inherited from generation to generation, and unique to particular societies and groups (Bennett 2015). In South Africa, twentieth-century discussions of culture have seen the concept as bounded in problematic ways, but some scholarship has worked to complicate the idea by reminding us that culture is constituted in particular places at particular historical moments (Boonzaier and Sharp 1988). For the purposes of this book, I see culture as including these previous ideas: culture encompasses all the practices, behaviors, and beliefs of a particular society but is not isolated or bounded. Instead, it is inextricably linked to other cultures, is always intertwined with political and historical processes, and is experienced differently by different members of a group. This will become obvious as the book progresses and we see the many ways rural South Africans, educators, and NGO employees think about culture and cultural belonging. Tradition, a related concept, is the intergenerational, shared practices that fall under the umbrella of culture.

The type of "freedom" experienced in democratic South Africa (not to mention elsewhere in the postcolonial world) has meant a perhaps ironic rise in violence and crime (Comaroff and Comaroff 2000, 299; Ferguson 2006). What many scholars have called neoliberalism has brought with it "liberation" via decentralization of government, corporatization of services, and a culture of individual consumerism that has heightened wealth disparities and maintained de facto segregation in devastating ways for most South Africans (Bond 2014). Though the country in many ways resists easy categorization as "neoliberal" because of its rise in social welfare programs (Ferguson 2015), there nonetheless exists a very real emphasis on increased privatization of many former government services and participation in global free market trade structures; the strong influence of Soviet communism in much apartheid-era political protest dissipated by the time Mandela rose to power in the 1990s (Beinart 1994). For young Black people in particular, these trends have meant a dearth of employment opportunities, which makes it increasingly difficult to fulfill the obligations of social reproduction as prescribed by culture, such as payments for marriage. This is certainly visible in Kamva, where throngs of unemployed or underemployed young people wander aimlessly along the streets and residents frequently cite alcoholism, crime, teenage pregnancy, and drug use as the biggest challenges facing young people in the community today. In 2014, one young man asked me as I waited in line to pay at a local grocery store, "Mandela promised us all jobs. Where are those jobs?"

These ruptures in normative processes of social reproduction have more than just economic consequences; they have direct and indirect ties to discourses of tradition. As individual consumption and accumulation become universal aspirations that structure notions of value, family relations are radically altered and cultural practices are renegotiated. For instance, young people getting married in rural South Africa today are far less likely to live with their relatives in extended kin groups, instead favoring nuclear family models in urban environments that support new employment opportunities and offer close proximity to consumer culture such as sprawling shopping centers. While such shifts are not necessarily integral to democracy as a system of governance, many people see them as part and parcel of political change. These ruptures and realignments, while not always explicitly connected to state politics, help illuminate why elders may reject democratic ideals in favor of apartheid-era structures of indirect governance that seemed to interfere less with cultural practices and ideologies in rural areas. Culture is suddenly in crisis, and traditionalism has become a way to frame a desired identity in the face of this threat.

South African political projects that aim to address cultural diversity also find themselves battling antiquated views of the African continent externally *and* internally. Much of Western discourse on Africa has been invoked only in its negation, the scholar Achille Mbembe (2001, 2) reminds us, "as a polemical argument for the West's desperate desire to assert its difference from the rest of the world." Colonial indoctrination and Western orientalizing discourses have become internalized in ways that contribute to complex cultural and racialized identities that anchor nostalgia for aspects of life under white rule (Bhabha 1994; Said 1978). Western forces that have long shaped hegemonic discourses on the African continent continue to characterize it by its lack, peering through the lens of Enlightenment rationality and coming up short for an explanation of local cultural variations. I have seen this internalization in my conversations with Fundani, a longtime friend in Kamva. He once questioned why "Africans don't make anything themselves" in a discussion of global production of goods like cars and computers. Rather than point out longstanding histories of structural inequality and racial capitalism, he wondered what might inherently be wrong with Africans to keep them from dominating the world's technological innovations. By taking into account how histories of inequality shape local knowledge systems, I demonstrate how the contemporary moment can be filled with a paradoxical combination of nostalgia for the past and future-oriented consumerism. Here culture is in crisis from both external and internal forces.

One of the best ways to enter into South African debates about culture after apartheid is to watch television—a medium that was only introduced to the country in 1976 (Krabill 2010). In 1996, just two years after the official end of apartheid, the South African Broadcasting Corporation (SABC) aired a highly popular situation comedy titled "Suburban Bliss." Although the show is no longer in production, the themes and challenges it raised remain relevant today. An early episode speaks volumes about South African entanglements of race, class, culture, and gender in the 1990s. The opening scene features a Black professional assertively yet politely asking his harried and unsympathetic white male employer for stock options in the company. He couches his request in apartheid-era terms of hierarchical respect, speaking quietly and with evident fear. The boss shouts back at him in stereotypically condescending ways. "I'm important to you!" exclaims the employee, as he becomes emboldened by the rejection and verbal abuse. To this the boss nastily responds, "So is my dog, but I'm not gonna give him a raise!" Cue the laugh track. Later that evening, the man goes home to the township and is greeted by his young Black wife, wearing a leopard print shirt and gold earrings, nail file in hand. She seems to have been impatiently waiting to hear the result of her husband's request at work. Disappointment and anger follow when she hears of his failure to secure the stock options, and an argument ensues pitting traditionalist yet timid and emasculated husband against consumerist and domineering wife. He explains that he longs for a future in which he has a large farm and cattle along a rural river far from the urban townships, and she corrects him on how capitalist desire is supposed to work: "The only bank I'm interested in is the bank that gives you the money to move to the white suburbs" (Se-Puma, Sargent, and Heany 1996).

The heavy-handed tropes in this show evidence the social and economic categories left over from apartheid that continue to inform and structure much of South African life and demonstrate the inextricable linkages between economics and culture in the contemporary nation. The young wife longs for a life that was recently restricted to whites only but remains tantalizingly out of financial reach for most people. On the other hand, the husband waxes nostalgic for the markers of success his ancestors would recognize but are increasingly rendered irrelevant by liberal democracy and capitalism. The husband tries to assert his new rights as an equal citizen of the South African state by asking for company ownership in the form of stock options but meekly defers to his white boss in ways that evidence internalized, persistent racial hierarchies. The wife's assertiveness vis-à-vis her husband hints at the push for gender equality in the democratic state, yet the couple remains entrenched in "traditionally" gendered roles: husband as wage earner and wife as homemaker. The husband clings to tradition in a new reality that renders him relatively powerless and emasculated.

As this vignette makes clear, while postapartheid South Africa has prioritized multiculturalism and equality as central to the democratic project, for many people this has been a disempowering and debilitating experience. This is partly because the state has yet to truly address its continuing legacy of economic and racial inequality. The anthropologist Jemima Pierre (2013, 5), though she focuses on Ghana, is relevant here to remind us that "we cannot understand how notions of ethnicity, nation, or culture are deployed in racialized-as-Black African communities without recognizing the ways they are refracted through processes of racialization." In other words, ideas about African culture cannot be divorced from the experience of Blackness on the continent. In South Africa, the history of racialization extends back far beyond the Afrikaner National Party and its apartheid government; rather, the colonial project helped instantiate tensions between ethnic groups and sediment the beginnings of modern race concepts in the country. As is the case anywhere, race in South Africa is a political project rather than a biological one; this is evident, for example, if you look at the numbers of people who "changed races" each year during apartheid (Seekings 2008). Thus, while spaces such as the classroom may foreground cultural tolerance and ethnic pride, legacies of colonial and apartheid racial hierarchies continue to structure such concepts. Blackness still informs much of the way many rural South Africans perceive both themselves and the world and plays an important role in their political orientations. As Fundani once phrased it, "I believe in a broader society of Blacks." The contemporary ANC has prioritized discourses of postracialism while doing little to attend to the racist structures of inequality set in motion by its predecessors; the recent #RhodesMustFall and #FeesMustFall protest movements have been a direct result of this dangerous omission in policy and practice. Diversity is not synonymous with historical redress or inclusion. While the ANC allegedly works toward a nonracial meritocracy, its participation in neoliberal forms of capitalism ensures that wealth remains divided along primarily racial lines (MacDonald 2004).

These crises of culture and tradition bring us to nostalgia—a form of memory distinct in its longing to return to an imagined and reconstructed past that may never have existed (Stewart 1988). Those who perceive culture and tradition as under threat turn to nostalgic feelings of loss for the predemocracy era. Since liberal democracy stresses—at least in rhetoric—the broad recognition of equality and equal footing for all cultures, many interpret it as lacking a unifying, cohesive value system (Brown 1998). Without a clear set of morals, many Black South Africans reject current instantiations of democracy because they regard them as amoral and sinful. For those struggling to accept democracy's amorphous ideology, nostalgic renderings of the past can provide a firm and familiar ground on which to stand.

EDUCATIONAL SPACES AND THE PRODUCTION OF DEMOCRACY

Central to this book is the recognition that democracy is not an entrenched ideology but rather a set of processes that take place in particular local institutions—educational spaces being one such institution. I seek to understand what democracy actually means for young rural Xhosa people who are inundated with specific discourses of nation building from both state and nonstate actors such as public schools and NGOs. What can we learn from these young people's experiences about democracy's contradictions and problems?

NGOs play a formative role in the economic and political fabric of the postapartheid state, including in processes of democratic and human rights education. After the transition to democracy and the opening up of South Africa's borders to the larger international community in the 1990s, a great number of NGOs rallied around equal rights discourses central to conceptions of democracy and reflective of larger transnational ideologies of governance (Robins 2008). This influx was not solely ideological; the increasing privatization of social services, such as water (Von Schnitzler 2016), left a critical gap many organizations sought to fill. Now many South Africans find such organizations an essential part of daily life, whether to provide school lunches, subsidize libraries, or offer in-home maternity care in rural areas of the country.

This is certainly not unique on the African continent. On the contrary, many African nations have seen the rise of NGOs in practically every facet of social life, from daily service provision to ideological training and activism. As Charles Piot (2010, 135) states in his discussion of post–Cold War Togo, "It is [NGOs] more than the state that are now organizing the production of life." At the same time, NGOs are not entirely removed from state institutions and instead are inextricably bound up with governmental institutions in complex and varying ways. Many NGOs accept funding from different government agencies and departments, support government work, and/or work closely with government employees to achieve their goals (Markowitz 2001). They also work to hold government accountable when it conflicts with their own agendas, as seen in the example of South Africa's Treatment Action Campaign (TAC), an organization that fights the HIV/AIDS epidemic and models innovative forms of civic participation in order to challenge state institutions. In the late 1990s, the TAC became highly visible for challenging then-President Thabo Mbeki, who was vocal in his skepticism of widely accepted HIV/AIDS science (Robins and von Lieres 2004). Such intersections of state and nonstate actors are characteristic of this moment in late capitalism, in which the seemingly neat distinctions between government and non-government actors are increasingly blurred and the economic processes behind these relations obscured (Comaroff and Comaroff 2000). In fact, these blurred boundaries mean that the term "nongovernmental organization" may itself be a misnomer. Nonetheless, I use the term in this book for its utility in calling attention to institutions that operate with relatively minimal government oversight; further, organizations often use the term to describe themselves and the work they do.

Many NGOs prioritize and work toward access to state resources for historically disadvantaged populations (Robins 2008). In other words, claims for rights, something so prominent in South African legal frameworks, are often the best language in which to frame the desire for state attention or basic services. My own focus on the Sonke Gender Justice Network is a case in point, as this South African NGO strives to shift local ideologies through legal and political channels.[4] However, the nation is home to a diverse array of both domestic and international organizations, making it impossible to identify a "typical" NGO (Robins 2008; Van Driel and Van Haren 2003). I insist that we look beyond dichotomous understandings of NGOs as either "handmaidens of Empire" (Robins 2008, 23) or benevolent, neutral conduits for democracy, instead opting for more nuanced and complex representations of these institutions. This will become evident in my later discussion of Sonke, an institution that both draws from and replicates individual, Western notions of personhood in line with government agendas while at the same time challenging oppressive state policies that deny equal rights to all South Africans. Much of this work happens through their community programs to educate children and youth on what it means to be members of a democracy.

The other educational space this book examines is the South African public school classroom. Classrooms are of course always inherently political, in that they reflect larger local, state, and national ideals and projects. In South Africa, schools have a long history of supporting national politics. During the early days of colonial rule, Christian missionaries ran schools meant to convert native Africans while providing them with basic literacy skills in order to read religious texts. Later, during apartheid, segregated schooling and Bantu Education (discussed in greater detail in ch. 4) served to bolster white supremacy and keep Black South Africans in subservient roles by teaching them only the basic skills needed for menial labor. Today the national system of public education heavily emphasizes the importance of training students to be civically engaged, informed democratic citizens. The introduction of a national curriculum, just after the fall of apartheid, involved purging the system of racist language and infusing it with a student-centered, multicultural perspective on education that places universal human rights front and center (Chisholm 2005). Nonetheless, conflicts abound both in curricular design and in its implementation. Many South Africans feel strongly that schools are failing to properly educate their children and prepare them for the workforce, and the racial disparities in school completion and employment rates are a testament to the potential truth of such sentiments. South Africa has, for the past two decades or so, seen public schooling as central to its larger democratic project. What has this looked like on the ground in places like the rural Eastern Cape? What happens when teachers like the one at Heritage Day push back against messages of liberal democracy and multiculturalism, despite curricular mandates to promote them? These are questions that the following pages address.

OUTLINE OF CHAPTERS

This book roughly follows my own path to understanding the production of democracy among rural South African youth. Chapter 1 introduces Kamva, the small town in the inland Eastern Cape that is the focal point for this ethnographic account. By traversing this economically depressed area that was once part of the Transkei homeland, I describe the ways that apartheid functioned in rural parts of South Africa, as well as the precolonial and colonial histories that led to the unique qualities of this predominantly Xhosa-identified region. South Africa has what we might call a double burden of colonial history, the first from its origins as a colony of the Dutch East India Company and then the British Empire and the second from internal colonialism via the white minority rule of the Afrikaner National Party and its associated apartheid government that lasted nearly half a century. It is essential to make note of the ways in which the push for an inclusive democracy intersects with the reality of a colonial history that in many ways exists as much in the present as it did in the past (Gilroy 2005; Mbembé 2001; Mudimbe 1988). Eastern Cape youth in places like Kamva navigate a diverse set of sociocultural identities: Xhosa, Black, and South African, to name but a few. How has the history of this region contributed to the production of identity among contemporary young people? What does it mean to teach democracy in this particular local context? Answering these questions is integral to the discussion of democratic education among historically marginalized populations more broadly.

Chapter 2 moves to the urban offices of the Sonke Gender Justice Network in Cape Town, an organization that serves to highlight broader liberal approaches to democratic education and human rights advocacy aligned with the goals of the South African state, the United Nations, and related international agencies. Sonke in many ways epitomizes the liberal, postapartheid project of participatory democracy; it challenges alleged antidemocratic practices labeled "traditional," insists on participation in international human rights ideology dominated by Western perspectives, pays close attention to discourses of cultural pluralism, and prioritizes education as a prime strategy for strengthening democracy and civil society. The chapter shows how this happens within the organization's own walls, by inculcating staff members with Sonke's values and running specific programs that align with its agenda.

Chapter 3 returns to Kamva, showing the interaction of Sonke staff and program facilitators with local teachers, government employees, and youth. I look closely at Sonke's interventions in democratic education in the years 2008–11, when it offered a series of programs such as digital storytelling production, peer education, and community workshops. I reveal how local cultural practices intersect with Sonke pedagogical strategies in ways very different from those imagined in urban NGO offices; for example, former participants express ambivalence about Sonke's message of gender equality as well as anger and disappointment at what they see as the organization's inability to create self-sustaining models in the community.

In chapter 4, I use a composite ethnography of several Kamva classrooms in order to detail the history of education in South Africa, especially that of Black students. Race and racism have been fundamental drivers in educational experiences throughout South Africa's history, from the earliest days at the Dutch Cape Colony until today. From Christian missionaries in the Eastern Cape in the 1800s to the infamous Bantu Education of Apartheid to today's National Curriculum Statement, the story of education in South Africa is also a story of colonialism, apartheid, and racial capitalism. The chapter examines Life Orientation classes, a product of recent educational redesigns that hope to craft active, engaged, and responsible citizens reflective of the nation's postapartheid agenda. But the official South Africa Department of Basic Education discourse and curricular materials surrounding this effort contrast greatly with the subtle and not so subtle everyday practices in the classroom that ethnographic fieldwork makes visible. Teachers filter course materials through the lens of Xhosa cultural identification and sociopolitical dissatisfaction in ways that promise to have consequences for young people's future political subjectivity.

An exploration of the discrepancies between national curricula and local teaching soon led me to the pervasive nostalgia for elements of life under apartheid among a variety of residents. Chapter 5 shows how people articulate frustrations with postapartheid democracy through nostalgic renderings of a past seemingly free from the tyranny of liberalism and the perceived failures of democracy. Crucial to this analysis is an understanding of the apartheid state's homeland system, which by design allowed for the illusion of cultural autonomy on the local level in rural areas. This is discussed in contrast to the seemingly intrusive rhetoric of national liberal democracy, which is articulated as an outside force threatening Xhosa culture and African identity. For example, the chapter includes a section that details teachers' fond memories of a time when corporal punishment was legal in school classrooms, insisting that the practice is integral to notions of traditional Xhosa culture and essential for teaching youth. My research also makes clear that this nostalgia will not end with the older generation: I show how Kamva youth are parroting the nostalgic narratives of their parents and grandparents. What emerges in this chapter and in chapter 6 is a portrait of youth who are deeply ambivalent about South African democracy in ways that promise to bleed into future political processes and identity formation.

Do rural South Africans actually seek freedom from liberal democracy rather than through it? I conclude the book with a larger, global discussion on recent ambivalences toward democracy and liberalism and the concurrent rise of support for authoritarianism and cultural traditionalism. My hope is that we can learn from places like Kamva and begin to take a more sustained and critical look at youth education and its connection to democracy. If children are receiving ambivalent and disparate messages about democracy—as highlighted by the Heritage Day speaker discussed in the opening of this chapter—it is likely to have profound effects on future political alignment.

CHAPTER ONE

Being Xhosa, Being South African

*I don't care who wins anymore. Zuma, Motlanthe . . . neither of them
are going to build me an indoor bathroom.*
> —Kamva woman, speaking about the
> 2012 ANC presidential primaries

ENTERING KAMVA

During the year I spent living in Kamva, I traveled to Cedarwood's Primary and Secondary Schools in the same manner as kids like Tando.
Every morning, this lanky teenager would hop into a *kombi* (minivan)
paid for monthly by his family, ride squashed and without a seatbelt between other students from his small village into town on the N2,[1] walk
across a field with cows grazing on yellowing grasses, climb down a steep
ravine covered in loose gravel, and then over a brook that is intermit-
tently clogged with trash and broken furniture from heavy downpours—
often necessitating a treacherous hop across the rocks onto the other side.
Cedarwood is a public school that was once private; today it retains its
Catholic heritage but sits on publicly owned land and receives Department of Basic Education funding. Unlike educational systems in other

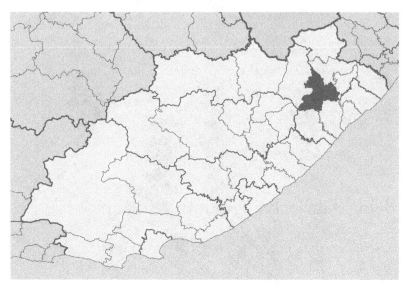

FIGURE I.I   Map of the Eastern Cape Province, with Kamva's municipality highlighted. Wikimedia Commons, 2016

countries, in South Africa school fees do not necessarily indicate that a school is private. The parents of Cedarwood students opted by majority vote in their Parent-Teacher Association to pay modest school fees in order to increase new teacher hires and thus educational quality. Cedarwood is known for having relatively involved parents, many of whom are gainfully employed, in contrast to much of the general Kamva population.

Tando's mother died when he was twelve, and he lives with his extended family that is already stretched thin on resources, so private school is not an option. He was extremely close to his mother, and the emotional trials of her illness and consequent death were likely the cause of his need to repeat a grade. He has been playing catch-up ever since. In 2012, when he was sixteen, he already towered over the other children in his class, many of whom were younger by a year or more. Although he may stand out physically, in an area with low exam pass rates and comparatively scarce educational resources, being held back a grade is not uncommon. Tando is bright and curious about the world, but like so many South African children his educational options are limited. Indeed, many of the students I know who once participated in Sonke's community programs in the area while in secondary school are now out of work, despite having various degrees in higher education. The seemingly

FIGURE 1.2   Exterior of Cedarwood Primary School. Photo by author, 2012

insurmountable legacies of colonialism and apartheid are particularly striking in parts of the country like Kamva.

I chose this small inland town along the national highway as the site
in which to navigate the central problems explored in this book: democracy, nostalgia, education, and youth. This community is simultaneously
fairly distinct and nondescript, providing a portrait of the lives of many
rural Black South Africans today. On the one hand, the town and its surroundings bear the unique history of the Mpondomise clan, a prominent
cultural affiliation and distinctive identity marker within the larger population that now is lumped together under the umbrella "Xhosa" (Peires
2003). The area also is in close proximity to Nelson Mandela's birthplace,
Qunu, a place that looms large in the national imagination. This notable
background has served to bolster Xhosa pride in the region as the birthplace not just of Mandela but also of many notable Freedom Fighters
during the antiapartheid struggle such as Steve Biko and Oliver Tambo.
(This history also means the area is a stronghold of the ANC, making
the nostalgia for the apartheid era chronicled later in this book particularly notable and troubling.) And yet Kamva is illustrative of a typical
rural South African town that remains far from the tourist circuits and
geographic portraits of the country that comprise the national and international imaginary of the postapartheid nation. In general, residents take

great pride in these ancestral homelands but also resent what seems like a government that has turned its back on them. The area suffers from profound social, economic, and political inequality.

While this book begins in Kamva, it does not stop at the town's opaque and somewhat sleepy borders. Instead, it meanders through nearby rural hilltop villages hidden away on dirt roads, passes the quiet port city of East London to the south, gives a nod to Johannesburg's sprawling and highly segregated suburbs several hundred kilometers north, and spends time far away in the shadows of Cape Town's majestic Table Mountain, exploring the wealthy urban environs of that city's Central Business District where NGOs like Sonke are headquartered. Much in the way that Charles Piot's *Remotely Global* (1999) portrayed the seemingly isolated and yet deeply intertwined rural communities of northern Togo, I envision Kamva as a root system that anchors a vast network of people and places around the country rather than some sort of rural backwater. This interconnection is essential to grasping how local understandings of democracy depend on larger national and global processes.

In 2012, I lived in Kamva for most of the year, embedding myself in the local community by living with a local family and doing hundreds of hours of participant observation in public schools. This took varying forms: sometimes I shared crowded desks at the back of classrooms with students, and at other times I sat in teachers' lounges having casual conversations about everything from curricula to discipline. When I first told my Capetonian friends that I would be doing fieldwork in this small rural Eastern Cape town, they were both incredulous and full of pity. "Why would you go to one of those dusty places? There's nothing to do," said a friend who had worked hard to escape such parts of the country and start a new life in the city years earlier. Kamva is a place that most people experience as a blur through a car window on the N2. In a country still deeply divided by race, it is a place that white people in particular tend to pass through without slowing down. And for its five thousand or so residents,[2] Kamva exists as a place in between: in between urban and rural, in between the past and the future, in between love and hate. You can walk from one end of town to the other along the N2 in about ten or fifteen minutes. Along the way, you will see a few large supermarkets, some small shops selling clothing and imported cheap electronics, a pharmacy, a health clinic, a doctor's office, and a few banks. If you choose to turn onto one of the handful of side streets, you will pass family-owned shops offering everything from cell phones to shoes to haircuts, all in one room, and that room will often be a converted shipping container. Continuing along these side streets, lines of caravans offer hot meals for modest prices. Mountains of trash line the edges of green trash cans, with signs exhorting residents, "Keep the Municipality Clean." The taxi stand, with its fleet of minivans that are characteristic of South African cheap public transportation, doubles as a central meeting place where gossip is exchanged, girls are cat-called, and flyers are posted advertising traditional healers specializing in penis enlargements, late-term abortions, and love potions. Despite the town's relatively small population, the streets are constantly thronged with people. In an area with staggering rates of unemployment, the crowds are relentless. In the larger municipality, 48.9 percent of all adults were unemployed in 2011. This is particularly troubling given the number of young people in the area: that same year, 38.3 percent of the population was under fourteen years of age. These bleak statistics help explain why people are fleeing the area to look for work; the municipality had a negative growth rate of 0.75 percent as of 2016 (Statistics South Africa 2016a).

While there are a few immigrant store owners and teachers from other countries, 94.3 percent of the municipality's population identify themselves as native Xhosa speakers. Most of these people live outside the town center, in one of the numerous hilltop villages dotting the relatively treeless, green landscape of rolling hills. The area was cleared long ago to make way for agriculture and pastoral subsistence, with a few man-made lumber fields the only exception. These villages are characterized by central outdoor taps where residents gather water for drinking, cooking, and washing, in addition to the large, bright green rainwater buckets attached to most house gutters.

In 2011, a mere 2.9 percent of residents had flush toilets connected to a sewer system (in an age of increasing neoliberal privatization, those few wealthy families that can afford it pay an independent company to install indoor plumbing). Homesteads usually have small vegetable and fruit gardens, and there are still large swaths of mostly empty government-sponsored houses that were constructed as part of the Reconstruction and Development Program (RDP) enacted soon after the fall of apartheid. Most villages have at least one family-owned tavern where primarily men and teenaged boys drink cheap beer and pass the time (Beinart 1981). By residents' own accounts, alcoholism is something of an epidemic here,

FIGURE 1.3   Village outside Kamva. Photo by author, 2012

FIGURE 1.4   Kamva, as seen from the National Highway in spring. Photo by author, 2012

obviously connected to the lack of jobs. Most people live with extended families on the same land for many generations, and kinship patterns loosely follow the traditional patrilineal and patrilocal descent and residence patterns of the past (Wilson 1982). It should be noted, however, that this is rapidly changing as teenage pregnancies, deaths from HIV/AIDS, and rampant unemployment increasingly push women and grandparents into the position of household heads and subvert more traditional patterns of patriarchy.

HISTORY OF THE TRANSKEI AND XHOSA IDENTITY

While it may be surprising that the residents of a former apartheid homeland wax nostalgically for elements of life under a racist regime, understanding Kamva's rich history of political resistance and complex experiences of colonization puts this contemporary dissatisfaction in perspective. The Eastern Cape was incorporated into the Cape Colony in 1870. Conflicts between British colonists and local African clans were bloody and lasted decades in a series of violent battles now referred to as the Xhosa Frontier Wars. In 1880, two local chiefs rebelled against the government and killed a white colonist, escalating interracial violence. Seeking vengeance for the murder of one of their own, as was the case across colonial Africa, they created factions among locals and purposely fomented exaggerated ethnic divisions between clans while lumping others together (Beinart 1981). In the process, the British greatly reduced chiefly powers, spread devastating diseases, and took control of farmland (Crais and McClendon 2014; Soga 1930; Thompson 1990). As I explain below, these events helped solidify a more uniform "Xhosa" identity that belies a far more complex picture of precolonial ethnicity.

Since Xhosa society had previously relied on cattle herding and farming, the transition to a market-based capitalist economy and loss of land-ownership were devastating to local barter economies and sparked the early stages of dependency on Western capital and commodities. Though they occurred nearly two hundred years ago, these events remain relevant in a province characterized by extreme poverty due to lack of employment and ceding of the most arable land during apartheid. An examination of the economic norms that existed within Xhosa communities of the rural Eastern Cape prior to colonial encounters in the 1800s further explains the disjunctures between established social norms in Kamva and the changes wrought by capitalist, consumer culture. Before colonial contact, wealth in Xhosa communities of the Eastern Cape centered on cattle; a family's value was determined not just by the number of cattle owned but also by their quality, using a barter economy that made the turn toward a market-based economy dependent on notions of private property somewhat alien for most people (Comaroff and Comaroff 1990). Cattle was a familial marker of personal wealth, but Xhosa chiefs acted as stewards of communally shared land, and any uninhabited tracts were public grazing ground, not private property. As Monica Hunter recorded in the 1930s, an owner's personal possessions were allegedly destroyed on his death, and thus significant differences in inheritance practices caused widespread resistance to the colonial inheritance laws instituted in the early 1900s (Hunter 1936). People understood wealth and status during this period in a way that greatly contrasts with colonial and contemporary South Africa, where the elite are now recognized by their expensive cars, their large houses in urban areas, and their ability to enrich the status of family members and friends rather than their community as a whole (Jeske 2016).

Therefore, colonial interventions in the economic life of the Eastern Cape, as in the rest of the colonized world, had drastic effects on the daily lives of Xhosa individuals as well as larger community structures. An oft-cited example of this phenomenon is in the dramatic and devastating Xhosa Cattle Killings of 1856–57, in which firmly rooted epistemologies of witchcraft and spirituality coincided with the impact of a recently introduced and foreign market economy. As historians have pointed out, contact with white settlers during this year brought about a lethal and widespread cattle lung disease that devastated herds across the Eastern Cape region. Several Xhosa prophets at the time understood this event as the work of witchcraft plaguing the community, though they also blended these beliefs with recently introduced concepts from Christian missionaries, suggesting that the evils wrought on the community were punishment for sinful behaviors. One young female prophet, Nongqawuse, returned from a long journey and reported meeting three of her ancestors, who insisted that all crops and remaining cattle be destroyed in order to start anew and save their people. Large-scale slaughter of livestock soon followed her prophecy; historians estimate that approximately

400,000 head of cattle were killed intentionally, leading to widespread starvation among the population that led to the death of some 40,000 Xhosa individuals (Peires 1989; Thompson 1990). One of the major long-term consequences of this event was increased economic dependency on the nearby white settler communities for trading of goods, which further pushed rural villages into a market-based cash economy and secured the frontier for the British.

The Xhosa Cattle Killings and related historical events provide useful evidence of the contrasting economic and spiritual systems that existed between Xhosa and European settler communities in their first years of contact and also shows the ways in which the introduction of a market economy extensively transformed, and in many cases devastated, rural societies (Hunter 1936). So great were these differences, in fact, that the South African anthropologist Monica Wilson (neé Hunter), known for her rare ethnographic portrait of twentieth-century Eastern Cape life, suggested in 1936 that the increasing rift she observed between generations of Xhosa males could be explained by these drastic economic changes. She saw young boys gaining new forms of economic independence through the market economy that she hypothesized were eroding traditional mechanisms of social control within the household and larger community (Hunter 1936, 178). Wilson's observations have clear parallels to my own descriptions of the ways in which new rights discourses and worldviews are challenging and perhaps inverting established social hierarchies, as detailed in later chapters. One interesting example is the male circumcision ritual traditionally used to indicate entrance into adulthood and readiness for marriage and ownership of private property. Today the ritual may look the same, but it has different implications: the shift to a global market economy combined with the remnants of apartheid segregation means that initiates cannot depend on work or marriage to mark their transition. In reality, after circumcision many of these young men continue to live at home with parents, grandparents, or other caretakers. In addition, the ceremony that follows circumcision, the *umgidi*, has been transformed from the spiritual entrance into the community of men into what many people report is a spectacle of wealth accumulation. Many adults complain that an umgidi used to involve a few small gifts, some traditional beer, and advice for the initiate. Today the young man is lavished with relatively large amounts of cash, household goods, and store-bought alcohol—in addition to the more traditional rounds of advice, singing, praying, and food and drink. People have suggested to me that this dilutes the symbolic importance of the ritual, instead adapting it to the norms of a capitalist state.

Despite these massive changes in economic life, some of the precolonial forms of ownership and wealth accumulation persist into the present day in places like Kamva, albeit in ever-evolving forms and with constantly renegotiated meanings. The example of *lobola* (bride-price) is particularly visible and common in the rural Eastern Cape as evidence of practices that remain widespread. Although many families no longer own cattle and Christian missionaries worked hard to outlaw the practice of lobola altogether as an alleged example of paganism and subjugation of women,[3] the amount owed to a bride's family is almost always still negotiated in terms of the value of cows—even if this is done in rhetoric only. During negotiations, families discuss how many "cows" the bride is worth and must be given to her family—a practice still common even in urban families far removed both geographically and historically from pastoralist traditions (Mtuze 2004). Such instances remind us that the introduction of a global market economy does not necessarily dissolve local agency but rather intersects to form new negotiations of practices on the ground.

Other precolonial systems of economic organization continue into the contemporary era. For instance, in Kamva and other rural areas of the Eastern Cape many women have economic support networks in small village settlements that provide assistance to fellow members when they are in need, such as helping with the cost of a funeral or giving extra crops to a hungry family. These women's groups meet frequently, discussing internal solutions to community challenges and collecting funds for future use. They create a sense of community beyond nuclear family models and support previously established clan connections that emphasize communalism over individual accumulation. They also offer an accessible alternative to state-regulated banking, which feels out of reach to most poor rural residents. I often witnessed female neighbors exchanging goods with each other. When one woman had an abundance of a certain crop in her garden, she would give some to a neighbor whose crop had been poor that year. This was not explained to me in altruistic terms; rather, it was insurance against future hardship by creating debt relationships that are mutually beneficial. As Tando put it, "The good thing about living in rural areas is that people here help each other. When there is spinach here, and the neighbors are not doing well with spinach, we give them spinach. And then they give us the things we are not doing well in." We can read in these seemingly small, quotidian acts the persistence of communal identification practices and resistance to forms of twenty-first-century individualism that stand in stark contrast to the movement of capital and naturalization of private property in a neoliberal economy.

Falling into the broader Nguni language group, Xhosa is considered part of the historical category "Bantu" or "Nguni," a group of people who spoke a common language and spread from West and Central Africa to southern Africa in ancient times (Alves et al. 2011; Meintjes 1998; Soga 1931). Today the word *Xhosa* usually refers to a group of people who share a linguistic and cultural heritage. Despite the dangers of cultural essentialism, I use the term because it remains a significant marker of identity to millions of people in South Africa and is one people use readily in self-descriptions and as a source of cultural pride. Nonetheless, like any other identifier, *Xhosa* has a porous boundary that people move in and out of depending on context. Fundani once explained to me in a conversation about Xhosa circumcision and the controversy surrounding it today how the long-standing clan differences in the area have become largely erased in the national imagination. He referred to his clan membership in the Bhacas and used that position to express outrage over a rite of passage that endangers the lives of young men.

> I come from a different school of thought because I'm a Bhaca. Bhacas used to not circumcise. It's only now they have started. They adopted it, I believe, because they were influenced by the other tribes. I believe what changed them so much was that those who started to be circumcised were learning in St. John's.[4] Those who were in St. John's were influenced and were called *inkwenkwes*, which means a boy. And that's when they started to be circumcised. Now the whole nation, even the Bhacas, has this ritual.

As Fundani succinctly demonstrates here, Xhosa "culture" has of course never been monolithic and static, a fact to which plenty of historical accounts also attest (e.g., Hunter 1936; McAllister 1989; Mills 1992; Soga 1931; Wilson 1982). And yet most Kamva residents identify as Xhosa along with other forms of clan identification. The label "Xhosa" refers to a broad category of differentiated clan groupings that have over the centuries been pitted against one another and then culturally assimilated, to some extent, through British colonization and then apartheid. In the act of working to secure the frontier of the Cape Colony, colonists drastically reshaped social organization (Lester 1997). And yet many of the precolonial clan designations remain salient and distinctive today (Beinart and Bundy 1987). In ways similar to other ethnic designations across the postcolonial world, "Xhosa" is a political and historical category manufactured through and reified by settler colonialism and racial ideology that nonetheless is still central to the identities of millions of people.

Xhosa speakers historically divide themselves into successively smaller kinship units, a system still at least partly in use today (Mtuze 2004; Soga 1931), as illustrated below.

Nation → Tribe → Clan → Lineage → Umzi (Household)

While the *umzi* is the basic family unit, it should not be confused with Western notions of the nuclear family. A typical umzi consists of not just parents and children, but uncles, aunts, cousins, and grandparents; the HIV/AIDS epidemic has left many children to be raised by grandparents or other extended family members. Historically, the clan was defined as "a group all members of which trace patrilineal descent from a common ancestor" (Hunter 1936, 52). While marriage restrictions have changed over time and families have spread out geographically, the patrilineal clan unit remains a central concept in Xhosa identity practices and marriage is still largely exogamous. In Kamva, clan names are used affectionately in daily greetings, and those within your clan expect a great deal of hospitality, kindness, and loyalty as compared to others outside the clan. Xhosa people often refer to those within their clan as *bhuti* (brother) or *sisi* (sister) to indicate the familial closeness of this relationship and the mutual obligation of assistance and support. This further illuminates how Xhosa identity practices continue to rely on a communal, non-Western view of the family that has ramifications for child-rearing, material property arrangements, and social obligations (see, e.g., Hammond-Tooke 1985).

The economic shifts of modernity have had indirect but significant impacts on the makeup of Xhosa families (Weiss 2004). People in the Eastern Cape have increasingly moved to nuclear family arrangements, at times forsaking the umzi as the basic social unit. Previous generations of Xhosa sons would have been expected to marry and build a second

FIGURE 1.5 Typical *umzi* in Kamva. Photo by author, 2012

structure on the family property. Today many young couples move to homesteads away from kin or to urban centers and start new households nearer to employment opportunities. Fundani is an apt example of this. His mother, Tando's grandmother, wishes her son would put his salary toward an indoor bathroom for her rural home, something only a few wealthy families in her community have and that she desperately wants. But at the time of this writing Fundani increasingly resided in the city with his wife, son, and stepson and aspired to using any discretionary income to save for a vacation abroad rather than contribute to his ancestral home. Contemporary shifts in residence patterns such as this both arise from and affect social and economic realities, removing wage earners from the umzi and taking the power of social control over youth out of the hands of grandparents and great-grandparents. In many cases, today the umzi is a place children visit with their parents on school holidays, where they are inculcated with reified notions of Xhosa "culture" before returning to urban life.

Contemporary perspectives on kinship in the Eastern Cape provide an example of just how inadequate "tradition" is as a signifier for long-standing cultural practice and how much things have changed in the modern era. Kinship terms that denote respect, largely falling along gendered and generational lines, are still central to family formations; they structure the social roles and responsibilities in the family and delineate inheritance patterns. Although there are increasing shifts to teenage births and absent fathers, most people adhere to patrilineal rules for things like lineage, surnames, and land inheritance. In most Xhosa households, the mother's brother ranks highest when a father is absent, as is often the case today. This uncle is the authority responsible for almost all major decision making, a positioning that has deep historical roots but has been recontextualized in the age of AIDS (Soga 1931). Previous incarnations of the family would have seen the children's genitor as household head; twenty-first-century sexual, reproductive, residence, and labor practices have altered the way this cultural schema manifests itself, though they have certainly not dissolved patriarchal ideologies. Today a brother or grandparent often stands in for a father who is working in the mines, who has died of complications from HIV/AIDS, or who never took financial or social responsibility for the child because he or she was the product of an extramarital teenage sexual encounter; these are all relatively frequent occurrences. The change in family arrangements and residence patterns among South Africans is closely connected to the transition to a capitalist economy and the resultant lack of property among those living in poverty (Bourgois 1995; Goode and Maskovsky 2001). Furthermore, scholars have argued that the political protest movements of the apartheid era impacted intergenerational relationships and shifted young people away from official marriage arrangements, though this likely was more common in the urban areas (Bank 2011; Makhulu 2015). Still, these types of family shifts are evident in the ethnographic accounts of the anthropologist Zolani Ngwane (2001, 405), who witnessed the changes in the rural Eastern Cape town of Cancele in the late twentieth century: "The generational impacts I observed at Cancele in 1996 reflected shifts in power relations within local institutions of social reproduction precipitated by nation-wide labor cutbacks that peaked in the mid-1980s, leaving a lot of older men from Cancele unemployed and young men of school-leaving age with no job prospects." In Cancele a rise in unemployment radically altered the social structure of domestic spaces. Men were no longer able to maintain social and economic dominance over their families through labor, which had serious consequences for notions of masculinity and gender relations.

The role of the *magoti*, or daughter-in-law, provides a vivid example of hierarchy's continuing importance, as well as the recent shifts in terms of both age and gender in Xhosa ideology. In 2012, while I was living in Kamva, Fundani was negotiating lobola with his childhood neighbors and future in-laws, finalizing his impending marriage to their daughter. At the time, Buhle, the soon-to-be bride, lived almost full-time in the city of East London, where she worked as a medical laboratory technician for a large company. Buhle embodied the plural identities many Eastern Cape residents negotiate in the contemporary moment, and this became increasingly evident as she took up the role of magoti. On weekends or holidays when she visited, she dressed in traditional clothes reserved exclusively for this role, including a head covering, apron, and long skirt. She responded to a new first name chosen by her husband's mother, the matriarch of the household. Her days were perhaps the busiest of anyone's: she cooked all the meals, served her future mother-in-law in bed, and cleaned the house constantly. While we talked as she stirred a pot of *isidudu*,[5] she would excitedly tell me in whispers that she wore spaghetti-strap dresses in East London (clandestinely showing me photos on her mobile phone), worked out at the Virgin Active luxury gym, and had altered her diet to include low-fat items in an attempt to lose weight. "When I cook boneless, skinless chicken breasts," Fundani exclaims, "this is not meat!" Despite such seemingly fractious realities, Buhle does not seem conflicted or troubled. Rather, she is able to emphasize different parts of her identity depending on the appropriate context (Hall 2002). Buhle's dual existence illustrates the complex roles that Xhosa youth work to negotiate today as they balance rural kin commitments with new urban realities of the capitalist state.

The intervention of Christian missionaries from Europe, primarily in the mid-nineteenth century, played a significant role in transforming and renegotiating Xhosa cultural practices and social norms in what is now the Eastern Cape. While different Christian denominations varied in their positions vis-à-vis local customs, missionaries universally challenged precolonial practices when they clashed with Christian theology (Mills 1992). These early missionaries rejected widespread practices central to social life, such as polygamy, lobola, initiation, and ancestor worship. Xhosa communities were hardly passive recipients of Christianity, but they adopted some ideas more readily than others; in particular, conceptions of heaven and hell and the resurrection seemed to fill a gap in local cosmology (Peires 2003). In contrast, missionaries' desire to stamp out beliefs in witchcraft was met with fierce resistance, as it was instead locally interpreted as a call to let evil go unchecked. The varying success of individual missionaries effectively, though gradually, transformed household relations and family structures in ways that had significant consequences for local gender and generational relations (Hunter 1936). Crucially, chiefs often received and accepted missionary activity not because of a genuine change of faith but rather as a conscientious political strategy in the face of violent colonial incursions on their frontier. Even where missionaries failed to eradicate practices deemed pagan, they often transformed them in significant ways; efforts to stamp out ritual circumcision because it was deemed satanic may have failed, for example, but many historians suggest this opposition was a major factor in the relatively recent shortening of the ritual from months to weeks (Mills 1992).

Christian missionaries also played a central role in defining and entrenching what is considered tradition, both in the Eastern Cape and throughout the colonial world. Natasha Erlank (2003, 940) explains that "the missionaries viewed their efforts to reform African behavior as stemming from their Christian belief but, in doing so, however inadvertently, they were also contributing to the process of identity-creation. In focusing on African practice and custom . . . they participated in defining the cultural characteristics of the groups they were attempting to convert." This was especially true with regard to gender relations, which is highy relevant to my later discussion of resistance to liberalism's agenda of equality. In her work, Erlank describes how missionary campaigns to recast the female initiation ceremony, *intonjane*, and lobola actually shifted the entire burden of guilt surrounding sexual transgressions from the broader community to individual women and thus helped cast women in subjugated roles vis-à-vis their male counterparts. The historical underpinnings of contemporary social practices such as these are often obscured in the present day, leading many people to describe certain cultural forms as an essential feature of Xhosa identity when they in fact have far more recent origins.

Today towns like Kamva are predominantly Christian, though hardly uniform in terms of religious belief or denomination. In 2012, the town boasted an impressive variety of churches for a relatively small community: Methodist, African Zionist, Anglican, Roman Catholic, Lutheran, and Baptist. Although general Christian principles are a ubiquitous and constant presence, there is great variation in the specifics of how these ideological systems work and what they mean for everyday lives, as anywhere else. Residents in the Kamva area who identify with precolonial ancestral beliefs have lives structured in very different ways. Though 2011 statistics cite a mere 0.3 percent of the population as practicing "Traditional Ancestral Religion" (Lehohla 2011), this number likely does not account for those who blend precolonial and colonial religious systems in novel and hybrid ways and might not identify as such. In earlier periods, non-Christian believers were referred to as the Red Xhosa, as opposed to the School Xhosa, a group that included those who were more adapted to Western ways of life and attended government schools and missionary churches (Mayer and Mayer 1970). Today such binaries are far less useful for understanding moral and ethical perspectives.

More illustrative than these broad dichotomies are the actual ways people engage with religion in the twenty-first century. For instance, one day in 2012 I was transcribing interviews in the teacher's lounge of a local school. Suddenly, a teacher dragged in a fifteen-year-old student who was convulsing and shaking. Alarmed, I assumed she was having an epileptic seizure. Two of the teachers present promptly began to administer what I can only describe as an exorcism, rapidly repeating Christian prayers with appeals to Jesus and grasping the girl's hands tightly on either side. I implored them to let me take her to the nearby hospital for medical treatment. This was apparently viewed not only as unhelpful but also as absolutely hilarious.[6] The shaking and seizing eventually stopped, and the ritual prayers were declared successful. The evidence was considered irrefutable: had they not administered the rites and soon after seen the problem disappear? After the girl left, they explained to me that the many small, vertical scars on the girl's face were evidence of the demon struggling to scratch its way from the inside out. In contrast, someone at the school later informed me that her family adhered to ancestor worship rather than Christianity and that these were examples of ritual scarification meant to cure her debilitating condition. While the scene in the teacher's lounge reminded me of the widespread alignment with charismatic Christianity among many of the town's residents, the girl's less public reality at home also affirmed the continued presence of precolonial belief systems that centuries of missionary activity failed to completely stamp out and that remain integrated with Christian beliefs.

Historically, each Xhosa clan has a chief who is the senior male of the royal bloodline and inherits the position from his father. Although they still exist, the chief's role has changed dramatically through colonialism and subsequent political regime changes. Before the arrival of

Europeans in the Eastern Cape, the chief facilitated a kind of direct democracy, instead of acting as an autocratic ruler (Mtuze 2004; Soga 1931).
The community maintained a system of checks and balances through an
inherited Court of Councillors that safeguarded against at least some
forms of chiefly abuse of power. This is particularly interesting in light of
present-day Kamva residents' vocal disappointment with democracy; in
many ways, preapartheid Xhosa society may have been closer to the ideals
of democracy than current political incarnations. This once again suggests
that democracy is often a scapegoat for issues like structural inequality
and political corruption.

While the explicit kinship structures and performative aspects of the
chieftaincy may look the same as they did centuries ago, the realities of
a chief's position today are quite different. The South African Constitution explicitly protects the "right to traditional leaders," but the rest of the
document circumscribes such leaders' powers in significant ways. While
a Xhosa chief may invoke culture to resist state legislative power, he is
unable to overrule juridical decisions based on the constitution. In the
democratic state, then, a chief's position is much more ambiguous than it
once was. Today Xhosa chiefs maintain their titles and continue to settle
local disputes in traditional courts while they earn salaries for their appointments through the municipal government. The constitution sees
this as a way to recognize and respect local cultural systems in a pluralistic state. Precolonial Xhosa politics and social life frequently relied on
adherence to the cultural concept of *ubuntu*, which loosely translates as
"humanity." This concept remains crucial to many Xhosa speakers today.
Early chiefs were meant, at least in theory, to facilitate equal political representation rather than wield total authority.

What these portrayals and descriptions of Xhosa identity ought to
convey, then, is how culture is inextricably intertwined with historical,
political, and economic structures in ways that obfuscate any clear understanding of its alleged "origins." In South Africa's contemporary climate of multiculturalism and ostensible tolerance for diversity, Xhosa
identity remains a source of great pride for millions of people. History and culture are dynamic processes that affect the specific instantiations of democracy in contemporary South Africa, not to mention
elsewhere, in terms of both ideology and everyday practice. The architecture of apartheid that unfolded from the 1940s through the 1980s
demonstrates how entrenched systems of racial and ethnic classification

and increasing economic inequality played a role in rural household re-organization, kinship patterns, the naturalization of capitalism, and the privatization of social services.

CREATION OF THE TRANSKEI: THE APARTHEID YEARS

It hardly bears stating that South Africa's long struggle with racist apartheid policy continues to permeate the social, psychological, political, and economic lives of South Africans on a daily basis. This policy of separation based on a hierarchy of racial characteristics codified discrimination in an insidious legal framework, affecting virtually all facets of life for South Africans during the period from 1948 to 1994. Apartheid, an Afrikaans word literally meaning "apartness," was introduced to the country in 1948 by the National Party after it narrowly won elections that year. Previously, Black South Africans had been gradually disenfranchised until they were only eligible to vote in elections specific to segregated communities, or in rare cases of exception for property ownership. The National Party's electoral victory can be attributed at least in part to economic relations and class struggles handed down from previous administrations and colonialist histories, as well as the quirks of the country's "First Past the Post" electoral system (Southall 2001). The 1940s saw many white farmers complaining of labor shortages and fierce competition in international capitalist markets. Apartheid's design appealed to those whites wishing to alleviate the labor needs of commercial agriculture and decrease wage competition through strict control of nonwhites' physical movement within the country and suppression of their political and economic rights. Rather than abruptly alter life in South Africa, however, apartheid was a slow ramping up of legislation that took as its foundation earlier colonial histories of racial hierarchy and prejudice.

In the early days of apartheid, the National Party passed a series of legislative acts designed to control the influx of people into cities, colloquially referred to as "pass laws." These were especially oppressive because they restricted movement and separated people from their families (Posel 1991). Under the Population Registration Act of 1950, South African residents were deemed "white," "coloured," or "Native" (the category "Asian" was added later); people were separated according to clusters of physical characteristics beyond just skin color (Clark and Worger 2004).[7] In 1952, the Native Laws Amendment Act was passed, which expanded earlier legislation and required all nonwhite people to carry a reference book that temporarily authorized them to work and live in areas within what was then officially South Africa.

Black South Africans were denied equal education under the infamous 1953 Bantu Education Act, which consolidated control of schools—many of which were previously missionary run—under the government, isolating African students from other races and teaching them only the skills deemed necessary for vocational labor (see ch. 4). In 1976, a further blow to Black students legislated that they would now only learn in Afrikaans, banning native languages such as Xhosa and Zulu in the classroom. Beyond the classroom, nonwhites were forced to use separate facilities in public spaces, such as toilets, drinking fountains, swimming pools, and building entrances.

Later years of the apartheid regime saw the government capitalize on the earlier British colonial administration's African "reserves" from the Natives' Land Act of 1913, using legislation to forcibly remove non-whites from economically desirable urban areas in order to make room for white residents. In 1959, then Prime Minister Hendrik Verwoerd, considered one of the main architects of apartheid, announced plans to set up areas colloquially called "Bantustans" that were specifically for Black residents. Bantustans were meant, at least in theory, to act as separate African chiefdoms with their own ruling bodies removed from the South African state, and in 1976 the government declared four of these homelands independent (though the international community never recognized them as such). Though in government rhetoric this was to be "separate but equal," the effect was to trap Blacks in rural areas and give them almost no access to viable education or employment opportunities, forcing migrant labor into the low-paid and dangerous mining industries. Apartheid's architects found support for these segregated homelands in racist evolutionary theory. They deemed Africans biologically distinct from and mentally and culturally inferior to whites, therefore suggesting they required different environments in order to thrive (Pells 1938).[8]

Bantustan residents were stripped of South African citizenship and could only enter adjacent regions with passes based on employment that required frequent renewal and were difficult to obtain. This meant that many young people of working age migrated to cities such as Cape Town, Johannesburg, and Pretoria for jobs, effectively splintering families and subjecting them to violent police brutality for the virtually unavoidable and constant violations of pass laws. Many young men traveled from places like Kamva to find work in the extractive mining industry, which involved extremely dangerous labor practices, constant job insecurity, and poor pay. A consequence of this system of labor was that many women and children were left behind as men migrated to urban employment centers and mining communities. The older Kamva residents portrayed in this book remember needing a pass if they wanted to enter East London, a city only about three hundred kilometers away and at the time across an "international" border (Clark and Worger 2004, 65–66).

Kamva is located in what was once the Transkei Bantustan,[9] and thus its residents have histories distinct from their urban counterparts that were structured by apartheid, not to mention the events preceding it. The Transkei was just south of the independent nation of Lesotho and hugs the Indian Ocean coast (see front matter map).

Though racist ideologies of white supremacy served as an explicit justification for apartheid, materialist perspectives on this period in history illustrate how economic relations of the capitalist economy drove many decisions and cannot be separated from racial legislation. Segregation did not just separate out undesirable phenotypic characteristics; it also allowed a white minority to stay in power through the exploitation of cheap labor, profit maximization, and the maintenance of ownership over the means of production. The dissolution of the Black family unit through the migrant labor and pass systems ensured an ample work force and helped prevent insurrection. Moreover, Bantu education effectively curbed social upheaval and rebellion for years by providing inadequate schooling in separate native languages. Therefore, we see how apartheid relied on racist ideology in order to secure the country's wealth through the exploitation of Black labor and the formation of social classes along distinctly racial lines. Under apartheid, the homelands acted as labor reserves from which able-bodied residents would migrate for temporary employment in urban or mining areas. Anne-Maria Makhulu (2015, 8) aptly describes this system as paradoxical, in that it was "built on Black labor that was at one and the same time sequestered at a distance from those centers of industrial production that that very same Black laboring class helped to sustain." In other words, apartheid was structured on the backs of Black bodies while simultaneously relegating those bodies to the geographic, political, and economic periphery.

As a response to the economic motivations of the National Party government, the antiapartheid movement of the 1970s and 1980s relied heavily on the Marxist ideology of workers' unions, rebellion against the ruling class, and calls to seize modes of production that were in the hands of the very few (Chipkin 2007). As in many other countries across the postcolonial world, the conflation of race and class has had serious consequences for South Africans beyond the years of apartheid, creating a rationale that justified oppression and has perpetuated dependency relationships that continue into the democratic era.

Meanwhile, homeland residents in places like the Transkei survived under apartheid partly through subsistence agriculture that the government strategically and consciously prevented from transforming into a profit-making system. Specifically, agricultural production declined in the later years of apartheid, and some scholars attribute this to the South African government's increase in taxes and seizure of Black-controlled farmland. Such measures had the obviously intentional effect of forcing people into the migrant labor force on which white society had increasingly come to depend (Knight and Lenta 1980). The economics of apartheid created a sort of revolving door with respect to the homelands, to which people were often forcibly removed and in which they maintained part-time residences. In the cities, the legal restrictions of apartheid drove many of these would-be returnees to illegal squatter camps on the peripheries. Police frequently razed these camps, and their physical and social remnants underlie many of today's township communities on the outskirts of cities like Cape Town and Johannesburg (Makhulu 2015). Under apartheid, homelands like the Transkei were treated as reservoirs meant to retain Black labor under inferior conditions for the sole benefit of white capitalism (Thompson 1990). The end of apartheid may have transformed this ideology, but it did little for the racial and economic realities in such places. These historical events help us situate the struggles of young people like Tando and give perspective to the vastly unequal opportunities with which they are presented today.

This history of the creation of the "independent" Transkei and the subsequent conditions of life within it is central to my framing of today's nostalgia for the past on the part of Eastern Cape residents. Fundani told me that when he was a child he had no awareness that he was a member of an oppressed group. This was what the architects of apartheid had deliberately planned: white supremacy was ensured for decades via the carefully crafted illusion of political and social autonomy. Of course, this is not to say that residents of the Transkei easily acquiesced to domination or sat idly by as whites profited from Black labor. During the height of Bantu Education, chiefs found ways to continue propagating native African languages in classrooms. In the 1950s and 1960s, a widespread agrarian social movement arose in the form of vigilante groups seeking to control rampant cattle theft; some of these individuals eventually aligned with and became part of the ANC (Crais 1998). Although these groups were notably violent and their tactics bordered on something of a witch-hunt (at times in the actual sense of the word), they can also be viewed as an incipient form of class consciousness and political organizing in the area that sought to resist economic oppression. Nonetheless, these acts of resistance were often invisible to people like Fundani who were children at the time. At the same time, some chiefs collaborated with the apartheid government, as in the notable example of the Matanzima brothers who controlled the Transkei for decades and became exceedingly wealthy in the process (Thompson 1990; van Niekerk 1987).

While underground organizing and resistance occurred throughout the apartheid era, by the 1970s resistance had become especially violent. What followed was a nationwide fight against the politics of white supremacy that galvanized the support of the international community and led to apartheid's fall in 1994. Young people made up a critical portion of the resistance against the apartheid government in later years of the regime,[10] often through membership in the ANC and its associated Youth League (ANCYL). The latter was founded in 1944 and then banned by the government in 1960, along with its mother organization, as conspirators against the state. Nonetheless, these political bodies continued to work underground toward a nonracial society; many members went into exile abroad where they continued their work. The ANCYL served as a radical faction of young Black people who constantly challenged the party to align their protests with the "grievances and interests of the masses" (Posel 2013). In this sense, the Youth League retained decision-making autonomy while existing under the political umbrella of the ANC (de Beer 1991). During the antiapartheid movement, protest activity was increasingly carried out by young men with violent force, constructing a politics of aggression and hypermasculinity as a method of resisting disenfranchisement and entrenched racism. Even Mandela, famed for his long adherence to nonviolent protest, eventually declared that violence would be necessary to dismantle the apartheid government (Mandela 2007). During the last decades of apartheid, many ANC and Youth

League members went abroad to communist countries such as the Soviet Union, East Germany, and Cuba to receive military and ideological training from allies. Mounting external pressures from other nations, including the United States, played a critical role in toppling the apartheid regime for good. For instance, in 1986 the U.S. Congress passed legislation that mandated a boycott of new South African investments, bank loans, air links, and many imports. Many international universities stopped inviting white South African academics to speak at their schools. South Africa was banned from participation in the Olympics for nearly twenty years.

The Transkei played a historic and legendary role in antiapartheid politics. Many of its famous Freedom Fighters worked underground during the apartheid years (Mandela perhaps the most famous among them). These individuals relied on regional networks that had links to national ANC organizing, though it should be noted that the boundaries between antiapartheid organizing and regional Bantustan leadership (working for the apartheid state) were porous and sometimes ambiguous (Gibbs 2011). Many of the ANC comrades working underground during the apartheid years were educated at rural missionary schools, further demonstrating the importance of educational institutions in South African political history.

The former Transkei looms large in the history of South African ethnography and the field of Africanist anthropology more broadly. A great deal of early twentieth-century South African anthropology arose from racist beliefs in separate development and links with colonialism and apartheid, most notably in the racist *volkekunde* school, where pseudoscientific views on race provided justification for separate development and oppression (Mamdani 1996). There were, however, pockets of progressive African scholars committed to anthropology's examination of culture as a way to resist the apartheid government. At Fort Hare University in Alice, Eastern Cape, the anthropology department was a meeting place for liberal and often-subversive scholars of South Africa, such as Monica Wilson, Hilda Kuper, Godfrey Pitje, Livingstone Mqotsi, Max Gluckman, and Jack Simons; the department was racially and culturally diverse, highly unusual for its time. These scholars rejected the volkekunde tradition in favor of studies that emphasized African nationalism and agency and were interested in questions of social cohesion and change (Bank 2016). In many ways, this book revisits some of those early topics but in a very different social and temporal setting.

THE POSTAPARTHEID EASTERN CAPE:
INEQUALITY AND IDENTITY POLITICS

After years of violent resistance to the apartheid government, the transition to democracy in 1994 was, by many media accounts and compared to fearful expectations, remarkably peaceful (Clark and Worger 2004). It included the drafting of a new constitution with wide protections for all citizens. This document outlines such extensive and thorough human rights legislation that it is often considered the most liberal, progressive, and inclusive constitution in the world (Robins 2008).[11] Part of what I challenge in this book, however, is the document's inclusivity; instead, I illuminate how Western framings of liberal democracy are at the heart of South African legislation post-1994. I also wish to draw attention to the tremendous loss of life and bloodshed that followed after the fall of apartheid, particulary in Black and coloured communities: in fact, the "peaceful transition" heralded in the media often referenced the lack of *white* bloodshed.

The enduring legacy of apartheid is obviously a huge hurdle in the construction of a free and equal society. Despite the incredibly "liberal" South African Constitution and its legislative commitment to a pluralistic and racially integrated society, the majority of South Africans experience unofficial geographic, educational, and social segregation along racial and cultural lines. For instance, Kamva's municipality today is 99.4 percent Black, and 94.3 percent of the population identifies as Xhosa, a demographic makeup that hardly reflects the national population (Lehohla 2011). The 2011 census identified 79.2 percent of the entire national population as "Black African," a designation that lumps Xhosa speakers with other African groups such as Zulu, Ndebele, Sotho, and Pedi.

In South Africa, then, systemic inequality and de facto segregation using previously established racial classifications have carried over into the twenty-first century in numerous ways. South Africa's violent and traumatic history necessitates a detailed understanding of and attention to the ways in which cultural and political realities constantly intersect with and are structured by racial ideologies. Racism in South Africa continues to present itself both subtly and explicitly on a near-constant basis in urban and rural areas alike, despite the nation's sustained rhertorical barrage of postracialism. As a white person in South Africa, heavily prejudiced whites often view me as a confederate and commiserate with me about the perceived innate inadequacies of Black people. Often without hesitation or embarrassment, people tell me that Black South Africans are "lazy," "unappreciative," "unintelligent," and "incapable of learning," to name a few disturbing and essentializing examples. At times, they distinguish the successes of Black Americans from those of Black South Africans, insisting on innate differences based on geographic separation over time. Such instances serve to remind us of the ways in which apartheid racial categories continue to structure the political, social, and economic present, not to mention transnational racial projects cemented during the colonial era. Undergirding such attitudes are histories of a pseudoscientific approach to human diversity that corrupted evolutionary theory and employed it to show race as a hierarchy from inferior to superior, with whites invariably at the top. These tenacious ideas were part and parcel of the colonial project, and they persist in contemporary postcolonies in numerous ways. Thus transnational histories of race and racism intersect with local expressions of identity in places like the Transkei, where residents simultaneously identify as Xhosa, African, Black, and South African, among other things.

Particularly in cities, class mobility across racial lines is growing and shifting the traditional lines of inequality in the country (Ashforth 2005). As a Black meritocracy emerges and nonwhites rise to leadership positions in the corporate sector, previous notions of communist wealth redistribution have been replaced by socialization to global neoliberal ideals of individual accumulation, free market trade, and ever-increasing consumer desires (Chalfin 2010; Robins 2008). In short, by many accounts the ANC has become another handmaiden to global capitalism, a part of Mandela's presidential legacy that celebrated accounts of his life often ignore (Comaroff and Comaroff 2004a, 521). Recently, large swaths of the voting population have abandoned years of ANC loyalty in favor of rival political parties, such as the Economic Freedom Fighters (EFF) and the Democratic Alliance (DA), which have crafted platforms on issues like wealth redistribution and land reform. This is not to say that the apartheid government did not rely heavily on capitalist modes of production—it certainly did, as I have shown—but rather that the postapartheid ANC came to power alongside a particular brand of neoliberalism that has dramatically heightened wealth inequalities and seen market forces gain increasing control over world political processes.

Along with norms of capitalist consumption in South Africa have come widespread reports of corruption in recent years that contribute heavily to current dissatisfaction with the ANC and its leadership. For example, consider the 2014 political and media scandal over Jacob Zuma's Nkandla estate in Kwa-Zulu Natal Province, which included the spending of R206 million on "security upgrades"—including an in-ground swimming pool allegedly designed for fire prevention—and led to a legal investigation and demands for him to pay back a portion of these funds (Evans 2014). This is not unique to South Africa, of course; across the continent, radical independence and Pan-Africanist movements of the 1960s through 1990s have shifted toward normalizing privatization, elitism, and corruption while obscuring their roots in colonial and postcolonial conditions (Apter 1999). For instance, private contracting companies now increasingly provide services that might otherwise be considered the purview of the state, such as indoor plumbing, road maintenance, and housing construction. This shift in norms of governmentality has significant implications for the lives of South African youth (Strickland 2002) and has led to questions about the roles and responsibilities of private organizations such as NGOs in processes of political socialization, constructions of civil society, and service provision (Comaroff and Comaroff 1999). For many, the ANC has lost its radical edge on rising to power—a trend that the 2016 and 2019 elections confirmed as a loss of voters compared to past contests was reported (Robins 2008, 3).

This ideological and economic shift has larger structural causes beyond South Africa's borders. The World Bank and the International Monetary Fund have instituted economic policies that foster financial dependency in the Global South and naturalize neoliberal capitalism not just as an economic system, but as an ideological framework for nationhood and citizenship (Goldman 2005). Many political analysts and journalists see the economic tensions along lines of race and class in South Africa as a tinderbox ready to catch fire at any moment (Mufson and Raghavan 2014). Indeed, during my fieldwork in 2012, Eastern Cape residents often told me that Mandela's death would herald riots against the ANC and break long-standing ties of allegiance with the party. While this was not an obvious or immediate reaction to Mandela's death, the recent #FeesMustFall protests against university tuition increases and #RhodesMustFall efforts to rid institutions of their colonial trappings might be read through this framing.

Today one need not dig deeply to find the remnants of historical inequalities. In the postapartheid period, the Kamva area continues to suffer from startilingly high rates of unemployment and a relative lack of government support.[12] The Eastern Cape struggles with one of the country's lowest provincial life expectancies,[13] a reality that goes hand in hand with the continued presence of one of the world's worst HIV/AIDS epidemics.[14] Cattle theft is still a real problem, though not on the massive scale of the 1950s and 1960s. Vigilante justice, local political organizing, varied forms of Christianity, and distrust in national government are all visible and audible parts of daily life. Though the area as a whole suffers from systemic inequality, class distinctions are not absent in Kamva. Houses vary from temporary metal shelters unconnected to the electrical grid to permanent concrete-and-brick painted structures complete with porches, multiple levels, and double-car garages. Admittedly, the latter lavish abodes are still rare and are the subject of much discussion among jealous and often perplexed residents. Such pronounced class divisions are the products of recent shifts in the decades since apartheid's end; as new career fields have opened to nonwhites, a Black elite employed in real estate, medicine, construction, and other fields has grown substantially. In fact, Kamva demonstrates the kinds of rapid economic, political, and cultural shifts occurring in rural South Africa in recent decades, allowing a vantage point from which to enter the larger discussion on democracy and nostalgia after apartheid. Many Eastern Cape residents continue to rely on chiefs for governance in the absence of easy access to state democratic participation and in the midst of feelings of the ANC's failure to represent all South Africans. Long-standing political institutions such as traditional courts and tribal chieftaincies remain influential in the rural Eastern Cape in ways that are less amplified in the diverse, multiethnic settings of urban townships.

This complex history of racial, ethnic, and class inequality in rural South African towns like Kamva both make evident why organizations like Sonke are insistent on staging their interventions in such communities and convey the incredibly difficult work they have in front of them. The messages of liberal democracy, equality, and Western-based human rights often stand in stark contrast to the illusions of cultural autonomy under the homeland system and contemporary experiences of political and socioeconomic disappointment after apartheid. But first, let us turn to the internal workings of Sonke as a way to highlight the broader ethos of democratic liberalism.

CHAPTER TWO

The NGO as Moral Compass?

Culture isn't static, it's very fluid, and we get to shape culture. That's what our work is about.

—Michael, Sonke staff member

PREACHING DIVERSITY

Every Monday, the Sonke Gender Justice Network staff in Cape Town gathers in their spacious, sun-drenched boardroom overlooking a main thoroughfare of the Central Business District of the city. Employees casually trickle in with their morning coffee from one of the nearby hipster cafés, sleepily taking a seat in a circle among colleagues from across the NGO's divisions. These weekly gatherings alternate between trainings led by external facilitators, reports on internal programs, future planning sessions, and general all-staff meetings on the overall well-being of the organization. As is always the case in a diverse group of personalities, some people clearly relish the opportunity to speak while others tolerate what they perceive as a bureaucratic annoyance keeping them from their desks.

During one such Monday meeting in February 2012, a team of employees led a report on Sonke's work in prisons. The focus was the epidemic of sexual violence and HIV/AIDS in South African prisons and the organization's decision to take a direct role combating it through a variety of programs.[1] The subject was a difficult one and elicited tense reactions and conflicting perspectives. In what was clearly meant to be an act of goodwill, a middle-aged man stood up and proposed an ice-breaker in the form of a group sing-along. Unsurprising to those who knew that the man is also a preacher in his community, he started leading the room in singing "Fishers of Men," a song about following the path of Jesus Christ. Almost everyone joined in, though a few staff members were politely (and somewhat conspicuously) silent. Like all Monday meetings, this one concluded with a self-reflective discussion of the positive and negative elements of that day's session, listed on a giant white paper pad in colorful markers. Nora, a young, politically liberal woman who tends to be fairly outspoken, took the stage. With some irritation, she identified herself as staunchly nonreligious and complained about "Fishers of Men" being sung in a place of business that she felt ought to remain secular. The preacher fought back; he maintained that in this context the song was not meant to refer to Christ, that it was an apt metaphor for Sonke's work, and that he often uses it in his community engagement to rally and encourage participants, a great majority of whom are Christian. For him, religious sentiment was a tool to be employed in the process of democracy building; for her, it was an oppressive barrier to liberal social change that functioned to reproduce long-standing hegemonies. Nora pointed out that the song's words have not changed from its Christian origins, that it had an overt religious message, and that it had no place in a professional environment that prides itself on cultural inclusivity and openness to diversity.

This argument continued for some time, until Michael, one of Sonke's directors, cautiously stepped in. In a soft yet firm tone, he diplomatically reminded everyone that "we need flexibility around the religion issue" and encouraged his staff to continue being honest with each other about how such instances make them feel. He offered no resolution, only a reminder that there should be tolerance on all sides of a contentious issue. The meeting adjourned, and everyone went back to their respective departments and offices.

This incident, which took place early in my fieldwork with Sonke, was remarkable to me for several reasons, and I have come to see it as emblematic of the way Sonke handles conflict both inside and outside its walls. I was surprised, as a secular American academic, to hear the song in the first place. I, like Nora, did not want to sing along. I was impressed with the meeting wrap-up and the way different sides of a very personal issue emerged in a professional setting. And I was also surprised that Michael did not use his leadership position to draw a firm line or offer concrete guidance but only to gently encourage more talk. Ultimately, there was no clear resolution about whether religious practices were allowed in the workplace.

I relay this story to show how Sonke toes a dangerous line. Unlike the passively observing anthropologist in the corner of the room furiously scribbling notes, Sonke unabashedly steps right into the fray when it comes to conflict over culture and tradition. This can entail discussing the role of religion in the workplace, or, as I discuss later in the chapter, it might involve adopting a controversial stance on ritual male circumcision in rural parts of the country. Either way, such instances of tension demonstrate the unresolved challenges of trying to find a bottom line among a group of people with extremely different backgrounds and ways of life. Sonke confronts a variety of sensitive and controversial issues in its work and must decide what stance to take when these arise.

How do NGOs like Sonke conceive of their role within larger projects of civil society construction and youth socialization to democracy, particularly in multicultural environments? This chapter tackles this question by examining what occurs within the organization's walls. After a brief background on the organization's history and ideology, I explore the ways in which Sonke builds a community of employees and volunteers through ideological training in line with Western liberal human rights agendas and the broader politics of the South African state. I ask what these processes say about larger issues of power, dependency, and cultural change in South Africa and how the politics of culture are invoked by NGOs, and to what end. I argue that Sonke insists on a reorientation to the individual rights-bearing citizen in order to create what it considers a functioning and healthy democracy.

This reorientation of the self is especially evident in people's stories about how they first became involved with Sonke. I look closely at the rhetorical strategies in these narratives, which I suggest bear remarkable parallels to stories about personal religious conversion. This may seem unrelated to a discussion of NGO interventions, but I demonstrate that it provides a framework that helps illuminate Sonke's reliance on linguistic practices and unconscious behaviors, such as emotionally charged speech and personal stories, to achieve its ideological goals. Much like a religious experience, Sonke aims to convert program participants to a specific perspective aligned with Western liberalism and democratic ideals that often are initially foreign to most of the people involved. For many employees, this process begins with a personal transformation that sets the stage for their future programmatic work and becomes unconsciously embodied in their everyday speech and practices. Close analysis of these narratives provides a crucial understanding of Sonke's methodology and ideological underpinnings before I move to their on-the-ground work with youth in the rural Eastern Cape.

More broadly, I contend in this chapter that many NGOs in South Africa and elsewhere rely on a critical moral framework that is based on specific Western notions of human rights, freedom, and civil society in ways that are relevant to larger discussions of citizenship production (Englund 2006). This chapter and the next, which looks at several of Sonke's interventions with young people in the Kamva area from 2008 to 2011, demonstrate the ways in which dominant narratives that paint a portrait of globalization and Western liberalism as a homogenizing force obscure local responses to hegemonic discourses. In reality, the varied interactions with global liberalism are a product of differing cultural, racial, and historical perspectives and lead to heterogeneous outcomes. In other words, NGO discourses conceptualized in urban offices look very different when translated to rural people in local contexts, and individual agency plays a critical role in constantly renegotiating the reception of organizational messages. Although Sonke's interventions involve processes of educational filtering similar to those in public school classrooms, there are critical differences in the ways nonstate institutions approach cultural difference.

ORGANIZATIONAL BACKGROUND

Michael was with the Sonke Gender Justice Network at its inception in 2006 as a nonpartisan, nonprofit NGO that "works across Africa to strengthen government, civil society and citizen capacity to support men and boys in taking action to promote gender equality, prevent domestic and sexual violence, and reduce the spread and impact of HIV and AIDS" (www.genderjustice.org.za). At the time of this research, the organization maintained two primary offices, one in Johannesburg and one in Cape Town. The airy and light Cape Town office on which this chapter focuses,

FIGURE 2.1   Wall art in Sonke's Cape Town offices. Photo by author, 2012

and where I did several months of ethnographic fieldwork, is instrumental in constructing a particular image for the organization. Staff members represent different ethnicities, races, genders, and social classes, implicitly and explicitly demonstrating the emphasis on multiculturalism in the organization and its work. Large color photographs lining the office walls capture community participants in moments of ostensible empowerment: a raised fist, a smiling face, a marching line of men wearing the NGO's signature program T-shirts, "One Man Can."

Sonke's professional environment encourages a specific vision of civil society in which a diverse citizenry challenges its elected leaders and actively participates in the construction of a multicultural, multiracial democracy. The organization works to mirror its goals for a free and democratic society in its office culture; everyone's salaries are common knowledge, and the organization's finances are discussed openly at staff meetings.

Though the organization has an explicit focus on gender inequities through work that targets men and boys, it tackles a wide array of related human rights injustices in its programs and continues to broaden its programming and activism beyond gender justice and even beyond the borders of South Africa. I examine Sonke's emphasis on gender here because it serves as an incisive example for larger discussions of human rights violations and the production of civil society in democratic South Africa. Sonke distinguishes itself from many women's rights and feminist organizations in that it promotes gender equality by working specifically with men and boys. The rationale is that it is more effective to address the perpetrators of gender discrimination and gender-based violence than to simply mitigate the symptoms. Importantly, gender does not function in isolation for Sonke but rather is seen as a central arena through which to tackle structural inequality and build democracy more broadly.

Many theorists have explored the phenomenon of perceived democratic failure within neoliberal states, showing how the privatization of social services has led to a proliferation of NGOs taking up the battle against inequality and injustice (Nel, Binns, and Motteux 2001, 5). Organizations like Sonke see themselves as playing a crucial part in spreading democratic ideals and keeping the government in check. Employees quite explicitly see their role as holding government institutions accountable for preserving the promised tenets of democratic equality and making good on promises of societal betterment for all people. As Michael explained to me, "We have hopefully conveyed the message to politicians, and male politicians [in particular], that if they say things that are sexist, misogynistic, or demeaning, we're likely to come after them. I would be surprised if people in public positions don't know about Sonke." This is not necessarily hyperbole: many Kamva educators stressed to me the importance of NGOs such as Sonke, saying how crucial they are in supporting school programs and providing much-needed equipment at their schools. Importantly, however, the organization is also constantly negotiating the seemingly contradictory positions of alignment with the government and democratic watchdog, which is a balancing act not uncommon among NGOs.

Sonke works with a variety of other organizations and often partners with national, provincial, and municipal governments to work toward its goal to create an equal and just society. Such alliances serve as a reminder that the term "nongovernmental organization" is often a misnomer that belies the complex connections between government and external institutions (Markowitz 2001). As the anthropologist James Ferguson (2010, 168) pointed out, "Social policy and nation-state are, to a very significant degree, decoupled, and we are only beginning to find ways to think about this." Thus many social services that were once intimately linked to the nation-state are being rerouted to other channels, such as NGOs and corporate bodies, and not just in South Africa but also across the globe in countries dealing with neoliberal economic policies that emphasize privatization.

Sonke's fearlessness in the face of state institutions is one of its defining characteristics. One of Sonke's greatest victories along these lines occurred in 2010, when it won a case against the controversial political figure Julius Malema. Former president of the ANCYL, Malema is now known for having founded the Economic Freedom Fighters party and remains a divisive figure in South African politics for his outspoken and often radical ideas. At the time of the lawsuit, Sonke charged him with hate speech for his sexist and demeaning remarks about a woman who accused President Jacob Zuma of rape. This stemmed from an incident in 2005 when Zuma—not yet president—was accused of raping the daughter of a family friend. He was found not guilty of the charges, and Malema publicly stated that the woman had not been raped but must have "enjoyed herself" since she stayed for breakfast and asked for taxi money home. The case against Malema was tried in South Africa's Equality Court, and he was found guilty of hate speech and discrimination. This was a major public victory for Sonke, and it provides an example of their desire to take government leaders to task on the grounds of gender discrimination, even at the highest levels. The court ordered Malema to issue a public apology for his comments and pay a fine of R50,000 to a women's rights organization (Sonke Gender Justice Network 2011). Such highly visible events help construct Sonke's public identity as a champion of democracy, equality, and civil society. Nonetheless, part of what this and the next chapter illuminate is the hidden ideological contradictions in work that both promotes equal recognition of cultural forms and seeks to radically transform "culture" in definitively subjective, and sometimes dogmatic, ways.

Sonke funding comes from a fairly diverse array of partnering organizations, corporations, private donors, and governmental bodies, such as the MacArthur Foundation, the Ford Foundation, the South Africa Development Fund, Save the Children, the Swedish International Development Cooperation Agency (SIDA), the United Nations High Commissioner for Human Rights (UNHCR), and the First National Bank of South Africa. The organization's main philosophy is based on a "spectrum of change" model that depends on interconnected ideals of participatory democracy, community education, and government partnerships, as seen on the Sonke website (https://genderjustice.org.za/about-us/about -sonke/). The model emphasizes community involvement and pairs it with government accountability, which plays out in programs at the local, national, and international levels. For example, the Child Rights and Positive Parenting Unit supports individuals through trainings on fatherhood and sexual reproductive health as well as advocating at the government level for better parental leave rights for men.

WHY SONKE?

While there are many NGOs doing youth education work in South Africa, Sonke has a broad focus on ideological change at multiple levels of scale. Many NGOs are devoted to providing basic social services, such as food, medicine, or textbooks, but Sonke strives to inform young people about their constitutional rights and empowers them to take leadership roles in their communities in order to create long-term ideological change. In this sense, Sonke plays a pivotal role in the lives of many young people, shaping their views on human rights protections and enactments of democracy in ways that supplement classroom learning. By extension, Sonke has the potential to transform whole communities, particularly in terms of the dynamic between genders and generations. Nonetheless, Sonke operates within a particular framework of democracy and liberalism that at times stands in opposition to its rhetorical embrace of cultural diversity. This tension makes it a compelling example of the complex role of NGOs in South African society today.

Sonke uses tactics to achieve its goals that many consider novel within the NGO field. Programs such as One Man Can tackle sexism and misogyny by working primarily with men and boys in community workshops to transform ideas about gender. Brothers for Life, a program for men over thirty, discusses the risks associated with multiple sexual partners and the importance of what Sonke calls "responsible fatherhood." To achieve its goals, Sonke employs diverse methods, ranging from more traditional tactics like pamphlets and condom distribution to less common approaches such as training children in video production in order to profile issues such as sexism, child abuse, and HIV/AIDS in rural communities (Reed 2011; Reed and Hill 2010). Sonke's ability to capture the attention of a broad public means its programs are potentially transformative and have far-reaching implications throughout the country. Indeed, I contend that Sonke, along with other NGOs, is playing a crucial role in defining and transforming South African conceptions of citizenship and democracy. Sonke also approaches social injustice on multiple societal levels, both working on the ground with community members and advocating at the national and international levels for legal reform and increased recognition of constitutional protections. Furthermore, they conduct research on topics such as condom use and gender-based violence in order to identify gaps in policy and make future recommendations, thereby supporting their efforts through data-driven evidence.

A project I became acquainted with while doing fieldwork with Sonke neatly encapsulates the organization's commitment to a particular vision of democracy—as well as the obstacles it encounters in a pluralistic society like contemporary South Africa. In 2012, Sonke partnered with other local human rights organizations in order to fight the proposed Traditional Courts Bill (TCB). The TCB, according to Sonke, was "set to severely limit the rights of rural people to seek legal justice in the formal courts of South Africa, a right enshrined in our nation's Constitution."[2] Sonke worked with the Alliance for Rural Democracy, which was specifically created to combat this bill proposal. The original version of the bill would have placed much greater power in the hands of Traditional Courts, which are rural institutions headed by chiefs. It also would have recognized only one leader at the courts, and that leader would almost always be male. Women would not be allowed to represent themselves, putting them at a serious disadvantage and further entrenching gender inequality in rural communities. The bill also would have made it impossible to opt out of Traditional Courts and seek justice in the national legal system regardless of cultural affiliation, meaning that even tourists passing through rural parts of the country would have been subject to it. Sonke saw the bill as antithetical to a healthy democracy in its entrenchment of patriarchal gender roles and its challenge to the national justice system. (Despite the fact that the majority of South Africa's provinces disliked the bill, Parliament sent it back to provincial legislatures. In 2014, Parliament dropped the bill when it became clear that most provinces would be voting against it.)

Unlike many other smaller-scale organizations, Sonke has a visible impact on South African politics and activist movements, making it especially worthy of critical scholarly attention. In recent years, it has expanded its gender equality and civil society interventions to other countries on the African continent, including Rwanda, Uganda, and Sierra Leone. My examination of Sonke looks at what makes it unique in South African civil society building projects as well as how it represents a larger movement of liberal NGOs educating youth within nascent democracies. In this critical examination of Sonke's work, I reveal how the organization helps mirror and instantiate hegemonic discourses on democracy and the liberal subject in ways that work to build very specific types of citizens—work that starts within the organization's own walls.

Organizations like Sonke rely on specific ideas of what constitutes freedom. Here freedom is intimately linked to an international human rights agenda that depends on democratization for its functioning. This agenda is based on larger transnational conversations with institutions like the United Nations, with which Sonke maintains close connections. Thus the focus of Sonke and similar institutions when pushing for "freedom" is based heavily on democratic liberal ideals: gender equality, children's rights, sexual freedom, and individual citizenship. Echoing Harri Englund (2006, 13) in his examination of NGOs in Malawi, I am interested in how "the narrow definition of human rights as political and civil freedoms emerges through a profoundly undemocratic process of translation." For me, these processes of translation occur in rural Sonke programs that unapologetically assert a specific vision of what freedom should look like, even when it contradicts local cultural understandings of morality and ethics. Beyond this, Sonke assumes that freedom is a basic priority for all people, despite the fact that—as later chapters show—this concept is a negative signifier for some rural South Africans depending on the context. For people in Kamva, not to mention elsewhere, the type of freedom Sonke promotes can force local cultural processes of social control to unravel. Lila Abu-Lughod (2002) is useful here in her discussion of "saving" Muslim women from the practice of veiling after 9/11. She interrogates cross-cultural notions of freedom and argues that the concept has drastically different significations depending on the context and furthermore that it is not necessarily a goal to which all people aspire. I now turn to employees' personal stories of adopting the Sonke message, a process that depends on this assumption of the shared human goal of democratic freedom.

CONVERSION NARRATIVES

Luke is a quiet man who grew up in the rural Eastern Cape and whose first language is Xhosa. He is one of several Sonke employees who come from that province and because of this is often called on to lead programs with Xhosa speakers and travel to the area. He is responsible for coordinating various programs in both rural and urban communities, and by the time I met him he had already been working at Sonke for about five years—after initially serving as a volunteer. Luke explained that he sees Sonke's goals as "to build a movement of men who uphold other men and make sure we create a society and homes where women and men and children can live safely and free. And enjoy their rights that the constitution of this country promised them." When he talked about how Sonke works to achieve these goals, he used terms bearing resemblance to narratives of religious experience. The NGO enters a community, adopts a role akin to a missionary, and works to convert the masses to a new worldview deemed innately superior. For instance, Luke described challenges in his facilitation of some Sonke community workshops: "We have those people who are extremely difficult. These are the kind of people that we want to work with. We don't want to work with [someone] who has already been converted, you know? We like to work with people who are not converted, people who understand women as subhuman." On the first day of a community workshop for One Man Can, for example, a man told Luke that his hope for the experience was that "women will learn that they are women." Four days later, Luke said, the man reported that he had been "exposed to what women go through." Luke saw this as a tremendous success; for him, the "unenlightened" are the primary target of Sonke programs. Luke summarized Sonke's overall goal as "striving to change mind-sets."

Many Sonke employees cited their own experiences of personal transformation as reasons they wanted to join or partner with the organization. These powerful and emotional stories, in which individuals spoke of the many ways in which they changed their views on issues such as gender equality, the stigma of HIV/AIDS, and violence also read like conversion narratives, in the sense that individuals have taken on new beliefs and values that now guide their lives and their interactions with others. The frequent presentation of these narratives both to me and in public gatherings constantly asserts and reaffirms a specific sense of self and follows a fairly consistent structure. In other words, individuals use these stories in order to align themselves with specific identification practices that reorient their sense of belonging and community, a process that often hinges on specific linguistic choices and behaviors (e.g., Baquedano-Lopez 1997;

Hanks 2010; Harding 1987). Religious conversion acts to "shape aspirations and reorient social life" through a continued set of practices that involve a search for some type of ultimate guiding truth by which to live (Austin-Broos 2003). The comparison of employee experiences with religious narratives provides a framework for understanding and making sense of Sonke's strategies and ideology. The anthropologist Peter Stromberg has argued that identity transformation through ideological language is not limited to the sphere of religious experience alone, showing that this can be a useful model to understand other forms of "conversion." Referencing Bourdieu, he states, "Behavioral change wrought by ideology is not due to a one-time transformation of some aspect of psychological structure, but is rather the result of an ongoing practice that allows one to act consistently in a certain manner" (Stromberg 1990, 43). In this sense, frequent rhetorical practices that reference a moment of conversion work to construct identities and consequently behavioral changes.

My primary contention in this chapter is that Sonke and its employees rely heavily on conversion to liberal, democratic perspectives of equality, civil society, and individual human rights in order to achieve their programmatic and advocacy goals. Embedded in this process, rhetorical choices and behaviors work to create citizens more aligned with a particular set of national and transnational ideals, even when this means pushing back against cultural identification. For some employees, their own ideological shift can be traced directly to their first involvement with Sonke as participants themselves. For others, personal transformations before connecting with Sonke led them to advocate for a specific vision of freedom and civil society.

In the same conversation, Luke described the path that initially led him to his job with Sonke.

> I was exposed to violence from a very early age. I'm speaking to you, but I might have been in jail by now, or I might have been six feet underground, or I might have been in a wheelchair. I've lost a lot of friends to violence. Some of them are in wheelchairs, some of them are in prisons, some of them have passed on. . . . I used to be violent. I am not a person who talks too much. [In the past] if you disagreed with me, you would expect to be punished. And that's the community I grew up with. The mere fact that I cannot remember the last time I committed violence means that I am indeed that change agent.

Here violence is cast as antidemocratic, whereas talking is a form of democratic and morally righteous civic participation. Such experiences with personal change bolster optimism and perseverance among the staff during Sonke programs, reminding them that their goals are in fact achievable. Stories like Luke's are also demonstrative for program participants who are new to Sonke ideals of gender equality and liberal human rights. Luke is deeply committed to the organization: "This work is not highly paid. It really requires a personal journey of the individual. In the process of doing this work, you realize that you are on this journey on purpose." Such notions of faith, identity transformation, and destiny closely echo transformative religious experiences. Even the language Luke uses reflects his realignment with Sonke; phrases like "change agent" are common refrains within the office walls and in their promotional literature that are adopted by staff members. He stresses the role of the individual in societal transformation, which is analyzed elsewhere as reflecting Western democratic values and often at odds with African communal social organization (Hickel 2015; Nyamnjoh 2002).

Unlike Luke, his colleague Pierre, an immigrant from the Democratic Republic of Congo, is very talkative and infectiously enthusiastic. He glows when talking about Sonke and is happy to tell you about its work. His own personal transformation occurred soon after moving from the Congo to South Africa. Shortly after arriving in Cape Town, he got involved as a participant in Sonke workshops in his community that focused on immigrant issues; the spates of xenophobic attacks over the past decade have been a big focus of their interventions in the area. During Sonke workshops, Pierre befriended an HIV-positive woman who lived alone in his neighborhood. She was in bad shape when they first met, heavily ostracized by her community for her viral status and very close to death. As Pierre recounted to me in an emotional tale, the woman had contracted HIV while escaping the Congo as a refugee when the man leading the group of refugees to freedom raped her repeatedly along the journey. Pierre defended her when community members maligned her for her status, and he began taking her to hospital appointments and checking that she took her medicine regularly. In large part because of his dedication and support, he explained to me, her viral load became undetectable within a couple of years, and the community ostracism stopped. He was deeply moved by this experience, especially his ability to create change through his individual actions: "I said from the experience with that woman, I *must* engage myself in this community. After you receive a Sonke training, you won't feel comfortable [witnessing ostracism and stigma]. You take it personally." He attributes his lifesaving actions to his Sonke trainings, which were happening concurrently and motivating him to take a stand on behalf of the woman. He remained involved with the organization and eventually secured employment with them. Today he sees himself as a changed man: "I realized that there's a *lot* of things that need to be changed. There are a *lot* of men that need to be changed! They need to change their behavior. I grew up in a family where by the age of seventeen or eighteen my father was telling me you have to treat a lady like this and this and this. And now I've recognized that he was telling me some bad things. I have to change that; I don't have to go down that road that my father went through, where he was beating his partner." For Pierre, individual action is essential to societal betterment, even when it goes against established norms. Sonke has hired many people like Pierre who were participants in their community programs, relying on the fact that their personal transformations will make them more empathetic and effective facilitators to the uninitiated. Beyond their ability to help others, this transformation is mutually beneficial in that it aligns the individual's identity with a desired moral framework and makes them able to relate to future community participants.

Garai is a young man from Zimbabwe who conducts research for Sonke's international programs, traveling frequently to other parts of the continent. As he explained to me, "[In workshops] we reflect on our personal issues, our personal failings, and so forth. Then that's how we start to see a little bit of shift in terms of thinking and attitudes, and in terms of certain practices.... A behavior is learned, so it can also be unlearned." Here he highlights how Sonke reshapes social norms such that they fall in line with a specific version of society and how many of the people doing this work on the ground have undergone such radical shifts themselves.

Importantly, this realignment of unconscious and conscious social norms does not just occur through narrative practices. The physical embodiment of specific ideologies also play a role in reshaping personal identities, such as a fist raised in solidarity at a Sonke rally that is meant to encourage participation and also reference a gesture once characteristic of antiapartheid protests. In the Monday meetings described in the opening of this chapter, proceedings always begin with a "check-in," during which employees are encouraged to bring up any personal news or issues in their lives outside of work. At times, these depart significantly from the activities of daily work and turn emotional, such as the time I heard a woman talk about reuniting with a long-lost friend over the weekend. Though such actions may appear trivial, they are a crucial part of how Sonke builds community beyond the materiality of labor. Employees are encouraged not just to think of Sonke as a job, but as a sort of family that shares a common ideological commitment. In this way, the organization intentionally blurs the line between the private and public spheres. Staff members learn to use their personal lives strategically to craft particular narratives and conversations that aid their work. Even seemingly quotidian practices, such as dress, play a role in this project: the staff comes to work in a brightly colored and eclectic mix of "traditional" dress from various regions across sub-Saharan Africa, jeans, Sonke T-shirts, and formal business wear. For Sonke, then, identity is defined precisely by its multivocality and commitment to cultural and racial pluralism. By fusing the intimate and professional space, the organization encourages staff to see their role as an ideological mission rather than simply a job to pay the bills. These verbal and nonverbal tactics create loyal subjects who then proselytize the same message they once received to local communities.

Continuing his story of conversion, Garai cited his childhood experience with domestic violence in Zimbabwe as the motivation to get involved in gender equality activism both in previous employment and at Sonke. "I was touched quite a lot in terms of domestic violence," he explained. "The way my father used to treat my mom, I wasn't comfortable with that. He used to just buy all these [messages], saying it's culture, I'm the head of the family, I'm the father, you have to listen. So many excuses! So I had a personal passion to at least start to talk to men." Here Garai retrospectively recodes previous experience as sexist and violent and now views their justification on the grounds of culture as unacceptable. Questioning the cultural authenticity of a particular attitude or behavior therefore becomes a strategy that allows Sonke to demand that it be stopped. The NGO takes on the role of recategorizing what it sees as mythical or ahistorical beliefs on the origins of certain behaviors and ideologies, which I elaborate on later in the chapter.

Both within the organization and outside its walls, employees repeatedly described their goal as conversion to a more gender-equitable society, which they say begins with individuals undergoing "gender transformation." To paraphrase Sonke employees, this term refers to a

FIGURE 2.2   Visibility through dress at a Sonke rally in Gugulethu, Cape Town. Photo by author, 2012

process whereby an individual shifts his thinking to not just see problems with the treatment of women in society, but to completely reorient how he understands women and men in relation to each other and all the associated behaviors and practices. Staff members, therefore, want to see more than a man who just stops beating his wife. They want to see this man view his wife as his equal and partner in all ways, to transform his perception of how gender operates in the world and how he should relate to members of the opposite sex as well as other men. Some Sonke staff members openly identify as former misogynists and/or abusers themselves and have gone through this process of gender transformation. They use their own experiences and backgrounds as a parable from which workshop participants can learn and model their own behavior. Though tied into community conversations, this transformation has the distinctly individual dimension of interior reflection and personal transformation.

Much like a religious experience, Sonke's message often has to be taken, at least at first, on faith. Many of the people with whom I spoke described their initial resistance to the idea of gender equality. This conversion also requires a broader reorientation of the subject's identity, something with a long historical precedent in missionizing Christianity (Buckser and Glazier 2003). While the foregrounding issue in such conversions centers on gender, the larger context for this work is the advancing of democratic liberal values as a form of political subjectivity and way of life. Beyond discursive alignment with ideals of gender equality, Sonke employees work to reorient bodily practices in much the way religion uses prayer to direct the body toward God. For instance, Sonke expects men to take up physical labor around the house as a way of actively displaying gender transformation, not just talking about it.[3]

Sonke is acutely aware of the lack of cultural sensitivity that plagues many humanitarian organizations. It strives to appropriately pair facilitators with the cultural, racial, and ethnic settings of the programs they are running as much as possible in order to mitigate this. If a workshop is held in the Xhosa homelands of the rural Eastern Cape, Sonke will most likely send a Xhosa-speaking staff member who has an intimate understanding of that community but has at the same time adopted the organization's rhetoric and beliefs. When a news article appeared in 2012 profiling a camp for Afrikaner boys with white supremacist undertones, they assigned Harry, the only Afrikaans man on the staff at the time, to speak publicly on the issue. He took this as a serious obligation. "I feel as an Afrikaans white man I want to speak out against racism and for a less violent masculinity," he told me. It should be noted, however, that such facilitators may not be representative of the communities in which they work. While a Xhosa staff member may have grown up in the rural Eastern Cape, his personal transformation into an activist and a feminist often sets him apart from the perspectives of many in this region. Harry explicitly acknowledged this problem in our discussions, saying he often feels pressure to represent an entire culture for the organization despite the obvious impossibility of this task. My own work in the rural Eastern Cape exposed some of the discrepancies between workshop facilitators and local youth, even when facilitators also identified as Xhosa. Particularly among boys, there was often great difficulty in accepting the idea of men and women as equals regardless of who conveyed this message to them and whether or not they were Xhosa. In fact, those who mirrored liberal democratic values like gender equality were sometimes talked about as though their Xhosa identity had become diluted or even nonexistent.

CHANGING "CULTURE"

In many interviews with Sonke employees, I was told that their job involves changing cultural beliefs and practices, or at the very least making people more aware of the origins of such practices rather than blindly following "tradition." Observations during Sonke meetings also reiterated the idea that Sonke is in the business of "changing cultural norms." As the opening quote of this chapter illuminates, staff members continually communicated to me the idea that many practices labeled "traditional" and thought of as rigid and timeless actually have much more recent histories than people believe. They see these histories as crucial to creating ideological shifts and instead see culture as fluid and dynamic. As we sat chatting in a Cape Town park one day, Michael spoke of this idea in reference to gender.

> [Often] what we think of as cultural practices are quite recently established. It's not as though we lived in some romanticized past where there wasn't gender inequality but that colonial systems shut down spaces for contestation between men and women. Precolonial systems did not centralize leadership in a figure in the ways that colonialism did. So spaces that were available for women to challenge misogyny and sexism shut down under colonialism. What many people view as culture and cultural practices now are relatively recent adaptations. There's a real reification of culture in some quarters. There's a quite sophisticated saying that you can't use culture as a traditional weapon . . . and I think we're reasonably unabashed that even if something *is* a cultural practice, if it's antidemocratic, if it's oppressive, then we challenge it.

"Tradition," in this perspective, is a subjective category shaped by historical circumstances and power dynamics rather than something that is firmly established and immutable (Hobsbawm and Ranger 1983). Michael highlighted the example of gender relations under colonialism, saying that colonists had a large role in concentrating power in male hands and closing down avenues for women's voices in rural South Africa and that many South Africans do not realize the historical roots of their sexist attitudes and practices. Still, he emphasized the fact that even if something *does* have a long history as "cultural," Sonke will not hesitate to challenge it if the organization deems it antidemocratic. And while he articulated the view that culture is flexible, he also suggested that its authenticity depends on being able to point to an ancient, precolonial history.

Michael's views on culture and his interest in questions of authenticity are supported by many anthropologists who do work in Africa. For example, Charles Piot's (1999) work in rural Togo illuminated the ways in which the rural Kabre people are not nearly as isolated as it might appear but instead have been extensively subjected to the forces of colonialism and postcolonialism in ways that might at first be invisible to outsiders. Jean-François Bayart (1989), in his writing on African politics, contends that many of the fixed ethnic identities of contemporary African people actually have relatively recent roots and were far more flexible in precolonial times.

Nonetheless, for many South Africans today, this notion of traditionalism is considered critical for identity practices and a sense of belonging in the face of devastating structural inequalities. John and Jean Comaroff, in their book *Ethnicity, Inc.* (2009), show how quests for "authentic" culture often intersect with late capitalism. They tell us that the illusion of authenticity becomes central to creating value and that this perception is strategically deployed by Africans who sell culture in the form of souvenirs, art, and the like. For Sonke, culture often presents itself as an obstacle to civil society construction, but in the work of scholars like the Comaroffs we see the possibility that such practices might actually be a way to preserve cherished identities otherwise threatened by modernity.

Sara is a young American lawyer who relocated to Cape Town and worked for Sonke's legal team at the time of my fieldwork. In particular, she has done a lot of work in Sonke's programs with men in prisons regarding HIV/AIDS and rape. She, too, was aware of the delicacy of issues around cultural authenticity in working with different South African communities.

> The naive [me] used these kinds of slogans, like "Culture is dynamic." And we can change culture; it's not static. And if somebody comes with a cultural legitimization of a certain behavior, that's fine! Because it's dynamic! Let's change your culture! But now I'm much more aware of the power of a white-funded NGO coming into a community saying, "Let's change your culture." I think we do [that], but I think we try to at least have more of a peer relationship in the communication of that kind of change.

As Sara's words demonstrate, Sonke struggles to address its power imbalance vis-à-vis local communities in its various programs. It works to model collaboration with community members rather than dogmatic power relations that impose culture change on historically oppressed communities.

Another young employee, Mary, also expressed this idea: "Sonke is sensitive, in certain ways, but they also challenge. They work very closely with traditional leaders and with the local people, but I think Sonke's not scared to challenge either. And I think that that's good and healthy, because if you're too okay with everything, then you're not really going to change any cultural norms." In other words, Sonke explicitly sees its role as changing social norms such that they fall in line with the tenets of South African democracy and its associated human rights ideals.

Beyond just changing the language individuals use around gender, Sonke expects behavioral transformations within domestic spaces, such as a man who cooks dinner for his family and washes the dishes afterward. It stresses that it is not enough to work for discursive shifts; rather the idea of transformation rests on behavioral changes that reorient household and community gender relations in everyday life. Sonke programs strive to make conscious those embedded, unconscious parts of a person's habitus as they relate to gender norms (Bourdieu 1977).

At the heart of liberal projects of democratic education are fundamental differences in how people understand and disseminate knowledge. Sonke's community workshops often revolve around discussions of the historical circumstances through which ideas and practices arose rather than focusing only on future change. If these "false histories" can be exposed, the organization's reasoning goes, then it will be much easier to convince individuals to discontinue what it sees as harmful cultural practices. According to Garai, "[People] take advantage of certain cultural practices to justify abuse, or to justify certain imbalances between genders." Importantly, the entire concept of false history relies on values of the rational, truth-seeking subject. Sonke techniques thus employ Enlightenment ideals of truth, despite the reality that many of the communities within which they work have very different epistemological systems.

When speaking of strategies for debunking historical claims on culture, many Sonke employees argued that practices are often mislabeled as cultural when they should be recognized to have individual, psychological explanations. I encountered this viewpoint again and again when telling Sonke employees about a specific and memorable interview from my research in Kamva. In 2009, I met a teenaged girl named Noluvo who was vehemently pro-life and homophobic. Bright-eyed and curious about the world, she was incredibly passionate and steadfast in her beliefs, expressing great pain about what she saw as the erosion of Xhosa culture because of the incursion of democracy and liberal human rights.

When I met her again in 2012 outside a doctor's office in Kamva, I expected Noluvo might have softened her staunch antidemocracy stance in the intervening years. She had moved to Johannesburg and was attending a college there.[4] What I found was quite the opposite: she had become more entrenched in her belief that life under apartheid was better and democracy could be blamed for society's ruin. Culture was at the heart of her argument. Noluvo emphasized that what she deemed "un-Xhosa" practices are destructive to traditional values and beliefs that she held dear. She also tied the emergence of such practices explicitly to the rise of the democratic state in ways that mirrored most of the adults around her: "Democracy gives too much equality to children. They said that abortion should be legal. I just think abortion was not supposed to be made legal. . . . I was raised under a Xhosa tradition. When you are raised under the Xhosa tradition, you follow the rules and the principles of it. . . . This democracy has destroyed the coming generation." Noluvo felt that "new" practices, such as abortion and same sex marriage, were ruining Xhosa society and normative modes of social reproduction in ways that deeply disturbed her. For Noluvo, specific ideas of motherhood, gender roles, sexuality, and marriage practices were embedded in her identity as natural, regardless of their actual origins. Contradicting ideologies therefore challenge the established order in deeply threatening ways for many people.

When I told the story of Noluvo to Sonke staff back in Cape Town, they were surprised and almost universally skeptical about whether practices such as abortion and homosexual relationships were actually new at all. Rather than simply focus on their disagreement with the young woman, they emphasized the potential origins of such beliefs as the key element of the tale. Susan, a staff member at Sonke who was responsible for communications and program evaluations, told me, "I would be interested to know what's going on behind [her views]. There's something that's triggering that . . . something about identity, or insecurity, or something else." Here we see how Sonke encourages its employees to find ways to unravel ideas many consider cultural, suggesting people recategorize them as the product of personal life experiences. This truth-seeking mission is paramount to the NGO's methodologies and practices. Many Sonke employees were similarly insistent that Noluvo must have had a more personal connection to the issues of abortion and same sex marriage, such as a past traumatic experience, to make her feel so strongly. Whether or not this is true, it demonstrates that unpacking the entire concept of culture and convincing people that culture is not static or neutral is central to the Sonke philosophy and methodology. If we understand culture as a kind of unconscious and naturalized map that directs individuals through their social lives, then Sonke challenges people to read this map from a new perspective or even rewrite the map completely (Bourdieu 1977, 2). Sonke's teachings also assume that there is only one *correct* way to read the map; history is seen as a linear and inherently knowable reality rather than a collection of subjective experiences open to interpretation.

Jean and John Comaroff, in their own analyses of postapartheid South Africa, refer to this problem of differing ideals and values as "heterodoxy" in order to demonstrate the limits of the liberal democratic state in accommodating cultural differences (Comaroff and Comaroff 2004b).[5] This is a useful concept here, as Sonke walks a delicate line between challenging heterodox systems and working to respect their legitimacy in the postapartheid state. NGOs must find a way to recognize multiple worldviews while promoting what they see as the best course toward a specific version of society. Luke articulated it this way: "Culture plays a big role. We have to respect the culture of the people [we work with]. If they're saying we don't talk about this man, see the benefits of not talking about him. If it's important to talk about, you have to show them why it is important, even though their culture doesn't allow that. But let them say their opinions and say your view too. And at the end of the day, they will benefit." Sonke workshops try to create a safe space in which participants' ideas are valued and explored rather than simply discredited. John, a vocal longtime staff member who works extensively in both urban and rural communities, told me, "You've got to acknowledge what they're saying. But try and engage them to see the other side as well."

Despite these attempts at inclusivity, in discussing moments of friction Luke made clear there is a bottom line when it comes to human rights—a perspective echoed by many of the other staff members at Sonke.

We ask, "Who told you about this culture?" I'm saying that the culture is playing a big role in destroying our future too! Because as a man [in Xhosa society] you are expected to have a wife at the age of twenty-five. You don't have money, you don't have anything, but you should have a wife. How are you going to support that wife? Because they say after you came from the [traditional circumcision ritual] you must take a wife. And if you have a wife, they are expecting you to have children. How are you going to support these children? Some people say we are disrespecting their culture, but they are the ones who disrespect their culture.

Luke explicitly referenced the fact that people have resisted Sonke's messages on cultural grounds. This is something I also heard from some former Sonke participants in Kamva—that the push to change norms on gender relations was disrespectful to Xhosa culture, for instance. In such tense moments of their work, Sonke staff members try to explain to participants why certain practices labeled as cultural should be discontinued. Sonke deals with both debunking what it sees as false histories and deciding when and where it must advocate against things that it understands as part of a people's culture and that it believes must go. "Culture is an idea that is shared by a group of people, and it's changing," Luke continued. "It's dynamic. And to the extent that what we practice is cultural, as long as it is not toxic and harmful to the next person, we'll continue to do that. But once some of the cultural elements are toxic and harmful, they definitely need to be challenged." Though in their rhetoric liberal organizations like Sonke stress that democracy is characterized by the freedom to follow multiple ideological pathways, perhaps these examples show a cognitive dissonance among staff members that ultimately leads to certain ideologies being deemed unacceptable and incorrect. To be clear, this is a problem much larger than just Sonke: the state confronts this problem every time cultural systems of belief come up against national law.

So how does Sonke, or anyone else, define what is harmful within a culture? This question gets to the heart of anthropology's long and contentious engagement with the concept of cultural relativism and the difficulties of its application (Abu-Lughod 2002; Scheper-Hughes 1995). I brought this idea up while talking to Luke, as he told me about his decision not to force his son to attend circumcision school. He explained that he saw the constitution as the primary arbiter of right and wrong: "[As for] the traditional customs and cultural practices in the country . . . as long as they uphold the constitution, which is supreme and above all cultures, then that should be fine." He detailed practices defended on cultural grounds that were in violation of the constitution, such as forced marriages of legally underage girls. Ultimately, his approach to culture held the constitution as the primary benchmark for notions of a healthy civil society and democracy; this document has strong influences from international human rights law and is part of much broader conversations about democracy and civil society.

How does one handle a situation in which the markers of a "harmful" practice are subtle and vary depending on individual opinions within a culture and are not addressed explicitly in the South African Constitution? When we look at cultural practices such as female genital mutilation or honor killings across the globe, it is easy for many people to label them as harmful. However, Sonke also deals with everyday practices that are much less clear-cut and far more difficult to define as good or bad. Who decides whether it is harmful to a family if the girls start herding cattle, a job reserved strictly for males in almost all Xhosa families? How do communities and families decide on whether it is culturally appropriate and beneficial to encourage boys to cook, when they might be ridiculed by their peers? In fact, such gender role transformations can create friction within communities and subvert gendered and generational hierarchies that the short tenure of most NGO interventions often miss. This is not because of a lack of concern on the part of organizations like Sonke; rather it is often the result of poor follow-up and program evaluation that could shed light on the subtle consequences of NGO interventions.

These observations contribute to larger theoretical questions concerning the consequences of outside organizations seeking to change cultural norms and socioeconomic realities (Fisher 1997; Markowitz 2001; Timmer 2010). For instance, Erica Bornstein's (2001) research in Zimbabwe on the Christian charity World Vision illustrates how seemingly benign child sponsorship efforts of North American donors have contributed to wealth inequality, provoked witchcraft accusations based on jealousy, and promoted individualism over established communal identity practices. What this previous scholarship rarely covers, however, is the ways in which young people are affected by NGO interventions that focus on ideological and political socialization rather than social service provision. Instead of just providing basic living necessities, Sonke works to socialize youth into specific incarnations of democracy and civil society by challenging local conceptions of culture and tradition in radical ways. Their work engages directly with the paradoxes of a commitment to specific ideas of equality within a culturally diverse state.

Take the example of Xhosa male circumcision, mentioned earlier. Organizations like Sonke have been very active in efforts to medicalize the ritual, as it frequently leads to infection and even the death of initiates. Xhosa boys between about seventeen and twenty across South Africa almost universally participate in this rite of passage.[6] Initiation schools are usually held in rural areas removed from boys' homes, and they stay there anywhere from weeks to months (Gwata 2009; Mtuze 2004). The initiation begins with a ritual circumcision performed without anesthesia. During the healing period that follows, traditional healers treat the initiates and socialize them into Xhosa ideologies of manhood and generational respect. After attending an initiation school, the boy is recognized as a full adult in Xhosa society. This transition is not merely rhetorical: the initiate is now able to marry, own property, and participate in community meetings meant exclusively for men. The new rights and responsibilities accorded to the young man have spatial implications as well: only men are allowed in the *kraal*, or cattle corral, and many rituals have spaces reserved only for those recognized as adult males. While the contemporary South African state considers eighteen the age at which people reach adulthood, rural Xhosa life histories are built on a very different understanding of what makes a child and what makes an adult (Gwata 2009). It is important to note that these initiation schools have undergone many changes throughout history, including shifting notions of their importance and consequences for everyday life.

It is likely that the primary driver of initiation has changed in recent decades, as demonstrations of masculinity among peer groups have superseded the importance of gaining adult community rights and responsibilities. More broadly, traditional chiefs and community leaders are in agreement that the historical mechanisms structuring the sexual socialization of Xhosa youth have largely broken down (Meintjes 1998, 101). At one time, circumcision schools played a big role in the sexual socialization of boys. Today scholars suggest that circumcision is regarded as a gateway to sex rather than the point at which responsible sexual behavior ought to begin (Vincent 2008, 433). While previous incarnations of the ritual's purpose focused on property inheritance and participation in local political structures, today it primarily centers on the demonstration of a specific form of masculinity as sexual prowess and conquest. As more young people move to urban areas upon marriage or shift to a nuclear family model, property inheritance loses much of its cultural significance. Furthermore, traditional Xhosa political structures have lost substantial powers of social

control in the face of national democracy and municipal government structures, as mentioned previously.

Despite the physical risks, boys face strong social pressure from peers
to attend initiation schools. Although most Xhosa families have converted
to Christianity, I have yet to encounter a young Xhosa man who did not
participate in this rite of passage. Boys who are not circumcised, or who
wait until a later than normal age to do so, are taunted and treated as inferior within peer groups. *Inkwenkwe* (Boy) is a frequent taunt leveled at
age mates who are still uncircumcised. In 2012, Tando had yet to undergo
circumcision and was frequently ordered around by his older, circumcised
brothers (in Western kinship terminology, cousins) and treated as a child
rather than an adult. The brothers, only a few years older, were given freedom to move around the village without adult permission and were considered beyond the control of family members. Their grandmother was
constantly annoyed at these two young men for what she considered their
disrespectful behavior (arriving home late at night, getting drunk in local
taverns, and being unhelpful around the house), yet rarely took pains to
discipline them, explaining to me that they were "grown" and mostly beyond such punitive measures.

In recent decades, these initiation schools have come under intense
media scrutiny. Traditional circumcision practitioners often have no state
medical training, and some have actually been exposed as con artists looking to make quick money. Conditions are rarely sterile, and infections are
common. During the initial recovery period, initiates are not allowed to
eat or drink water, save for a corn porridge, and dehydration is a constant
and sometimes even fatal threat. A 2010 *Los Angeles Times* investigation of
Xhosa circumcision practices stated that often the ritual involves a single
kitchen knife that is not sterilized between uses, thus spreading HIV infections in a country with some of the highest rates of prevalence for the
disease in the world (UNAIDS 2019). Many boys have lost part or all of
their penises from complications related to the procedure, such as the tight
wrapping of the penis in cloth for weeks after the initial ritual (Dixon
and Pienaar 2010). Every year at circumcision "season" (which, in contemporary times, corresponds with school holidays) these extreme cases
of botched circumcision receive national media attention and reignite the
flames of debate over the practice.

One proposed solution to this controversy is medical circumcision,
something for which Sonke has actively advocated. Medical circumcision

is where a doctor conducts the procedure at a hospital using Western medicine to prevent infection. The frequent media reports of deaths or mutilations resulting from initiation school circumcisions have sparked nationwide roll-outs of interventions to encourage boys and their families to select medical circumcision as a more appropriate alternative (Venter 2011). Another motivation is the scientific finding that circumcision confers some protection against HIV transmission (Vincent 2008). The debate over medical circumcision illustrates some of the enormous difficulties Sonke encounters in rural South African communities.

Even though it might be seen as a better option, boys usually reject the alternative of medical circumcision. What is more, they often tease those who seek it out as weaker and less able to endure pain, which many consider an essential aspect of the ritual. Xhosa boys are expected to prove their ability to act as men and command respect by bearing the pain that accompanies ritual circumcision. The physical risk inherent in the practice is actually central to its meaning, and those who do not survive circumcision are sometimes said to have been rejected by the ancestors as unfit for manhood. Medical circumcision, under this logic, denies the ancestors their right to oversee the construction of adulthood and dissolves entrenched methods of social control central to Xhosa kinship ideology, creating significant spiritual insecurity (Mtuze 2004). Many boys told me that medical circumcision is the less "manly" option because it does not involve as much pain or risk. Xhosa masculinity is primarily based on the values of stoicism, strength, and independence—values that become particularly challenging obstacles for NGOs like Sonke that strive to overcome entrenched gender hierarchies and norms of sexism and misogyny. Many young boys have described feelings of extreme rejection and social isolation when they were perceived to have "failed" the circumcision ritual by seeking medical attention (Mavundla et al. 2010). As some teachers in Kamva mentioned to me, peer pressure plays a significant role in this resistance; boys laugh at those who choose hospitals instead of the "bush." Beyond such taunts, performing the ritual under culturally accepted norms has historically been considered a prerequisite for property inheritance from fathers to their sons (Mills 1992). Despite the fact that inheritance is based on less traditionally gendered lines today, these unconscious historical connections to the ritual remain important to many people. Efforts to sanitize and control this cultural practice may actually deprive it of critical symbolic value and therefore dilute or even negate its efficacy within social structures.

Sonke's interest in medicalizing Xhosa circumcision falls under its larger mission to advance children's rights and combat alleged forms of toxic masculinity. Sonke has encountered fierce resistance to these efforts. In a conversation about tradition one day, Fundani surprised me with his liberal—and unusual among rural Xhosa South Africans—views on circumcision for his own son. He also demonstrated why so many people have problems with efforts like Sonke's: "Even if you are not circumcised you are a man! These boys, they fight. You are categorized as not man enough if you go to the hospital. They need them to see that pain. If it were up to me, I would just take my son to the hospital. But because I want this guy to be acceptable, I must find a way of doing it their way and making sure that it's safe." Here we see that Fundani has struggled deeply with the need to stay within the bounds of normative social reproduction despite his own views on masculinity. As Louise Vincent (2008, 434) points out, "Male circumcision rites are symbolically saturated: the enhancement of masculine virility, the performative enactment of the separation between men and women, preparation for marriage and adult sexuality and the hardening of boys for warfare are typical themes." In this way, cultural capital is lost when circumcision is performed in a hospital setting, devaluing the ritual and removing its most salient social feature: the creation of a particular type of masculine subject. The hospital setting also removes the clearly delineated phases of separation, transition, and incorporation from the original ritual, which are elements of central importance to the completion of a rite of passage not just here but elsewhere (Gennep 1960; Gwata 2009; Turner 1967). In this sense, we should understand circumcision's social significance as much more about process than physicality. The intersection of biomedicine and cultural authenticity in medical circumcision can be compared to efforts to combat female circumcision elsewhere in Africa (Christoffersen-Deb 2005). Western-oriented biomedical and activist perspectives often disproportionately focus on the physical aspects of these rituals, ignoring the more deeply embedded, invisible symbolic work that is at play.

Beyond the challenge to physical aspects of the ritual, medical circumcision poses an ideological problem because it pushes people to reorient their notions of belonging toward the nation-state instead of the family, clan, or larger Xhosa community. By succumbing to medical interventions in the practice, young men must abandon elements of the ritual seen as central to Xhosa identification, such as social isolation and traditional treatments. As Susan, a Sonke employee, explained, "There's a big tension between traditional circumcision and medical circumcision. And it made putting together materials around medical circumcision *really* difficult. You can't say the word *safer*, for example, because people might interpret that as 'safer than traditional.' It's that sensitive." Although Sonke does consider medical circumcision a safer alternative to traditional circumcision, it carefully chooses language that is meant to respect cultural practices and not incite anger among community members in ways that would alienate them. When I asked specifically, Susan explained that Sonke's bottom line on circumcision is that it can be done in traditional initiation schools but should be "regulated" by trained medical practitioners who use sterile equipment and know how to handle the healing process correctly to prevent infection. In other words, the state should oversee and manage cultural practices so that they fall in line with and do not violate human rights legislation.

Notably, however, Sonke is not pushing for abandonment of circumcision altogether. Instead, the organization advocates medical circumcision for all boys as a strategy for reducing HIV transmission rates (Bell 2015). It approaches this issue in various ways, from pamphlets explaining the scientifically proven benefits of medical circumcision to infusing their messages in the story lines of young adult novels published nationwide in an effort to spread awareness among youth.

These efforts perhaps miss the point of ritual circumcision in the contemporary era. In an age when many other mechanisms of successful social reproduction have been eroded through neoliberal norms of the state and increasing wealth inequality, rites of passage serve to socialize young people into Xhosa ideologies and mold preferred identities vis-à-vis the nation. Increased rates of unemployment and estrangement from previous modes of household reproduction make ritual activities and beliefs all the more important in maintaining some semblance of social continuity with past generations (White 2004). In this sense, resistance to medical circumcision can be understood as logically consistent with the need for social reproduction into the next generation, especially where other methods have been rendered obsolete. It is another instance of Sonke being perceived as trying to change culture in problematic ways.

Ideologies surrounding fatherhood provide another example of resistance to Sonke programs on cultural grounds. Sonke has long run a program called My Dad Can, a play on the wording of their hallmark

FIGURE 2.3   Sonke pamphlet promoting medical circumcision. Photo by author, 2012

One Man Can program that focuses on gender equality from the perspective of men. The newer program, often broadcast on Father's Day each year, encourages men to act as responsible fathers by highlighting positive stories of fathers throughout the country. Through partnerships with local radio stations in eight different provinces, Sonke's program asks children to nominate their fathers and answer the question, "What makes your father special?" Susan described the backlash to the radio program that year: "Callers to the show just latched onto this idea of the nuclear family being a Western concept. And they were *incredibly* defensive! Every single caller to the show spoke about the same thing, saying, 'This is a Western concept that you're bringing in, this is our cultural norm, and you're challenging us.'" Sonke's response to such criticism has been to emphasize that the "Dad" in One Dad Can is a metaphor for any significant person in your life and is not meant to foster a single vision of a healthy family or promote the nuclear family as an ideal model (some children write about their uncles or brothers, for example). Nonetheless, a variety of cultural norms are often packaged along with Sonke programming regardless of the sensitivity of staff members to such issues, which is something NGOs working in diverse contexts seemingly cannot avoid. For instance, although the fine print allows for recognition of any significant adult in a child's life, One Dad Can appears on the surface to exclude lesbian households, despite their protection with extensive rights and marriage equality in the South African Constitution. It also potentially, though not intentionally, sidelines other males who are the primary caretakers of children, such as uncles or older siblings. As these instances showcase yet again, many rural Xhosa citizens feel threatened by what feels like the imposition of Western values.

All these instances of encountering cultural difference really start at home for Sonke, as the opening story about the song "Fishers of Men" suggests. As Sara explained to me, "Those issues about cultural translation, it's even a problem internally. These things really play out not just in the communities we're working in, but in the way we interact with other organizations. Like, are you gonna work with me? Oh no, they're led by a white woman, they're gonna participate this way. . . . This means that when we go to this setting, these people aren't going to listen to us." The staff must constantly take into account their own backgrounds—race, gender, ethnicity—when working in various community settings, with the understanding that they will be perceived differently depending on the circumstances. Nora, a young South African woman who grew up in Britain, recognized this: "I think [our diversity] is a strength mainly because we're in South Africa, so you have to have it. It would be wrong to just have one race, or one age or one gender. So, yes, it's an asset in that we have people who understand all sorts of different walks of life in South Africa. But I think it's one of Sonke's biggest problems as well. There are certain barriers due to a wide variety of differences that get on my nerves, and I know get on a lot of other people's nerves." Along these lines, some staff members complained to me in interviews that the gender transformation process Sonke preaches was incomplete among some male employees. Speaking of one experience during a program, Amelia, a young woman who was relatively new to Sonke at the time, told me about a particular social interaction among the staff: "It was a *complete* boys' club. [Staff members] spoke derogatorily towards prostitutes. You just don't do that in a gender organization! You should know better! I feel like there's something wrong with the way members within Sonke interact. I think there needs to be a lot more training." Though Amelia cushioned her statement with the caveat that only a minority of Sonke employees held such attitudes, she was not alone in her dissatisfaction with the levels of gender transformation *within* office walls. Thus diversity within the NGO was seen as both an area of strength and an area of potential weakness in reaching civil society goals, which is also reflected on the national level.

Examining the personal narratives and embodied practices of Sonke employees in Cape Town makes it evident that the organization works to convert people to a specific view of society, one in which the basic tenets of South African democracy are upheld regardless of gender, race, culture, religion, ethnicity, or sexual orientation. By employing a host of rhetorical strategies and community programming, Sonke promotes its ideological perspective through personal narratives that encourage empathy and emotional connection. I have argued that this conversion process starts with Sonke's staff, who then enter diverse communities to proselytize the concept of gender transformation and spur further conversions by leading with their own examples.

As the opening anecdote in this chapter illuminated, Sonke aims to create dialogue, transparency, and respect regarding cultural, racial, and religious difference in ways that can lead to resolution and understanding while minimizing conflict. Beyond these innocuous goals, however, they often challenge the very definition and origins of practices labeled as cultural, questioning both their histories and their authenticity in ways that are controversial. These discursive practices on the part of the NGO assume a type of Western-based rationalism aligned closely with the values in the South African Constitution. Sonke workshops, despite the emphasis on respect for diversity, are fraught with issues of power and dependency between the NGO and local communities. Since NGOs are not required to adhere to the government curriculum or Department of Basic Education standards of evaluation in their work with youth, they are able to challenge societal norms in ways that public schools might find impossible. The idea of "changing culture" or exposing "false histories" has far-reaching consequences for young people and how they identify culturally and politically. Sonke's interventions have the potential to affect how the next generation will negotiate what it means to be Xhosa. Ultimately, Sonke aims to align identification processes with notions of individual citizenship and nationalism even if it means challenging Xhosa worldviews and practices. In short, rural South Africans are encouraged to align with the democratic state, a process that sometimes comes at the expense of "tradition."

In the next chapter, I connect this inside glimpse of the NGO climate and rhetoric with Sonke's work in rural Eastern Cape communities such as Kamva, examining the impacts of using local Xhosa residents as facilitators to implement programs with young people. I wish to cast a critical eye at issues of translation, sustainability, and cultural sensitivity through an ethnographic portrait that demonstrates the central importance of cultural politics for Kamva residents. Sonke represents part of a larger trend in South Africa toward Western models of equality, citizenship, and democracy while at the same time differing from governmental institutions, such as public schools, in notable ways. Sonke also relies on complex notions of what constitutes authentic culture in order to convince individuals to discontinue practices the organization deems undemocratic and harmful. Rather than treat the NGO as a separate body completely disconnected from the state apparatus, I situate the organization within complex networks involving governmental institutions on the international, national, and local levels; global capitalism; and the politics of culture. Sonke, in this instance, is but a node in a larger web of nation-building institutions and stakeholders.

CHAPTER THREE

"Thinking Outside the Box"

Sonke in Kamva

*I think [Sonke] must be checking up on how things are going here. I don't
see them doing that. It's like they just said, "Okay! We preached and are
just going to the next church."*
                            —Mangaliso, former Sonke program participant

SONKE AND WAMKELEKILE

Lina's cake habit is certainly not helping her lose weight, something
she desperately wants. "I must be the only person not getting skinny from
HIV. It's not fair," she tells me as she unwraps the giant piece of cake
covered in sticky sweet frosting from its shrink-wrapped styrofoam tray.
We're sitting across from each other in the back room of a doctor's office, huddled around a paraffin heater topped with a tin of boiling water.
Kamva winters may not be snow-laden, but it gets cold up here in the
mountains without indoor heat. Africa isn't always warm.

The office in which Lina works is located at the end of the main
stretch of the National Highway that cuts through Kamva. This is the

FIGURE 3.1   The doctor's office out of which Wamkelekile operates. Photo by author, 2012

space out of which Wamkelekile,[1] an HIV/AIDS support and advocacy organization that serves the local community in a variety of ways, does its work. Started in 1999 by the doctor who works on the same property as a way to combat the burgeoning epidemic in the area, this nonprofit partner of Sonke has promoted the ideals of gender equality and run community programs to educate people about HIV/AIDS prevention, treatment, and stigma. Wamkelekile gets its funding from a variety of governmental, nongovernmental, and private sources and remains a champion of the Sonke model today, even though Sonke has finished its work in the community. The organization offers services like support groups, home care visits, and anti-stigma trainings for the local community.

People like Lina, who are openly HIV-positive, work to reduce stigma relating to the disease and help those suffering from its devastating effects. Lina is passionate about her work: during dry spells in funding, she has done it without being paid. She was around when Sonke ran various programs in Kamva between 2008 and 2011. She witnessed firsthand their One Man Can program that encouraged local men to rethink their ideas of masculinity and the treatment of women. She was in the office as they

FIGURE 3.2   A rural school where Sonke worked in 2008–11. Photo by author, 2012

sent facilitators to teach youth to make digital stories that highlighted challenges in their community. She is on a first-name basis with some of the Xhosa staff members from the Cape Town and Johannesburg offices and frequently asks about them.

In 2012, I dug through records and computer files with Lina and other employees in Wamkelekile's office, trying to compile a list of local students who had been involved in Sonke programs in recent years. I hoped to meet them and hear more about their experiences with the organization. But finding comprehensive records of these interventions was challenging to say the least, as Wamkelekile has gone through difficult periods in which it received no funding. Though I managed to collect a dozen or so names of former participants, I soon realized I had an incomplete list. Word of my presence in the area began to spread, and other young people at local schools started approaching me to say that they had also been Sonke participants through Wamkelekile and wanted to talk to me.

One day, I approached the entrance to a high school and a bunch of students I had already been working with told me a boy had been eagerly looking forward to speaking with me. When they took me to him, he shyly explained that he had been a Sonke participant along with his peers. His story was moving: his mother had died in the intervening years since Sonke had last been in the community, and he was not coping well. He mistakenly took me for a Sonke employee and assumed I had come to resurrect the Peer Educator Program of which he had been a part. He expected me to help him manage the loss of his mother. It quickly became clear he was completely distraught, felt he had no viable support networks, and did not know how to go on in life. He was desperate. Though I kept explaining that I did not work for Sonke or Wamkelekile and was actually there to conduct research, he kept pleading with me for help. It seemed that he viewed me as his last resort in the midst of an insurmountable life challenge. Although his school had trained Department of Basic Education psychologists for exactly this purpose, he was still hopefully and anxiously awaiting the return of the NGO for help he felt he could not get anywhere else in his community. While trained and caring, school psychologists are overloaded with work and have a virtually impossible job description. I interviewed one such woman working as a psychologist for the Department of Basic Education, and she told me that she was the sole professional in her field responsible for students at 256 schools. Nonetheless, I referred this young man to her and alerted his teachers to his distress—the most I could offer at the time by way of help.

The dependency and expectations at play in this young man's sad story are not unusual in the realm of those individuals, especially young people, who have had meaningful relationships with NGOs such as Sonke. I highlight this example here because it hints at the complexity of Sonke's relationships with rural communities, demonstrating both the organization's ability to play a significant and seemingly positive role in youth socialization and psychological support and its potential to set up problematic one-sided relationships that are expected to continue after the NGO's inevitable exit from a community.

Sonke's temporary presence in the Eastern Cape advanced the organization's broader project of creating a world in which communities have transparent support networks based on the values of equality, liberalism, and democracy. In Sonke trainings, rural participants learned the organizational philosophy and pedagogical strategies to become program facilitators. This model is meant to create long-term sustainability and cultural change that continues after Sonke employees leave the area. Usually the organization focuses on community leaders, activists, and teachers as appropriate and ideal targets for such facilitation. For Sonke, building a healthy democracy requires mobilizing people on the ground to push for societal change, especially with regard to gender relations. The liberal norms of individual empowerment, self-determination, and agency are crucial to this mission. But from what kinds of histories and power dynamics do such goals arise? How do rural citizens, far removed from boardroom discussions of civil society and governance, receive such projects on the ground? And what happens to local facilitators like Lina and youth participants like the motherless boy when the NGO packs up and goes home?

In this chapter, I take up these difficult questions through a portrait of how Sonke's messages of equality and rights are challenging for rural Xhosa residents to adopt. Sonke's programming in Kamva was undergirded by assumptions of Western liberalism that remain alien to and are unwanted by many people there. Democratic ideologies crafted from Western understandings of personhood and identity, presented by NGOs or other conduits, compel individuals to shift their alignment from local cultural modes of belonging to a framework of nationalism and South African citizenship (Hickel 2015). While people are of course able to and frequently do maintain multiple identification practices in complex ways, I use examples of Sonke programs in this chapter to show how many Kamva residents view the particular self-conceptions encouraged by both the NGO and Xhosa cultural ideologies as diametrically opposed in seemingly unresolvable ways (Hall 2002).

Despite using terms of cultural inclusivity, as discussed in the previous chapter, Sonke programming nonetheless relies on Western liberal ideals that are at odds with many Xhosa norms. Adopting Sonke's brand of civil society and personhood often entails subverting gender and generation hierarchies in ways that uproot local modes of social reproduction and does not appear to offer a viable alternative by which to maintain community cohesion. In this sense, Sonke challenges the status quo and works to transform the behaviors of rural people in ways that are innovative and problematic all at once. While Sonke employees and volunteers rarely seem to view their messages as an ultimatum between democracy and traditionalism, many Xhosa residents in the Eastern Cape clearly perceive them as such.

This chapter also demonstrates how, by using local facilitators to do their work, Sonke's messages are adapted to fit local cultural contexts. Kamva educators and program facilitators found ways to renegotiate and adapt liberal discourses to fit local cultural models in unanticipated, and likely unwanted, ways. In other words, the seemingly unidirectional transfer of information is transformed as it moves from urban NGO offices to rural communities. By adapting discourses of equality and democracy in culturally strategic ways, individuals are able to maintain and uphold long-standing identities, renegotiating official views of what it means to be a South African democratic citizen. Embedded in these difficult negotiations are troubling but essential questions of the sustainability of community interventions, as temporary NGO programs have the very real potential to create one-way dependency relationships and challenge historically disadvantaged populations to fill in the gaps once the organization exits the community.

More broadly, this discussion again demonstrates the ways in which dominant narratives of globalization as a homogenizing force, through conduits such as nongovernmental agencies, make local responses to national rhetoric invisible. In other words, media perceptions of South African citizenship obscure individual agency and the nuances of cultural resistance. Through the residents of Kamva, we see that NGO interventions that depend on unequal power dynamics do not rule out the potential for local agency and creativity but instead often spur it on in unintended ways. Here is an arena in which the ethnographic method offers something critical that many other research methodologies do not: the ability to understand and assess liberal projects beyond surface-level readings of curriculum statements or NGO planning materials, taking account of the multidirectional flows of information that occur in the real world.

To be fair, most people who worked directly with Sonke seemed to feel the organization had benefited their community, improving gender relations and reducing youth violence and drug use in the area's schools. In fact, at times it seemed as though residents hesitated to speak negatively at all about any aspect of the organization's work with me, for fear that they would not work with them in the future. This sentiment was expressed time and again, and several people even asked me if I could get Sonke to return to the community. Usually, any criticism of the NGO emerged later on in my conversations with research participants and revolved around a particular set of issues dealing with cultural change and sustainability. Such hesitant and ambivalent confessions illuminate the complex and unequal power dynamics between NGO employees and community participants. Many people seemed to adopt an attitude of humility and gratitude, thankful for any work Sonke was willing to do in the community even if they found it flawed and incomplete. This should make scholars, NGOs, and educators alike question whether appropriate programs offer outlets for community feedback and how they might be incorporated to better serve people along culturally sensitive and inclusive lines. It also illuminates the desperation many educators and other municipal employees face in the struggle to adequately serve rural, historically oppressed communities.

Lina's first encounter with Sonke was in 2008, when employees from the Cape Town office found Wamkelekile through the municipality's database of nonprofit organizations. She described to me some of her first encounters with Sonke while at Wamkelekile. In many ways, her words mirror Sonke employees' own articulations of its work, as illustrated in the previous chapter. "They said it's time to have a change," Lina told me. "So that men can be involved in the community and also in the household. When you have a bath, the man must be in there and they must be involved in helping a woman. So that as a woman you cannot do all the jobs and the man stands there, doesn't do anything, especially when a man is not working." Although Lina reported that she personally embraced these ideas of gender equality and social change even before her first encounters with Sonke, she hinted at her initial disbelief when she heard the organization's plans for spreading these messages to the larger Kamva community. Specifically, she took issue with their teaching methods. She cited culture as the prime impediment to gender transformation in her community, telling me that many people, especially in rural areas, felt that Sonke was attacking their culture. Though she herself stressed the belief that culture is dynamic and ever-changing, she nonetheless saw the organization's insistence on gender transformation as alien to most people in rural areas. As the interview progressed, she became more openly critical of Sonke.

I felt a little like it was imposing. We would go to these awareness campaigns with some people from Sonke, and they would say, "You should do this and this and this, it's the right thing to do," while people have been living their own lives. And you come up with something and say, "You should do this! You should do this!" And I felt it's not practical when a rural person is living in the rural areas. And you came once, and you said this thing, and then you said a man must help a woman with a birth. It's not for them!

While program leaders like Luke and Sara talked about facilitating discussion, Lina painted a picture of unequal and hierarchical power relations between urban NGO staff and rural participants. She also described a dogmatic approach to behavioral change. In my experiences with Sonke employees, they stressed open discussion and appreciation of local worldviews and diverse opinions in places like Kamva, but Lina's account made the staff appear uncompromising and prescriptive. Despite these initial reservations, however, she told me of her surprise when many people in the community seemed to actually accept the Sonke message of gender equality and even some *inkosis* (chiefs) showed up to participate in their workshops. Still, she seemed unconvinced of the breadth of change they were able to make. When I asked for examples of changes she had seen in her community, she mentioned meeting a man in a rural area who was helping his wife around the house with chores and seeing people in the area wearing Sonke's signature "One Man Can" T-shirts. Although she estimated that Sonke may have reached much of the local community, she explained that sustained change needed many years of trainings and interventions.

Many of the educators in Kamva who worked with Sonke appeared to adopt the internalized discourses of liberalism in ways that stood in stark contrast to many Xhosa identity practices. Asanda, a Department of Basic Education employee in Kamva who works with the elderly and disabled, raved about the successes of Sonke's work in her community: "Here in our communities I can say we were oppressed. Because we girls, we used to do men's jobs, but when it comes to men, to do the girl's jobs, they'd say, 'No no no, that's a girl's thing.' But when Sonke came here, that really changed." Despite her glowing review of the organization, we see a type of narrative conversion at work here similar to that described in the previous chapter with Sonke employees; she has taken on the semantic coding of not just the NGO but also larger national discourses by using terms like "oppressed" to characterize gender relations in her community that she previously did not question or label as such. When I asked her about her views on gender equality before her involvement with the NGO, she replied, "Before Sonke? We *never* thought of that. I can't lie." Thus Sonke does not just ask for behavioral change but also encourages people to recode the world based on the particular language of Western liberalism.

Such discourses of inequality and the politicization of culture tie into the vast body of literature on humanitarianism, which has suggested that we consider histories of colonialism, political economy, and racialization when critically examining aid projects in Africa and throughout the world (Bornstein 2001; Bornstein and Redfield 2011; Timmer 2010). How might Sonke and similar liberal political projects have been or continue to be implicated or complicit in larger legacies of colonialism and racialization? How do these nongovernmental interventions reify the nation-state as a primary organizing principle for personhood and identity? The complex relationships of gratitude, dependency, and resentment these local facilitators had and continue to have with Sonke evidence such possibilities and help us situate such projects in larger historical, political, and economic narratives. In many ways, NGO interventions that seek "culture change" push what we might call a neocolonial project that constructs understandings of morality around Western liberal constructs of freedom, abuse, and equality that do not always translate well (or at all) in local contexts (Englund 2006). Rather than simply point fingers at NGOs, however, I want to suggest that it is the very capitalist, Western-oriented system in which such organizations are deeply embedded that structure their actions and limit potential resistance to hegemonic powers. As these relationships and larger structures trickle down to rural classrooms, they become a naturalized and powerful invisible force in experiences of youth political socialization. In other words, Sonke does not actually aim to subvert the hegemony of liberalism because it is a product of that very system.

CASE STUDY 1: THE PEER EDUCATOR PROGRAM

Ms. Khumbule's entire face lights up when you mention the Sonke Gender Justice Network, and she soon asks about the various staff members from the NGO's urban headquarters who initiated projects at her rural Eastern Cape school years ago. She is part of a multinational government partnership, supported by the United Nations Children's Fund (UNICEF) and the Swiss Agency for Development and Cooperation (SDC), called Care and Support for Teaching and Learning (CSTL). Ms. Khumbule is a "learner support agent," meaning that she is charged with identifying and assisting "vulnerable" children, defined as those without parents or guardians, living in extreme poverty, facing abusive home environments, and/or suffering from HIV/AIDS. She feels a deep personal connection with this position, as she herself grew up an impoverished orphan in the same rural community where she now works.

When Sonke came to Kamva to initiate the Peer Educator Program with youth, Ms. Khumbule was a logical choice to facilitate at her school. After all, she already maintained lists of the population in which Sonke was most interested and she worked outside the normal curriculum with her students on issues the NGO wanted to cover in the community, such as gender inequality, domestic violence, and child abuse. Unlike many of her colleagues in the area, she staunchly rejects corporal punishment as a type of child abuse and has inverted normative hierarchical relationships in her close emotional bonds with children. These attributes made her a fairly typical choice for a Sonke educator: the organization seeks local residents who have access to populations of interest to their goals and already demonstrate some allegiance to the Sonke ideals. Sonke's Peer Educator Program was instituted in several local secondary schools from 2008 until roughly 2011 on a weekly basis. Teachers selected students or whole classes to attend regular after-school meetings over many months or years depending on the school, and Sonke-trained facilitators would use this setting to spread the organization's message. Afterward, the participants would be expected to transmit these messages among their peers. The model emphasized making use of preexisting peer networks in schools to spread awareness, stop abuse, and create change by means of a sort of domino effect.

Ms. Khumbule, in conjunction with staff from Wamkelekile, used Sonke teachings and activities with students even after the organization was no longer officially present in the area. "The students get more when they teach each other," she insisted in a conversation with me in 2012, explaining that the program with Sonke focused on issues such as HIV/ AIDS, safe sex, and domestic violence. This emphasis on peer relationships and open discussion is in stark contrast to the rote educational practices and rigid age hierarchies characteristic of many rural South African public school classrooms, as discussed in the next chapter. Sonke's work, therefore, was made easier by the fact that Ms. Khumbule already aligned with national models of Western liberalism and equality. In her work, she advocated for a specific conception of children's rights and gender equality that is mirrored in the constitution but often absent in local attitudes. Ms. Khumbule's initial response to the NGO's mission in the area was overwhelmingly positive: she loved having the opportunity to talk to students further about personal challenges and felt a cultural connection to the Xhosa-speaking Sonke staff members who visited the school periodically.

Ms. Khumbule, like Lina, did have some problems with the organization's chosen methods, however. She said that the Cape Town staff's approach during workshops was somewhat different from what she would have chosen for this community. "Sometimes they were rude to other people. In fact, they did not understand that we came from rural areas and have different backgrounds," she explained. This quote echoes the earlier comparison of Sonke's conversion-like approach to liberal human rights teachings, demonstrating that their messages were sometimes received as an intrusion into local ways of life. Many of the Sonke staff members to whom Ms. Khumbule refers actually *are* from rural Xhosa backgrounds and frequently *do* have extensive knowledge of the area, but they now live in urban environments and have clearly adopted a perspective that she sees as divisive and problematic.

Zinzi is a nineteen-year-old who was a peer educator trained by both Sonke staff and her secondary school teachers. Her parents are not alive, which was a common thread among all the students involved in the program at her school. Zinzi was a peer educator for three years. She was overwhelmingly positive about her experience in the program: "I learned a lot. I learned how to treat people who are in need and how to treat the elderly." The Peer Educator Program encouraged young people to be leaders and role models within their schools and communities rather than wait for their elders to intervene on their behalf. Once in a while during the program's existence, Sonke staff members from Cape Town or Johannesburg would drop in to observe sessions and speak with students about their progress, but the model relied on local facilitation to create lasting change. When we spoke, Zinzi highlighted her background as an orphan and explained how it influenced her experience with Sonke. She said that Sonke's program was especially helpful in teaching her to make peace with her identity: "As an orphan, I always thought, 'I don't have any parents, so what's there to live for?' Now I say, 'There is time to live, and even though I don't have parents, I can succeed.' The people from Sonke said that because I don't know my parents, I must pay more attention to my studies. And if my parents do come back to my life, they may find me successful." She mentioned that her grades improved noticeably after participation in the program.

The Peer Educator Program used nontraditional teaching methods, such as drama, poetry, and debate, to engage students and encourage a discussion-based environment that contrasted with daily lessons filled with rote lectures, written assignments, and examinations. As Zinzi explained, "We acted out stories about people who were orphans and were mistreated. And people who were raped. And what signs you see in a person who has been raped, like the person might not focus too much in class. He or she likes to sit by themselves." "While teachers often ignore what you say," she continued, "the people from Sonke Gender Justice pay attention to what you say. I didn't have a problem talking to them about anything, because they were friendly and spirited." Many students felt that Sonke's methods created a safe environment in which they were free to learn through discussions, express their opinions, and ask questions on any topic—often a welcome and surprising change from classroom experiences.

Luzuko, a teenaged boy who was another participant in the Peer Educator Program with Zinzi, explained to me when we spoke that some of his peers had recently stopped coming to school. Although the Sonke program had ended a year earlier, he drew on his experience as a mentor and confronted them: "I talked to them, and now they are promising to come back to school next year. I went to them and started chatting out of the blue, and I listened to what they told me. Then I gave them advice." He said that he would never have done this if it were not for what he learned as a Sonke peer educator. Stories like Zinzi's and Luzuko's were common among the former peer educators: students generally had extremely positive associations with the program, recalling fondly their experiences of belonging, support, and mentorship. One young man discussed with me how Sonke-trained educators from Wamkelekile convinced him to stop smoking cigarettes. Another young man said that the program encouraged him to use condoms during sex and treat his female peers with more respect and less anger: "It has changed my life. Before I was beating people when I got angry. Now if I get angry I just let it go." Many students I spoke with emphasized their appreciation for the knowledge gained through the program.

The Peer Educator Program model's logic, then, relied on reorienting passive youth subjects toward roles of active leadership and civic engagement in their communities. In particular, youth were encouraged to intervene in issues of central concern to Sonke: children's rights, the importance of education, and gender equality. Young people were encouraged to speak out or intervene in the affairs of others, even if this meant challenging their elders. This is where the program had potentially problematic elements. In most Xhosa families, young people are not encouraged to speak out or intervene in the affairs of others, let alone take up leadership roles vis-à-vis their elders. Indeed, there were cases where the Sonke method obviously created a conflict of interest for its young participants because of this inversion of normative age and gender hierarchies. For all of Zinzi's praise of the Peer Educator Program, she had trouble following the model: "I do help elderly people now, but I am too scared to help those my own age, because . . . I don't know how to talk to them. We were taught, but I am too scared to talk to young people." When I pressed her for an example, she said that she has a neighbor she would like to help: "She is fifteen or sixteen. She has to be at school at half eight, but at home she is beaten, so she is often late. She's an orphan, and so she gets beaten every time there's something that is wrong. If there is something stolen, they blame it on her." Zinzi felt that she could not intrude in this girl's home life without appearing nosy and rude. In such instances, it is apparent that deeply embedded age and gender hierarchies complicate the Peer Educator Program's seemingly straightforward message to youth, making it hard for them to take up non-normative roles in their communities.

Importantly, students' narratives of how and why the program operated differed in marked ways from Sonke staff members' expressed goals in the Cape Town offices. For instance, one student said that in one session of his Peer Educator Program run by a local facilitator "they educated the boys about what happens when you rape someone, that you could go to jail, and what happens in jail." He elaborated that the Wamkelekile employee told them that men rape other men in jail, which was clearly an effort to dissuade them from involvement in illegal activity. This was in marked contrast to Sonke's norms. As a case in point, while I was conducting participant observation in the Cape Town offices earlier that year, there was a meeting at which a recent television campaign aimed at dissuading people from drunk driving was discussed. Through suggestive imagery and acting, the TV campaign promoted the idea that if they were arrested and jailed, men and boys could expect to get raped there (Laing 2010). The Sonke staff, along with other advocacy groups and media outlets, were horrified by this stereotypical portrayal of prisons—and of homosexuality—in a way they felt violated their work on gender, LGBTQ equality, and the South African incarceration system. While local facilitators in Kamva cast prison rape as a useful deterrent to illegal activity, Sonke challenged such portrayals as dangerous to liberal democracy. It is hard to imagine that these kinds of lessons were what Sonke program coordinators in Cape Town originally had in mind.

While Sonke promotional material, offices, and staff discussions almost always revolve around the concept of gender transformation as an ideal of the democratic state and the primary goal of the organization, my conversations with young people suggested that local Kamva educators seemed to deemphasize or restructure this discussion in youth programs in ways deemed more culturally appropriate and less controversial. Many students did not remember learning about the topic at all in the program; others appeared unconvinced. Often I asked whether a student supported gender equality only to be met by a blank stare. This is particularly notable considering that gender justice is front and center in virtually everything Sonke does. In some instances, former participants recognized the idea of gender equality but demonstrated resistance to it. One teenaged participant in Kamva, for example, insisted that there should be equality between women and men, confirming that he had learned about it in the many months he spent involved in the Peer Educator Program led by local facilitators. When I pushed him to explain what this equality actually meant to him, however, things shifted. He could not hide his laughter when I asked if gender equality meant girls and boys could take on nonnormative roles in the house—a subject that was discussed loudly and constantly in the Sonke offices and in their many community workshops. "If a girl ever helped me with the cattle," this young man said, "people would say I'm a lazy boy. . . . Men and women can't do the same jobs because women are weak." His description of attitudinal changes regarding gender extended only to concepts such as ending domestic violence and abuse, not to the concept of transforming household roles. Lonwabo echoed this sentiment. Practically in the same breath as his fervent agreement with the portion of the Bill of Rights saying that women and men have equal rights, he said, "The man is the head of the house, so the woman should respect the husband." And Zinzi said she supported the idea of gender equality as presented by Sonke in the Peer Educator Program, yet made contradictory statements later on in our discussion. When I asked her if a girl could herd cattle, she laughed. She assured me that herding cattle was a task reserved for boys. "It's our culture," she said. In these instances, it seemed Sonke's message had not hit its intended target.

Though Sonke's message of gender equality and human rights might have been parroted back by youth participants because they felt it was expected of them, it is significant that Xhosa cultural ideologies seemed to override many of these messages in practice. Much of this, I contend, is due to the fact that trained community facilitators from Wamkelekile presented Sonke messages through the filter of local Xhosa value systems, thereby failing to challenge the status quo as Sonke might have hoped. Through discussions with teachers and reports from former participants, it became clear that this part of Sonke's message was frequently deemphasized. Of course, these instances of misalignment also illustrate how deeply ingrained cultural notions of gender and generation are and how difficult it is to subvert them in a relatively brief time.

While some students clearly disagreed with the notion of gender equality, others simply recast it in ways that fit into Xhosa frameworks of normative societal roles. For instance, one young man explained that he agreed with the idea of men and women being equal in the house. But when I pressed him on the issue of whether they could do the same jobs, such as herd cattle or cook, he said no. Rather than see this as a contradiction of the ideals of equality, however, he explained, "There's a part of the house where a woman can be in charge and a part of the house where a man can be in charge. For instance, a woman cannot go out and collect the cows because she might be raped." Thus he adapted the idea of gender equality to a familiar cultural framework that did not threaten normative modes of social reproduction in the household. He implied that domestic life should include both males and females working in concert to assist each other in separate spheres of the house, but he did not see these two spheres as inherently unequal.

Sonke's Peer Educator Program in the Kamva area, and by extension the local facilitators who adopted their model, focused primarily on a specific vision of children's and women's rights under a democratic state, encouraging young people to recognize violations such as child abuse, sexual crimes, domestic violence, and explicit gender discrimination and report it to authorities. Program leaders told participants what kinds of signs might indicate an abusive household, for instance, and pointed them toward appropriate adults in the community to whom they could turn for help. Beyond these specific interventions, the program broadly encouraged youth to be vocal in ways that remain uncommon for rural Xhosa children, especially girls.

In this sense, Sonke's model recognizes an egalitarian model of society in which children's voices are just as important as those of adults. Noluthando, a young woman who at the time was attending Cedarwood Secondary School, told me that in the Peer Educator Program she was taught "how to respect other learners and respect ourselves. . . . They taught about how to be a good father, how to treat your family. That you have to help with household work when you are not working. . . . I used to think men are not equal to women. Men are powerful, and I thought that they had more rights, more than women. They taught us that all people are equal. No one has the right to abuse others." Underlying such liberal messages are assumptions of what it means to be a "good" father, for instance, or what should or should not qualify as abuse. Due to these differences in definition, Sonke's human rights agenda was often at odds with larger community gender relations and ideologies, which had the potential to pit youth against their peers and older generations. Some young people complained that friends would laugh at their messages of gender equality, which they often recited because the program encouraged using their skills to teach others. In fact, some teenagers told me that they had radically changed the composition of their group of friends after involvement with Sonke, because they could no longer relate to friends who had not changed their attitudes about gender.

While Sonke programs in the Kamva area targeted cases of child and domestic abuse as a specific part of their missions, it seemed not all students agreed on a definition of what actions fall into these categories when asked. As a young boy named Xola explained to me, children in his Peer Educator class started calling things abuse that he considered routine, acceptable parts of everyday life: "Some people started saying that when teachers sent us to do something, like fetch water, it was abuse. And I did not agree." Interestingly, teachers and parents expressed fears that today's youth are unable to balance rights with the importance of responsibilities to their community. Many adults in the area worry that teaching children their constitutional rights will lead to unjustified outcries of abuse and will unravel essential methods of social control. Perhaps Xola's description of his classmates gives credence to these fears.

Some of the participants in the Peer Educator Program were skeptical of whether the program made a significant difference in the community. Imitha, a student at Cedarwood Secondary School the year I spoke with her, loved the Sonke program. She raved about how it allowed her a venue to talk about things her regular school classes didn't cover and said it changed her feelings about gender equality. She told me that she now herds the cattle at home, despite the fact that people sometimes stare at her for doing a traditionally male job. For Imitha, the Sonke program was transformative and life-changing. Nonetheless, she was frustrated with what she saw as its relatively small impact on her community compared to her initial expectations. For example, she discussed how the program focused on preventing teen pregnancy, something Kamva residents frequently cite as the biggest challenge facing youth today. "Some girls have changed, but some haven't. Some of the girls who were there in that Sonke Gender Justice program have babies now. But they were taught, you see? They don't want to obey, they don't want to listen, they don't want to think about what they were taught." Though there are certainly other explanations for the high rates of teenage pregnancy in Kamva, Imitha's disappointment reflects her perception that the program was not able to create widespread behavioral transformation.

This issue of sustainability was a central concern mentioned by Kamva youth and adults alike, and one mirrored in national and international conversations about NGO interventions. A big part of this problem is the dependence on ever-shifting donor funds that frequently push an NGO to leave communities or enter new ones. Sonke's work in Kamva ended when its funding for this particular program ran out in 2011, and in fact it had always been conceived as a temporary project.[2] This was not communicated well to most of the young participants who were involved, however. For many people, program discontinuation was abrupt, confusing, and painful. Noluthando reflected on this upsetting experience: "We were not even notified, it just stopped. . . . I was quite down, because they didn't tell us what happened. They just said it came to an end."

Mr. Wize, a middle-aged man who works for the municipality's Department of Basic Education in Social Planning and Youth Affairs, helps oversee government-sponsored student clubs in over 257 area schools. Because of his position, he was one of the local liaisons who worked with Sonke when it was in the Kamva area. He had very positive things to say about the organization, as it focused on social justice issues with which his department is particularly concerned: gender-based violence, child abuse, safety, and so on. In fact, he kept running his own version of the Peer Educator Program long after Sonke left the area. And yet he recognized serious sustainability problems in Sonke's model. When talking about the end of the program and its impact on students, he suggested, "I think the reason might be communication failures. . . . I don't know who was supposed to go and tell the learners that Sonke is not operating anymore." Mr. Wize emphasized the importance of NGOs like Sonke to the work he is trying to do, making this issue of sustainability especially critical to resolve. "I very much felt the loss when Sonke left. . . . Now that they are not here, I have to think of ways to sustain the program in those schools where they were." In similar conversations with teachers and administrators, I learned that even program facilitators were confused about Sonke's exit from the community, expressing the feeling that they had not been properly informed. Later in our discussion, after reflecting on his experience with Sonke, Mr. Wize offered a critique of NGOs more generally, as he has worked with quite a few: "They need some new strategies. They need to strategize more on the issue of sustainability. Because as soon as they leave, they leave the program with the municipality, and the municipality can't reach all the areas. So the impact after they leave is not sustained. Many programs do die because of that. . . . It's a problem in the system." Such issues with long-term sustainability do not necessarily arise from a lack of good intentions, of course, but rather exist within a larger system of neoliberal privatization and government corruption that places educators at the mercy of outside organizations to supplement their programs. Mr. Wize indicated recognition of this as well, as he attributed the lack of sustainability to a "problem in the system" rather than misguided intentions on the part of the NGO. For example, in 2012, the Eastern Cape Department of Basic Education was heavily criticized in the news for underspending its allocated budget, particularly in the area of infrastructure.[3] Forty-nine school buildings throughout the province had been earmarked for replacement that year, but only twelve projects had been completed. Corruption is a huge problem in South Africa, and education is not exempt from its effects; in fact, recent reports show an increase in all kinds of corruption in schools across the country: embezzlement of funds, teacher sexual abuse of students, and crumbling infrastructure that has led to children being injured and even killed (Breakfast 2018; Onishi and Gebrekidan 2018).

In this political climate, it clearly is not realistic to assume the Department of Basic Education will pick up the slack once Sonke leaves. Since the organization implements many projects simultaneously all over the country (as well as in other African countries), it is often stretched thin in terms of staff members, funds, and time. Frequently, projects are initiated through a particular funding source and then terminated when the money runs out. In Kamva, some of the local residents who worked alongside Sonke as program facilitators chose to create makeshift programs that replicated the Sonke model after the organization left to fill the absence created in its wake. This shows how the outsourcing of educational prerogatives to NGOs and extracurricular programs means the potential creation of dependency relationships between local teachers and these external bodies. Though in theory Sonke works to create self-sufficiency and train community leaders who will continue their work after the organization leaves, in reality many programs deteriorate after the NGO exits the community. This leads to variable amounts of ideological change among community members after Sonke interventions.

These issues of sustainability and impact are echoed in the work of other scholars examining humanitarian aid projects around the globe, particularly on the African continent. Erica Bornstein (2001, 598–600) discusses a World Vision project in Zimbabwe involving child sponsorship from overseas donors that ended in 1987 "in order to promote the self-sufficiency of the community." Describing the story of Albert, a boy who was sponsored by a World Vision donor, she draws our attention to the serious problem of sustainability among NGOs: he was not told directly that the project was coming to an end. "They just closed up the offices," he explained. He considered it a phase in his life, a chapter that ended. When the project closed, he lost contact with his sponsor. He described a feeling of loss without the fortnightly meetings or the gifts. Albert experienced World Vision's initiative of self-sufficiency as abandonment.

For some Kamva students who participated in Sonke's programs, activities came to a particularly abrupt and upsetting end. One locally trained educator and volunteer from Wamkelekile was convicted of the rape of his relative, a minor, in a rural hilltop community a short drive from town. His jail sentence, according to the students who were in his class, marked the end of that branch of the Peer Educator Program for many youth, though only some of the participants fully grasped the events that led to its demise. Noluthando knew all about the incident and discussed it with me, expressing confusion, sadness, and anger. It seemed she learned about it through community gossip rather than any explanation from school, Wamkelekile, or Sonke officials. Noluthando said, "The thing I didn't like about the program is that our Peer Educator, he's the one who told us about things that were wrong, see? But then after the program, we heard that he was in jail because he raped someone."

Around the same time, Noluthando used the methods she had learned in her Peer Educator Program to help a girl in her class who had been raped. She convinced the girl to speak out and counseled her through the difficult time and also helped her stand up to other students who teased her and stigmatized her for the rape accusations. Much to her surprise, Noluthando later found out it was the very same facilitator from her Sonke Peer Educator Program who had raped her friend. Though the man was found guilty and spent a year in prison, in 2012 he was once again interacting with youth in the community. Many of them mentioned running into him and feeling a difficult mixture of emotions, including pity, sadness, and fear. Some said they would still speak to him, while others took care to avoid him. Noluthando confided in me that she would feel very afraid when she saw him in public. Such an upsetting turn of events calls attention to the ways in which NGO messages have the propensity to change greatly when enacted in rural settings through community members and also suggests the complexities of choosing local facilitators to run programs. Furthermore, it reminds us of the troubling heterodoxy that exists in a multicultural state like South Africa, as certain discourses become widespread and public even if they differ sharply from embedded, unconscious ideologies and actions on the ground.

Despite the fact that local youth rarely depended on Sonke for physical support, such as food, water, or school fees, the story of the boy who lost his mother shows that many relied on the emotional and psychological support the organization brought to their community.[4] A girl named Sisa who had participated in the Peer Educator Program, for instance, told me that it helped her feel confident enough to do well in school, but when it ended, she failed twelfth grade and had to repeat it. She explained that while she was in the program, "her mind was fresh," and the facilitator was talking to her on a daily basis in a way that increased her confidence, focus, and performance at school. Even though the subjects she did poorly in were unrelated to the Sonke curriculum, she was adamant that the program had psychological benefits that went beyond the curriculum and expectations of facilitators. Such narratives suggest that we take a much broader approach to understanding the community networks in which NGOs become embedded, even if they are only present physically for a short time. Rather than isolated programs focusing on specific topics, NGOs such as

Sonke can permeate communities in ways that are invisible on the surface but have long-lasting effects on individuals and their social networks.

For some, Sonke's withdrawal prompted not just frustration or sadness, but outrage. One young man said in 2012, years after the program ended, "We were so irate, because it just stopped. They didn't tell us what was happening. We were angry at our teachers, and we are still angry." His words call attention to the question of responsibility among organizations that come into communities on a temporary basis. What, if any, are their ethical commitments to the people with whom they work? Should NGOs such as Sonke be held accountable in the same way that democratic discourses suggest we hold political parties and elected representatives accountable, or the ways in which the South Africa Department of Basic Education monitors—at least in theory—public school educators and curricula? While Sonke prides itself on keeping the government in check, who or what does the same for the organization itself?

CASE STUDY 2: "EMPOWERMENT" THROUGH VISUAL MEDIA

In 2008, Sonke partnered with the Silence Speaks program from California on a "digital stories" project in the Kamva area (in addition to other sites around the country) that trained youth in digital video production and culminated in individual short videos using mixed media that highlighted young people's challenges in their communities.[5] Much in the way that Sonke employees structure their alignment with the liberal message of democratic equality across lines of gender and generation, young people's narratives of community problems in these videos largely fit into Western modes of personal salvation, liberal enlightenment, and individual agency. Program participants uniformly spoke in positive terms about the program, and it is not my intention here to minimize the importance it had to those young people. Instead, I wish to analyze the ideological structure on which the Digital Stories program rested. The project relied on particular forms of narrative structure that crafted a story very different from the kinds of stories most young Xhosa people are encouraged to tell openly. Another facet of interest here is that reports of the program by former participants echo some of the same issues with sustainability as those of the Peer Educator Program. Mangaliso, a young man from the Kamva area who participated in the Digital Stories project, explained his experience with Sonke: "I thought [before,] 'Okay fine, a man can cook, but it's not important ritually.' And when I met with Sonke my mind completely changed. I mean if you are surrounded by people who are stereotyping, you end up also stereotyping. They say if there's only one potato rotten in a bag they all get rotten. And I don't think I can ever stereotype now, because everyone is equal. What you can do, I can also do." The young man describes those not yet reoriented to the Sonke message as "rotten potatoes" and structures his personal transformation around notions of democratic equality and gender transformation. His story profiles resistance to nontraditional gender roles in his community, particularly cooking. While in the beginning of the story he is ostracized for doing "women's chores" such as making dinner at home, by the end his peers have seen the value in his ability to cook and seem converted to this message of gender equality. He brings his food to school and earns praise from his friends. Some of them even begin to cook as well, saying that it will attract girls and increase their popularity. Mangaliso spoke highly of the experience in the program as life-changing and formative.

His thoughts on Sonke's long-term impact in the community were far more ambivalent, as the epigraph to this chapter suggests.

> I think Sonke made changes, but I would say maybe for those months [that they were here]. I expected a change that would stay there. Not for a period of time. I didn't expect the change would have a duration, I thought it would always be there. . . . Ever since Sonke came, I thought I was going to see changes when it comes to gender inequalities, but honestly? I haven't. Sonke played their role, and they did a lot, but I think maybe they should be checking up on how things are going here.

Ms. Zinhle helped select students like Mangaliso for the Digital Stories project at her school and then passed them on to Sonke and Silence Speaks for workshops and training. She was thrilled with the idea of the program when she first heard about it: "I liked it from the very first time I heard about it, because the involvement of children is a good thing. That is why I was not reluctant to choose learners. I just chose learners freely and with enthusiasm." Nonetheless, she told me, she was disappointed with the outcome after the program ended and the stories were made. In particular, she expected the production of the stories to lead to widespread dissemination to other learners who had not had the opportunity to participate. She assumed there would be extensive community screenings of the videos and schoolwide discussions on their themes. "Here at school," she explained, "the impact of it was never felt. There was nothing that changed, because they were not coming to report to the school. They were not giving any feedback." Interestingly, she mentioned that she not only did not understand why Sonke left the community but also had no idea what inspired them to come in the first place. Despite this sense of unmet expectations, she did say that Sonke never promised further community engagement beyond the Digital Stories project, and her disappointment was based on her own personal hopes after seeing the work the organization did with her students. Nonetheless, it was clear to me that such hopes for widespread change and community involvement were shared by many, if not most, participants in the various Sonke programs.

Amahle also participated in the Digital Stories project, creating a video about a friend who was raped and the impact of absent fathers on young women in the area. When I spoke to her several years after the initial project, she had extremely positive things to say about her experience with Sonke: "The Sonke experience was very educational. I think it helped me look at stuff from a very different perspective. You know sometimes when you don't know that certain stuff is happening around you, you don't think anything of that sort is possible. Or you don't think it matters that much. . . . But with Sonke, we learned that everyone is from a different set of homes, everyone has particular problems. . . . We learned to listen to people. We learned to *care*." This idea of learning to have empathy for those around you on a one-to-one basis is particularly interesting to me here, as it suggests Sonke encouraged youth to realign their sense of self vis-à-vis their local communities. Rather than passively accept societal norms, they were trained to question them and consider the ways in which people around them might be suffering. Amahle also talked about how she was trained to resist behaviors she might have otherwise treated as socially acceptable.

> If I didn't learn that abuse is a bad thing, if I had a boyfriend who did that to me, I think—like most women in our culture—I would have gotten used to the fact that it's just something that happens. Now I learned that you should never allow something like that to happen.

And if it happens, you do this. This is who you call. . . . My mom talks to me, but she doesn't talk about everything. And with Sonke, we got to know stuff that sometimes our parents wouldn't feel very comfortable talking about to us.

This emphasis on children's agency over familial and communal loyalty is discussed elsewhere in the literature on democracy in African contexts; across the continent there are examples of ways in which Western liberal norms of individual agency and the rights of children conflict with non-Western cultural practices. The Cameroonian anthropologist Francis Nyamnjoh (2002) describes this conflict not through a neat binary of agency/dependence but rather through a discussion of the differences between *independence* and *interdependence*. He sees this as encapsulated in the phrase "a child is one person's only in the womb" (see also Bornstein 2001). The Digital Stories project worked with children directly, out of the context of their families and larger communities. Though Amahle's mother has been very supportive of the work she did with Sonke, one could easily imagine another parent being not so happy about the encouragement of this type of children's agency.

Rather than a simple process of translation from government or NGO to rural residents, the production of civil society involves interconnected social, economic, and political webs that, to borrow the anthropologist Anna Tsing's (2005) term, result in instances of "friction" in unanticipated ways. These webs include diverse nodes of intersection, such as NGOs, state institutions, municipal employees, and local actors such as chiefs, teachers, administrators, parents, and youth. Equally important, to understand these webs we must pay attention to the differing values underlying varying notions of civil society as a guiding concept. What this ideal means to the NGO does not necessarily translate to local participants.

Sonke's programs with youth in the Kamva area, while well intentioned and generally beloved during their multiyear tenure, often glossed over or ignored crucial notions of generational and gendered hierarchies that continue to structure Xhosa social reproduction and community in meaningful and visible ways. Encouraging youth to speak out on issues such as domestic violence and abuse is a deeply political act that can threaten their delicate position in the social hierarchy. Nonetheless, Sonke employees adamantly defend their emphasis on culture change for the cause of civil society, stressing the need to abolish practices such as patriarchy and male domination that do not align with democratic, liberal notions of equality and individual personhood. Though the organization promotes the idea of cultural relativism and the plurality of identities in the "Rainbow Nation" through its media presence, program materials, and use of facilitators with local language skills, its alignment with the Western ideals of democracy and human rights nonetheless makes it difficult or perhaps even impossible for some participants to simultaneously maintain national and cultural allegiances.

In other words, Sonke upholds cultural relativism until the point at which it comes into conflict with democratic liberalism, and citizen production that adheres to ideals of democracy remains at the core of the organization's mission regardless of its potential to offend or disrupt. At a time when so many rural South Africans find state projects of democratic governance suspect, the concept of national unity through shared ideological values is far from neutral territory; to be fair, this is something of which Sonke staff are, for the most part, acutely aware. Sonke's community involvement in Kamva exemplifies the intensely political and potentially problematic nature of their work more broadly. But how does this type of political education compare to the work teachers are doing in public school classrooms? What does the state curriculum offer in the way of democratic, liberal education? It is to these questions that I now turn.

CHAPTER FOUR

Life Orientation as Democratic Project

CURRICULAR MISTRANSLATIONS?

One afternoon in November, I sat in the teacher's lounge at Cedarwood Secondary School transcribing interviews on my laptop while the teachers around me were buried in seemingly endless stacks of student work. Out of nowhere, the teacher sitting to my right paused in her work. "Amber, what do you think the cause of homosexuality is?" It turned out she was grading the results of an assignment she had given her Life Orientation students in which she asked them to discuss the "problem" of homosexuality and offer up a "solution." I countered that I did not see it as a problem. As we politely debated our differing viewpoints, she explained to me that homosexuality went against the teachings of the Bible. This assignment certainly was not in the national curriculum for Life Orientation but rather was her own interpretation of how to teach students about contemporary social issues and discuss how society might solve them.

This anecdote shows the often great disparities between the national curriculum on political and social ideology and what is actually taught by teachers in local contexts like Cedarwood. South Africa's liberal constitution is infused in student lessons on human rights and democracy, yet this is no guarantee of what makes it into actual classroom settings (Hues 2011). In this chapter, I discuss how democracy is translated and

FIGURE 4.1   Students line up for morning assembly at a rural Eastern Cape school.
Photo by Sarah Caufield, 2012

shaped in ambivalent lessons in the rural Eastern Cape. Western-based
educational practices, like discussion and active learning, are alien to many
Kamva teachers and lead them to negotiate the curriculum on an individual basis in order to meet particular cultural needs and understandings. In many ways, the educational system of the democratic state is less
familiar to Xhosa teachers and parents than anything that preceded it. In
fact, this chapter and the next show how elements of school life under
apartheid are actually held in high regard by many rural South Africans.
This is an unexpected result of the nation's path to and enactment of specific forms of democracy that are at odds with local realities and lead to
the kinds of nostalgic discourses discussed in the next chapter. Put another way, this chapter shows how apartheid-era education in many ways
aligned more closely with Xhosa intergenerational norms and conceptions of youth than the current democratic curricular mandate does.

Here I turn to a particular phase in the production of South African
democracy: how the state educates young citizens in the shadow of apartheid's end. I also ask how Xhosa cultural and historical worldviews act as
filters for larger political and moral discourses. Eastern Cape youth learn

about democracy and its attendant liberal human rights agenda through public school curricula that aim to create civically engaged citizens of the postapartheid state. But they also are subject to the ways in which local educators filter information through their own political, cultural, and moral ideologies.

This is anything but a simple process of translation. I also want to make clear that it would be reductive to portray teachers as traditionalists and the national curriculum as inherently modern and democratic; instead, this discursive binary emerges as a particular ideology held by many people (though, importantly, not all). A liberal national agenda is producing a backlash of traditionalism as a practice of resistance, though this does not necessarily indicate an actual desire to return to past ways of life. In other words, the idea that democracy should be equated with modernity while tradition is labeled as antidemocratic is a fallacy, albeit a tenacious one (Owusu 1997). African indigenous systems of governance had for centuries included democratic processes, even if not in name. For example, Judith van Allen (1972) writes about the practice of "sitting on a man" in precolonial Igbo societies in which women would shame men through collective protest. This exercise of women's political power was largely overlooked by colonists, to whom it did not appear as a recognizable form of political agency, especially because of the preexisting norms for Victorian women. To fully understand how democracy in Africa functions, then, we must contextualize it in particular histories and understand the ways in which historical narratives are constructed rather than simply reflect the past. This contextualization, unfortunately, is often missed by the South African public education curriculum; rather, the concept of democracy is presented as monolithic and universal even though this does not align with many local realities. Such assumptions mean that teachers are burdened with a curriculum that does not fully attend to cultural difference and youth receive mixed messages about what it means to live in a democracy.

Though state discourses on topics such as children's rights, gender equality, and freedom are embedded in the curriculum across provincial and cultural lines, teachers always present them through their own preexisting cultural worldviews and local perspectives—a phenomenon that is of course not unique to either the Eastern Cape or South Africa more generally. This means that the presence of a nationwide policy on teaching democracy hardly leads to the production of one type of democratic citizen. In many cases, practices in the classroom conflict with rhetorical and discursive strategies, evidencing disjunctures between unconscious actions and conscious narratives. My examination of in-class practices in this chapter illuminates the ways in which democratic values are locally negotiated in the classroom between teachers and students.[1] More specifically, I examine how daily actions and behaviors both unconsciously and consciously create, sustain, and reorient value structures, hierarchies, and political ideologies in local communities (Bucholtz 1999; Ortner 1984). Xhosa resistance to democratic ideologies is both a reaffirmation of previously existing social structures, such as rigid age hierarchies and discourses on respect, and evidence of local actors' agency in creating new societal formations. I show how my ethnographic encounters point to a rejection of national children's rights discourses primarily on the basis of cultural traditionalism and Xhosa identity practices.

EDUCATIONAL HISTORY IN SOUTH AFRICA

While the Bantu Education Act of 1953 may have codified racism, it certainly was not the beginning of racially motivated and segregated schooling in South Africa. Much like the rest of racist legislation under the National Party government, unequal educational structures extend further back than apartheid.

Educational experiences have varied greatly based on racial and ethnic designations since the earliest days of the Dutch settlers at the Cape, though they have always included deep power imbalances that reflected the larger experience of European colonization. In the early days of the Colony, the Dutch East India Company played a large role in education efforts, as did the Dutch Reformed Church. Until the late 1800s and early 1900s, the colonial government spent very little on nonwhite students, leaving them at the mercy of charitable missionary societies that took them on as part of their "civilizing" mission of natives. Where Black students were formally educated during the earliest years of the Colony, it was mainly in the service of teaching them Dutch as a tool for conversion to Christianity. Literacy was thought of as a necessary skill for religious participation, and children were taught to read in order to read the Bible. Over time, however, the focus of systematic educational efforts shifted increasingly to poor white children, and nonwhites were largely left behind (Abdi 2002).

As parts of what are now the Eastern Cape were annexed to the Cape Colony, missionaries began to found native schools connected to the church that worked to bolster literacy and integrate Xhosa people according to the ideals of Christian colonial life. This fomented internal divisions between School (Christian) and Red (pagan) Xhosa and newly fractured the community (Davis 1969; Mayer and Mayer 1970). Like elsewhere in the colonial world, such educational projects rested on the fundamental beliefs of native inferiority, racial hierarchies, and salvation through Christianity. Native schools rarely offered more than basic vocational training, as the colonists had specific labor needs that this education was meant to satisfy (Hansen and Twaddle 2002). Notably, however, many of the early iterations of these schools taught European missionaries' children, meaning that white and Black students learned in the same classrooms, unlike during the apartheid years. This is a salient reminder that the highly structured racial segregation of apartheid belies the full story of race in South Africa, which is far more complex and dynamic. Even where education was integrated racially in preapartheid South Africa, though, it was still deeply gendered. Up through the 1800s, mission schools were primarily for boys, which should remind us of the fact that Christianity played an instrumental role in crafting and entrenching gendered divisions of labor in ways that are now often wrongly attributed to precolonial traditionalism and essentialized notions of African culture (Healy-Clancy 2014). In the 1800s, the British began using schools as a way to anglicize the native population.

By 1903, as the British state took over education, racially segregated schooling became codified into law. While nationalized education meant more widespread Black education, it nonetheless relied on the belief in a hierarchy of races that was used to justify vastly unequal schooling. Of course, this justification also reflected the fact that colonists were ever fearful of the Black majority, especially an educated one that might be able to organize and seriously threaten white supremacy. Many South Africans at the time criticized mission schools for bolstering the status of Blacks in undesirable ways, and the broader international discourse of social Darwinism in the early twentieth century served to justify inferior education for nonwhite students across the colonial world. Native colleges like Fort

Hare in the Eastern Cape sought to meet increasing demands for higher education while keeping Black students out of white universities (Nkomo 1990). In addition, many rural Black schools were situated on white farmlands, meaning that white farmers had some measure of control over Black education—to the great detriment of these students (Abdi 2002).

By the 1940s, when schooling for Blacks was fully implemented nationally, the architecture of racial segregation was already firmly in place. This history set the stage for later legislative acts of racism in education under apartheid, as well as the massive protests centered on schools in the later years of that regime. A commission on native education produced a report in 1949 stating that Blacks needed separate educational facilities that would be specifically under the control of the Ministry of Native Affairs rather than the South African Ministry. This led to the Bantu Education Act, which halted state subsidizing of mission schools, where Black students were by and large previously educated. Then, in 1959, this segregated schooling was extended to universities. The Bantu Education Act was justified on the grounds that it was wrong to train Black students for careers that would never be available to them. Materials in the service of Bantu Education were replete with racist portraits of Africans and skewed perspectives of history in favor of white colonization, and native languages were banned (Clark and Worger 2004). Education was a central tool in the creation of obedience to the apartheid state.

Because of these legal acts, the ANC and related organizations increasingly recognized the importance of education as a rallying point in their movement for independence and racial equality. By the 1970s, overcrowding due to underfunded schools was a huge problem in Black education. Steve Biko, an activist who helped lead the Black Consciousness movement, founded the South African Students' Organization (SASO) in 1968, and soon students began to strike on university campuses nationwide. These protests came to a head with the 1976 Soweto uprising and the police killing of thirteen-year-old Hector Petersen, who quickly became a visible emblem of the bloody battle against institutional racism in South Africa—and, for many, remains so today. Schools were therefore at the epicenter of antiapartheid protests; rather than create an obedient workforce as it had intended, the apartheid state had inadvertently radicalized a generation of Black youth. This is particularly important to keep in mind when we turn to nostalgic narratives in the next chapter, as many of these hinge on a romanticized portrayal of Bantu Education.

POSTAPARTHEID EDUCATION

Although changing educational policy was at the heart of much anti-apartheid organizing, the postapartheid state's public education system remains mired in the legacy of apartheid. For many South Africans, the antiapartheid movement failed to establish equality in education. After 1994, control of education was divided between the national government and the nine newly created provinces. However, in line with other forms of neoliberal economic policy, the 1996 South African Schools Act decentralized control of education and gave much of it back to individual schools. This allowed school governing bodies, like parent-teacher associations, to set student fees that would enhance school resources and allow for new hires. What this has meant functionally is that wealthier areas have much better school funding than poorer areas. Unsurprisingly, this occurs mostly along color lines. As the education theorist Clive Harber (2001, 16) wrote of the early days of South African democratic schooling, "Admission on the grounds of race may now be illegal, but high fees may well have the same net effect." Recent census data show that 9.1 percent of Black South Africans ages twenty-five to sixty-four have attained a postsecondary education, compared to 38.3 percent of whites in the same age range (South Africa Department of Basic Education 2015). During the height of Bantu Education, overcrowded classrooms often contained seventy students with just one teacher. In 2012, Eastern Cape classrooms I visited frequently had similar numbers. In such conditions, getting the teacher's individual attention is often an exercise in futility. During the year I spent visiting Cedarwood Primary, a shiny new computer lab partly funded by an NGO donation sat unused because there was no qualified computer science teacher. Teachers and students alike struggle against an education system in crisis; reports of corruption in this sector are high, and materials meant to enrich classrooms frequently do not make it into the hands of local teachers and staff (Breakfast 2018; Harber 2001). In short, much of the Freirean radicalism inherent in antiapartheid approaches to decolonizing education gave way to a market-driven philosophy that did little to dismantle previously existing racial and class hierarchies in the field (Freire 1970; Harber 2001).

All this is not to say the state has not tried. Since the end of apartheid, South Africa has had a flurry of changes in educational design at the national level meant to democratize education and remove racism from its curriculum. The need to better prepare students for the workforce, increase matriculation examination pass rates, and infuse multiculturalism and democratic ideals into the curriculum have all driven these efforts. In 1996, the Department of Basic Education instituted Outcomes-Based Education (OBE), which focused on a "learner-centered ethos" and was originally developed in the United States (Botha 2002, 362). As the name implies, OBE is concerned with measuring student outcomes—in other words, how much was actually learned. In theory, this strategy was meant to ensure that students received a quality education that emphasized critical thinking and trained them adequately for future careers. What OBE meant in practice, according to many teachers and administrators, was an overwhelming and unwieldy workload, involving frequent mandatory progress reports and learning assessments. Teachers felt like they were saddled with mountains of paperwork that took time away from teaching. Because of this extensive backlash, the state refined this program in the National Curriculum Statement (NCS) in 2010 and in 2011 added the Curriculum and Assessment Policy Statements (CAPS), which mandates fewer learner projects and written assessments for educators (CAPS is meant to amend the NCS rather than replace it) (Cobban 2010; Jones 2013).

Despite these changes, teachers still frequently lament what they see as an unbearable load of paperwork and assessment-based exercises that keep them from focusing on teaching. Ms. Legodi is not a teacher, but she can certainly relate to their frustrations. An older woman serving as deputy chief education specialist in Kamva, she is intensely frustrated with South Africa's education bureaucracy. Her job is attending to the area's special needs learners, and although she has been in the position since 1995, she told me that she still feels unable to get a grasp on it. Much like Ms. Mbodi, the psychologist who was discussed earlier, Ms. Legodi laments how underresourced and overworked department employees are. She is the sole person responsible for special needs learners for 250 schools. Though she cares deeply for the students, her work is clearly a source of great stress. As she has been working in the school system for a long time, she can recall clearly the days of OBE: "With the introduction of OBE, there were a lot of terms that were confusing to teachers. Then it was streamlined to NCS. Still, the teachers complained that there's a lot of written work. This makes it so they don't have enough time to teach. They are always busy writing, preparing for us departmental officials, . . . so they are busy writing instead of doing their actual job of teaching." Though this may be true, critiques leveled against the South Africa Department of Basic Education also reflect cultural differences and personal perspectives on pedagogical strategy and classroom norms. Xhosa teachers often define the act of teaching very differently from liberal democratic pedagogy.

LIFE ORIENTATION

In 2002, in alignment with the nascent democratic state, the South Africa Department of Basic Education pioneered a course mandatory for all students in Grades 7 through 12 called Life Orientation. Picking up where Life Skills, taught in the earlier grades, leaves off, this course covers a wide range of topics that are not dealt with in the rest of the school day, from nutrition and physical education to gender equality and child abuse (Prinsloo 2007). Life Orientation class takes up two instructional hours per week in both the Senior phase (Grades 7–9) and Further Education and Training phase (Grades 10–12) (South Africa Department of Basic Education 2011a). I have observed Life Orientation lessons that trained children to understand the difference between healthy and unhealthy foods, encouraged them to exercise by doing jumping jacks in class, and informed them of their basic human rights as enshrined in the South African Bill of Rights. Put another way, the introduction of Life Orientation has meant that "schools had to be concerned with the development of the whole person"— a far cry from the education offered Black students under apartheid (Diale, Pillay, and Fritz 2014, 83). Life Orientation asks educators and students to both celebrate and embrace cultural diversity and enforce the constitution as the ultimate authority on questions of law and rights. These two imperatives are frequently at odds with one another, as I demonstrate below.

Much like Sonke's programs, I situate the Life Orientation classroom as a microcosm of larger state discourses on democracy, since one of its primary goals is producing thoughtful and engaged citizens who participate fully in the democratic process on both the local and national levels (South Africa Department of Basic Education 2011a). This educational priority reflects the postapartheid national rhetoric of an inclusive state based on equality and universal civic participation. It is also grounded in the assumption that children and youth should inherently possess specific rights and responsibilities in the democratic state and that they have the capacity to act as engaged members of civil society even before reaching what the law defines as adulthood (in South Africa, eighteen years of age). Prioritizing engaged citizenship presumes a specific vision of political action that insists on active rather than passive participation (Abdi 2002). But Life Orientation in practice does not offer a microcosm of an *ideal* democracy. Instead, it shows the realities of implementing a democratic curriculum in the midst of complex cultural tensions. In the Life Orientation classroom, we have the opportunity to see both the great hopes and the spectacular failures of South Africa's democratic project where it begins.

Officially, the South Africa Department of Basic Education defines the purpose of Life Orientation in the following terms, which are worth reproducing here in full.

> Life Orientation equips learners to engage on personal, psychological, neuro-cognitive, motor, physical, moral, spiritual, cultural, socio-economic and constitutional levels, to respond positively to the demands of the world, to assume responsibilities, and to make the most of life's opportunities. It enables learners to know how to exercise their constitutional rights and responsibilities, to respect the rights of others, and to value diversity, health and well-being. Life Orientation promotes knowledge, values, attitudes and skills that prepare learners to respond effectively to the challenges that confront them as well as the challenges they will have to deal with as adults, and to play a meaningful role in society and the economy. (South Africa Department of Basic Education 2011a)

The ambiguity of the rhetoric advocating learners to "respond positively to the demands of the world" and "make the most of life's opportunities" leaves a wide margin of interpretation for individual educators, which is of particular interest here. What should we consider the "demands of the world"? Exactly what counts as "opportunities," and how do you "make the most of them"? Within the Life Orientation general goals, a portion of the curriculum more specifically addresses citizenship education: "It is important for learners to be politically literate, that is, to know and understand democratic processes. The importance of volunteerism, social service, and involvement in a democratic society [is] emphasized." Thus a close and critical examination of the South African Constitution and the rights contained therein is a primary objective of the Life Orientation class.

Beyond creating politically conscious youth, however, this educational objective prizes socialization to those values understood by the state as "democratic." As I show in what follows, this aim is met with varying results and teaching strategies in local contexts, precisely because of the difficulty of interpreting the state's objectives through one's own cultural lens. Many of the terms used by the state are not clearly defined and are open to multiple interpretations depending on the context. For instance, "rights and responsibilities" in the above official policy are alluded to without the provision of universal definitions for these terms. In presenting my ethnographic data, I show that people have very different views on what this should entail. Teachers and parents emphasize the "responsibilities" element of this language, and their understanding of what youth should be responsible for is structured around Xhosa cultural norms.

The Life Orientation curriculum also works toward the recognition of what it calls "indigenous value systems." This goal is meant to make explicit the need for respect in a multicultural state with a history of oppression of its nonwhite residents. The Department of Basic Education outlines this in its curriculum statements.

> In the 1960s, the theory of multiple-intelligences forced educationists to recognise that there were many ways of processing information to make sense of the world, and that, if one were to define intelligence anew, one would have to take these different approaches into account. Up until then the Western world had only valued logical, mathematical and specific linguistic abilities, and rated people as 'intelligent' only if they were adept in these ways. Now people recognise the wide diversity of knowledge systems through which people make sense of and attach meaning to the world in which they live. Indigenous knowledge systems in the South African context refer to a body of knowledge embedded in African philosophical thinking and social practices that have evolved over thousands of years. The National Curriculum Statement Grades 10–12 (General) has infused indigenous knowledge systems into the Subject Statements. It acknowledges the rich history and heritage of this country as important contributors to nurturing the values contained in the Constitution. (South Africa Department of Basic Education 2011a)

Taken together, these descriptions of the national curriculum leave one to wonder how you teach students to be rights-bearing, responsible citizens while simultaneously attending to the varying worldviews of different cultural groups. How do individual teachers prioritize the "rich history and heritage" of a multicultural, pluralistic nation while acknowledging state demands for the production of a specific type of citizen? What happens when particular cultural knowledge systems do not neatly align with South African legal frameworks?

In attempting to redress the horrors and injustices of apartheid, South African legislation seeks to promote recognition of cultural diversity on many levels. However, this venerable goal of equality across cultures is highly problematic to enact on the ground (Comaroff and Comaroff 2004b). While the above curriculum statement pays lip service to multiple ways of knowing, it ultimately prioritizes one official rhetoric—that of the South African Constitution. Put another way, cultural diversity is respected as long as it does not conflict with the constitution. When local ideas of right and wrong conflict with the Life Orientation curriculum, how do individual teachers deal with the resulting cultural tension? What governs their decisions in the classroom on a daily basis?

Rote versus Active Learning

Maybe the fact that she is relatively young and therefore has lived through less of apartheid-era education has something to do with the fact that Ms. Yandani has welcomed the introduction of Life Orientation. She teaches at a secondary school just down the road from Cedarwood and is passionate about education. She is especially interested in connecting on a personal level with her students in order to guide them through life's challenges—something you do not often see in rural schools with high student-to-teacher ratios. Her enthusiasm for the course garnered her a nomination from the school principal to participate in a two-year training program at Rhodes University that was sponsored by the Department of Basic Education, during which she attended occasional multiday workshops that used experiential techniques to train teachers in the Life Orientation curriculum. When we first met, she was working toward an honors degree in Curriculum Development, with the hope that she would later use it to teach education at the university level.

Ms. Yandani loves Life Orientation because she was acting as a mentor to students long before its introduction; in fact, her students had started to address her as "Mama"—a fact of which she is deeply proud. In this sense, the new curriculum mandate simply codified what she was already doing in practice. In her class, she leads discussions on various case studies, like teenage pregnancy or a child-headed family, with the rationale that she can check students' decision-making skills on the real-life issues many of them deal with regularly. She sees Life Orientation as an important supplement to traditional academic subjects, in that it takes a holistic approach to children's lived realities and experiences beyond the classroom. Nonetheless, it still includes national standards, objectives, protocols, and assessments. Ms. Yandani described her affinity to the Life Orientation curriculum: "I've always wanted a platform where one can speak freely to the learners. Especially at the high school level. Because they are the ones who are most affected by teenage pregnancy, HIV and AIDS, and all those issues." She painted a picture of her classroom as one free of indoctrination and open to multiple viewpoints, and in this she is somewhat of an anomaly in this area, where rote educational practices still have a firm grip on classroom norms and a diversity of opinions are not generally encouraged. In this sense, Ms. Yandani serves as a model of what Life Orientation is ideally supposed to be. "With Life Orientation, we take it as one is unique," she said. "And what you believe in, I don't have to believe in. So we don't have to indoctrinate them." This is a more discussion-based, nondogmatic approach to education. Yet it rarely matched the actions I observed in classrooms, and few of the educators I spoke with shared Ms. Yandani's perspective on teaching. In fact, *indoctrination* seemed an apt word for many Life Orientation classes I attended.

In my forays into Eastern Cape secondary school classrooms, the active learning, discussion-based environment advocated in the National Curriculum Statement was almost nowhere to be found. Instead, lessons that the Statement outlines as meant to foster discussion and creativity became lectures parroted back in unison by students, devoid of dialogue or critical thinking. Little space was made for questions, and "Yes, teacher" and "No, teacher" were clearly well-rehearsed lines by the time students reached secondary school. Classrooms can be characterized by a relationship of subservience. Children and youth are not only expected to complete in-class assignments and do homework, but they are expected to follow orders almost regardless of their content or relevance to academics. For instance, children in Kamva are often tasked with staying at the end of the day to clean the classrooms or with making tea and coffee for their teachers between lessons. In some instances, I witnessed girls commanded to stay after class to do their teacher's hair. While this portrait of schools may sound abusive or exploitative, neither teachers nor students appeared to see it that way. Instead, it was presented as part of the daily expectations of being a student.

One day, I was sitting among students in a Life Orientation class when the teacher handed out a worksheet. One side contained a list of basic human rights as seen in the South African Constitution, and the other side presented fictional violations of those rights. The teacher told students to work individually, drawing a connecting line between each right and its corresponding violation. Though the teacher presented this as a straightforward assignment, I personally found that many of the listed violations fit multiple rights definitions. For example, a case illustrating the rape of a child could arguably be considered a violation of the "right to freedom and security of the person," the "right to human dignity," and "the right to be protected from abuse" (Constitution of the Republic of South Africa 1996). Despite this ambiguity, the teacher had students recite their answers aloud and then scolded those who chose an answer that did not exactly match the one provided in the answer key. The teacher conveyed the message that these rights, as enumerated in the constitution, were unambiguous, objective, and transparent. She also had students engage with them through rote memorization. There was no discussion of how students arrived at their "wrong" answers or how alternative perspectives might see these issues differently.

This lesson stands in stark contrast to the wording in National Curriculum documents. For example, a major stated emphasis of the Life Orientation curriculum is the ability to dialogue across cultural and religious lines. Furthermore, encouraging critical thinking—as opposed to rote memorization—is clearly emphasized in the Department of Basic Education literature. In the Grade 11 curriculum description for the topic "Democracy and Human Rights," teachers are instructed to help students "identify and critically analyze various moral and spiritual issues and dilemmas, such as right-to-life, euthanasia, cultural practices and traditions, economic issues and environmental issues." In Grade 12, students should be able to "evaluate their own position when dealing with discrimination

FIGURE 4.2   Students are expected to keep the school clean, both during and outside class hours. Photo by Sarah Caufield, 2012

and human rights violations, taking into account the Bill of Rights" (South Africa Department of Basic Education 2011b). The worksheet activity presented students with the Bill of Rights, but the teacher did not give students the opportunity to evaluate personal circumstances that may have led to their answers. Thinking critically was not part of the lesson. These realities are also in direct contrast to the Freirean influence in antiapartheid educational policy; Paulo Freire (1970, 72) heavily critiqued what he called the "banking model" of education, in which students are perceived as empty vessels for teachers' knowledge. In my experience in Eastern Cape classrooms, this is actually a good descriptor for much of the pedagogical strategies still being used.

To understand the classroom interactions and dynamics in the rural Eastern Cape, we need to take a step back and understand how most Xhosa communities think about the role of children and youth within a broader social hierarchy. *Hlonipha*, which refers to a cultural practice of respect both in practice and in language, is a value of central cultural importance to both Xhosa and Zulu people in South Africa. It provides a set of crucial values that governs interactions between genders and generations, including taboos (Hickel 2015). Hlonipha clearly plays a role in classroom norms for students and teachers in rural schools. Children are taught from an early age that talking back to an elder is forbidden and will be severely punished. Children should receive things from adults by extending two hands cupped together, deferentially. They should address adults with specific gendered terms of respect. They learn that decision making is the purview of adults (and within that category, primarily men). This is demonstrated not only in compliance in the classroom but also in the ways teachers conceive of their role of guiding youth more generally. Teachers' choices to reframe or even omit elements of the national curriculum make sense in light of such Xhosa ideologies on generations and the role of youth (Harley et al. 2000), as well as their own educational experiences growing up during the era of Bantu Education. While the democratic curriculum wants students to participate actively and express their opinions in order to highlight diversity and foster individualism, Xhosa hierarchies of respect encourage conformity, communal values, and rote learning. As my friend Fundani explained to me one day, "When we grew up, we were taught that you do not ask questions to the elders." In this sense, Xhosa social relations between elders and youth actually align more closely with certain elements of Bantu Education, in that the latter encouraged a strict generational and gendered hierarchy and inculcated youth with obedience to authority and emphasized conformity.

Ms. Fodo is Cedarwood Primary School's principal and an English teacher since 1979. She is a kind woman who is exhausted by the many curricular redesigns she has witnessed. She calls the type of education I have been describing "traditional teaching." She explained to me that it would involve "standing in front of the class and teaching, giving class-work, marking, and having very little activity from the learners." While she may resist certain aspects of these former pedagogical strategies such as corporal punishment, she nonetheless laments the overall decline in respect for authority among her students. She describes today's South African classrooms as noisy and unruly, compared to the quiet and obedient classrooms in her early career. She believes the drop in matriculation examination pass rates that she has witnessed over her years of teaching is directly tied to this decrease in academic standards.[2] Despite the fact that the national curriculum is continually overhauled to include more active learning, Ms. Fodo teaches the same way she has always taught: "I teach English as I have been teaching it, and children have passed and passed it well. I only change the form of assessment. I can't really keep track of all the changes, and English remains English whether you involve the learners or you don't involve them. A tense will always be a tense. An adjective is always an adjective." While there are certainly practical reasons for the defense of rote education strategies, such as large class sizes and a lack of in-depth teacher training on curricular redesigns, there are clearly cultural and historical elements at play as well.[3] Put more simply, "active learning" is an imported practice that stands in direct contrast to both historical and cultural norms. Through the lens of Xhosa culture, it is illegible and ineffective as compared to the so-called traditional teaching of which Ms. Fodo speaks.

Mr. Hackula is the principal of a primary school outside of Kamva and also a teacher of Life Orientation. For him, the goal of this class is to tell students "what they should do and what they should not do." Interestingly, this is the initial way he described his approach to teaching the class. Soon after he spoke, though, he shifted his tone: "You must differentiate between what is good and what is not good. . . . I'm deciding for them. The learners decide for themselves as well. To take what is good for them." This quote implies a clear notion of objective morality that adults wish to impart forcefully to potentially misguided youth. At the same time, Mr. Hackula projected an apparent awareness that the postapartheid state curriculum encourages a more subjective and student-centered approach to the discussion of values and morals and quickly corrected himself to illustrate his alignment with these ideals, at least discursively. Such teaching philosophies and historical experiences of educational transition make for lessons that often switch ambivalently between dogmatic indoctrination and attention to cultural and individual difference. This was evident in Mr. Hackula's behavior as well. He decried corporal punishment in an interview with me, stating that it was ineffective in solving disciplinary problems and that he never used it himself. A few weeks later, I accidentally surprised him in the act of beating a misbehaving student with a switch in his office.

Many teachers expressed deep dissatisfaction with a curriculum that encouraged discussion-based learning, as it presented to them what felt like ambiguous learning objectives and an educational strategy foreign to previous modes of teaching in the community. Ms. Zinhle, a woman who was trained by Sonke and facilitated some of their workshops in Kamva, was born and raised in Kamva and has been teaching since 1983. She now teaches Life Orientation and has found it hard to weather the many shifts in educational design over recent years: "With the change of the curriculum, first it says you must teach the learners. Then they come with a curriculum that says, 'Don't teach. Facilitate.' You just facilitate, you just give them the topic and let them discuss." Ms. Zinhle found the mandate to "facilitate" learning not just confusing, but impossible. She did not see how it would contribute to student knowledge, nor did she seem to understand her expected role in a discussion-based educational model. In some cases, teachers rectify this confusion on how to act by simply doling out paperwork to students instead of lecturing on the material.

These stories make clear that a discussion-based classroom environment becomes alien and undesirable when recast in light of local perspectives. If youth socialization in Xhosa communities depends on obedience to authority and notions of hierarchical respect, how can an egalitarian classroom environment with "facilitation" instead of "teaching" be understood locally as a best practice? While the Life Orientation curriculum preaches the importance of learning about cultural diversity, such diversity does not structure the actual format of learning itself. Instead, the curriculum is modeled on progressive educational norms. In short, the content of Life Orientation might be diverse, but the methods are not.

Crucially, this emphasis on obedience to authority is not to say that rebellious youth are absent in places like the rural Eastern Cape or that all young people fall in line obediently behind their elders. Instead, rebellion and intergenerational tension surfaces in ways that tend to fit within prescribed cultural frameworks and may be invisible to outsiders. While children of all ages seem to be remarkably obedient when given commands, asked questions, or taught lessons, adolescents often rebel from the authority of elders indirectly through late-night drinking, inattention to studying, and a desire to distance themselves in later childhood and adulthood from rural, "traditional" lifestyles that they associate with the older generations. Thus youth rebellion is rarely exercised in direct confrontation with adults, making classroom debate and discussion highly unlikely in this context. In this sense, there is a major oversight in curricular design at the national level: it does not account for how cultural norms play a critical role in the process of teaching and learning. Such an analysis offers one (though certainly not the only) potential factor to explain the notoriously low exam pass rates in the rural Eastern Cape. In 2013, the province had the lowest rate of success on the National Senior Certificate exam: 64.9 percent, compared to the country's 78.2 percent.[4] The exam includes sections, for example, that ask students to critically analyze evidence, interpret information, and draw individual conclusions.[5] When most students are trained using memorization for a test that emphasizes critical thinking and the ability to argue one's own positions, it is easy to imagine why pass rates in places like the rural Eastern Cape are so low.

Rights versus Responsibilities

The Life Orientation curriculum emphasizes the notion of liberal human rights in a democratic state. By Grade 12, for example, students should be able to meet goals like "addressing unequal power relations and power inequality between genders" and "participating in discussions, projects, campaigns, and events which address discrimination and human rights violations" (South Africa Department of Basic Education 2011b). And yet almost every single teacher I met with or whose classroom I observed in the rural Eastern Cape felt the need to balance this emphasis with the importance of youth responsibilities. This is relatively absent in the national documents provided by the Department of Basic Education: there is some discussion of students' responsibility to participate in civic life and to foster environmental sustainability, but it is minimal compared to the extensive discussion of rights (Rice 2017). And when responsibility is mentioned in the official curriculum, it differs substantially from the kinds of obligations with which rural teachers and parents appear to be concerned. Tando explained, "They teach us how to take care of ourselves and to recognize our strengths and weaknesses." He told me that many children were taking advantage of the national emphasis on rights in the country: "Democracy has brought us rights, but sometimes I feel like people are misusing their rights. Like children in schools, they don't want to be punished. They say that it's their right. And some of them don't want to go to school. They say they can do whatever they want."

Much of the discussion of this imbalance between rights and responsibilities hinged on anxieties over cultural loss. Elders and youth alike stressed the importance of keeping Xhosa culture intact in the face of threats from democratic teaching. Adults frequently reported to me the areas in which today's youth are seen as distancing themselves from Xhosa culture: their inability to farm and tend cattle; their lack of knowledge of traditional Xhosa dance, basketry, and beadwork; their support of feminism; and their adherence to outside spiritual practices such as Satanism. One young teacher, Ms. Tyrone, told me, "The olden dances were performed by our fathers and mothers. Some people forget about their culture. When we are going to do our traditions they are not interested. Few people know those dances. What they see on TV, they think that is their culture." This emphasis on traditionalism reflects a growing fear that democracy will erode essential Xhosa practices and beliefs; in other words, concern with cultural preservation and authenticity seems heightened in the postapartheid moment.

I observed one Life Orientation class covering the topic of ubuntu, a uniquely South African term that is roughly translated as "humanity." The teacher had students recite the definition in unison, discussing how it allows room for different cultures and all races under one nation in its emphasis on mutual respect. She reminded students that "the good of the group is more important than the good of the individual." This lesson is more reflective of Xhosa communal identification practices than the current national political discourse. While ubuntu emphasizes the communal good, the national curriculum stresses individual citizenship and personhood. Teachers' discursive strategies emphasizing preferred cultural values are often at odds with state ideals of democratic citizenship.

FIGURE 4.3   In Arts and Culture and Life Orientation classes, lessons are often intended to preserve Xhosa cultural heritage. Photo by author, 2012

My conversations with students about the South African Constitution's Bill of Rights demonstrated this perspective on communalism over individual notions of personhood. When questioned about his agreement with the right to equality for all, one teenaged boy told me that "all people should be treated equal because a person is a person with other people." "A person is a person with other people" is the translation of a famous proverb, "Umntu ngumuntu ngabantu," and a telling reflection of how many Xhosa South Africans envision a healthy society. Democratic-based rights discourses, which emphasize individual agency, do not always fit within local South African frameworks of communalism (Robins 2008). Liberal democracy rests on the idea of creating individual citizens rather than emphasizing communitarian hierarchies, which is difficult to translate in many cross-cultural settings (Englund 2006).

Teachers' fears of cultural loss are not just about the neglect of responsibility but also the misinterpretation of the very definition of human rights and what they ought to entail. Thus many teachers and parents feel unable to maintain their authority over young people, understanding this phenomenon as the result of the latter's misinterpretation of democratic rights discourses imported from outside cultural contexts. In this sense, adults perceive young people's invoking of rights discourses as a way to empower themselves and challenge normative processes of social reproduction. Such statements on rights and responsibilities were so prevalent among my interviews and casual conversations with Xhosa adults that I began to wonder if media sources or local officials were feeding people a catchphrase or slogan; however, many people assured me this was not the case.

During a discussion with Mr. Hackula, he identified the lack of youth responsibility as one of the biggest problems arising from the transition to democracy. Everyone wants rights, but no one wants responsibilities. As the frustrated principal phrased it, "Students don't know what this word means, *democracy*. They are concerned mainly with their rights and not their responsibilities. I used to say to them, 'Please, learners, it's quite obvious that this is a democratic type of government. But this democratic type of government must not mean you only rely on your rights. These rights of yours are fine and good, but they must be accompanied by responsibilities.'"

Mr. Radebe is a middle-aged Department of Basic Education employee who runs extracurricular programs from the municipality offices in Kamva. He has been in this role since 2008 and before that was a teacher in a town about an hour to the south. Among other things, his job involves traveling around the area and leading awareness campaigns for people of all ages on the rights of children as enshrined in the constitution. Despite his job's emphasis on rights, he shares the larger community's concern with inculcating youth with a sense of responsibility: "Normally we make sure before we go [to a school] for an event, we need to educate people of the entire community on the rights of children. But we actually make sure that we do not say these are the rights. When we talk of the rights, we also mean responsibilities. We have to educate them specifically on rights and the responsibilities. When we go, we say what is right and what is wrong." Ms. Zinhle echoed this attitude on rights and responsibilities: "Learners, they like this thing of rights. Most of the time, the learners, they don't know that when they are having rights, they are also having responsibilities. They don't even know the meaning of human rights. They will say that, for instance, they cannot go to school. And you say, 'Why are you not going to school?' 'It's my right.' You hear them say such things . . . and that's not even a right."

By focusing on human rights without a corresponding focus on responsibility, democracy in this context seems to open the door to a host of alien practices and beliefs. Discourses on equality and multiculturalism appear amoral in their lack of a coherent position on right and wrong, so many Kamva educators introduce culturally appropriate moral standards in their lessons to fill the void (Brown 1998; Comaroff and Comaroff 2004b). The influx of un-Xhosa value systems in the age of democracy was a constant strand of conversation laden with fear as I talked with educators and parents. In one instance, a local teacher told me about a young girl who was called into the principal's office at her school for "worshipping Lucifer." The girl admitted she got this idea from an internet search on her mobile phone, which led her teacher to lecture me on the problems associated with twenty-first-century technologies: they bring unwanted worldviews into rural communities that interfere with Xhosa processes of cultural transmission from adult to child. In this way, contemporary social and economic norms that have accompanied the transition to democracy, such as the ubiquitous use of cell phones, incite spiritual insecurity that is deeply threatening (see, e.g., Ashforth 2005; West 2005). They also foster a fondness for rural life during apartheid, as the isolationism of the homeland system kept external cultural influences to a minimum. The apartheid government in fact propped up traditionalism through tribal leaders and an illusion of cultural autonomy while blocking access to international media and information in order to suppress rebellion. South Africans did not have access to television until 1971, and broadcasts in African languages did not appear until 1982 (Evans 2014).

Notably, teachers' antidemocratic sentiments and fear of outside influences stand in stark contrast to the Life Orientation curriculum, with its emphasis on rights like religious freedom and free speech. But teachers do not articulate these anxieties as a rejection of the Life Orientation class itself. Instead, they have found ways to blend their own ideological and cultural perspectives with the national curriculum. Life Orientation, in many cases, turns into a celebration of Xhosa cultural values justified by a curriculum that encourages attention to multiculturalism and diversity. As the opening anecdote indicates, this can mean a rejection of national projects to support gay rights on the grounds that they contradict interpretations of what it means to be Xhosa. In the classroom, Life Orientation is transformed into orienting young people to the kinds of lives teachers see as culturally and socially appropriate.

The perceived decline in responsibility is seen as having serious ramifications beyond the classroom. In fact, people link myriad social and economic ills to the alleged dilution of tradition and the espousal of democratic rights. For example, one of the biggest concerns among educators and parents in Kamva is the high rate of teenage pregnancy. People frequently pointed to democracy as the reason this has occurred. Inculcating children with a sense of individual rights and autonomy allegedly erodes mechanisms of parental control, encouraging young people to act out sexually in ways that elders previously would have prevented. In other words, democracy is blamed for encouraging teenage pregnancy by allowing young people to resist authority, challenge long-standing social norms, and absorb destructive outside influences.

A significant aspect of present-day South African rhetoric on democracy and human rights that pervades the Life Orientation classroom is the push for a more gender equitable society, seen as a fundamental tenet of a modern, "progressive" state. This comes into play in the classroom, where the curriculum encourages teachers to interrogate students' notions of gender roles and teach them about equality and feminism. The Life Orientation mandate to teach gender equality is often recast in ways deemed more culturally appropriate by Kamva educators. Depending on the teacher, students are either presented with lessons that challenge gender inequality within their communities or reinforce these norms under the justification of Xhosa culture.

Even for those teachers who agree with the idea of gender equality, it can be a very hard sell to rural youth. Ms. Zinhle cares deeply about today's political and social emphasis on gender equality, and it shows when she speaks about Life Orientation. She was raised in a traditionally gendered household, but her marriage involves a fairly equitable division of labor. When talking about her job, she told me with frustration that "gender equality is part of Life Orientation, but [the learners] take it lightly. They don't go deep . . . in a classroom situation, you cannot say everything . . . and it's important, because our culture still discriminates [against women]." She later discussed an example of the challenges of teaching gender equality.

> The students—especially the boys—will say no. I tell them what is said in the Life Orientation subject syllabus. That according to this subject, there should be no roles that are for men and no roles that are for ladies. I even told them that I went to a certain home where there is a young couple, and they have a two-year-old girl. And the father— the *father!*—it's a Xhosa man—he took the child to change her. And I told them in class, and the boys were saying, "No no no no, we cannot change nappies." . . . The challenge in teaching Life Orientation is that the learners take it as a joke.

As Ms. Zinhle explained, teachers encounter tremendous resistance from students to the liberal, democratic messages of the national curriculum, in addition to any resistance they might have themselves. They reported to me varying degrees of success and failure in convincing young people to accept the basic tenets of gender equality. Similarly, Ms. Yandani spoke with me at great length about the issue of gender and the role it plays in her Life Orientation teaching. She explained, "With the learners, it starts with them. In fact, I've just done a chapter with them on relationships and gender stereotypes. And the way they are brought up at home, how it affects their thinking of men and their thinking of women. And I find out that the boys think they are superior to girls. . . . In fact, you even notice it because when they call girls, they call them *abantwana* [children]." This example highlights the difficult intersections of Xhosa cultural and linguistic practices with the democratic values of the postapartheid state.

Mr. Xaba, an educational director since 2006 who works for the local municipality running various youth programs, explained to me that parents are simply no longer able to control their children, who are heavily influenced by foreign cultural values and rights discourses like Western feminism. "In our culture," he said, "girls used to know there are certain things they cannot do." While the state sees gender equality as a key element of democratic liberation, here these same rights are recast as a form of oppression and denigration of culture. In the same conversation, Mr. Xaba mentioned that democratic laws granting children rights have prohibited parents and teachers from beating children as a form of punishment. Similarly, this right is seen as threatening important processes of social control and cohesion in Xhosa communities. This brings us to perhaps the biggest area in which educators resist liberal democratic teaching on the grounds of culture—the illegality of corporal punishment.

CORPORAL PUNISHMENT

One day I sat in the back row of a high school classroom and watched a teacher who is known throughout the community for his more violent use of the switch beat several students for not completing their homework. Usually beatings involve a few lashes on the palm of the hand, but this man often hit harder or on other places on the body, such as the backs of the legs. I even heard rumors that he drew blood, provoking the ire of parents who otherwise support corporal punishment as a form of discipline for their children. Despite these extreme actions, he is celebrated at the school for greatly improving student matriculation exam pass rates (to which school records attest). While I sat in class on this particular day, he addressed me directly while his students wordlessly and fearfully lined up to receive their beatings. With pride and a smile, he informed me that I was witnessing "African love." With this comment, he was calling attention to my outsider status and his own cultural expertise. His theatrical display of the switch combined with his rhetorical strategies challenge dominant power structures of the state and subvert hegemonic political ideologies seen as infringing on notions of "African culture."

Corporal punishment is one of the most common ways Xhosa parents and teachers inculcate youth with a sense of responsibility and discipline both in schools and at home. The practice, usually accomplished with a small branch, combines both discursive and behavioral practices in the effort to control youth and reproduce desired social norms. Corporal punishment has been illegal in South African schools since 1996, with the passage of the South African Schools Act (as well as a more recent ruling that prohibits physical punishment in the home).[6]

Nonetheless, beatings in schools and homes remain ubiquitous and frequent, particularly in rural areas away from the constant watch of Department of Basic Education representatives. Many people reported to me that teachers know to hide their switches whenever government officials are nearby, but based on my observations the practice occurs on a daily basis at most—if not all—rural schools. Contrary to methodological concerns that people might act differently in front of an outside ethnographer, most teachers used their switches freely and often justified this decision to me with confidence. In other cases, students and teachers would tell me explicitly that no beating occurred at their school while I saw teachers openly carry switches. Most incidents of corporal punishment likely go unreported, and those that are reported often result in little or no consequences for teachers.[7]

Those teachers who expressed reservations about the use of corporal punishment said they felt that the laws against the practice stifled their ability to control classrooms and mold student behavior and supported beatings as a necessary evil in at least some cases. Ms. Smith is the mother of one of my teenaged research participants and in 2012 was a local elementary school teacher on the verge of retirement. She lives far outside town in a hilltop homestead with her elderly mother and is frequently burdened by physical ailments and a fear of crime in the area when her son is not around. She has raised an obedient and respectful only child who is deferential around the house and a diligent student. On a sunny spring day, we spoke in her living room over glasses of Coca-Cola while her son fried chicken in the kitchen for supper. "[Students] are not supposed to be punished today, and as a result you can't teach them," she complained. She told me how much she was looking forward to retirement, in part because she no longer understood the school environment in the era of children's rights and democracy.

Ms. Tyrone is a much younger teacher on the staff of Cedarwood; she started teaching in 2009 and currently teaches a class called Arts and

Culture that is part of the national curriculum. Though she was born in Cape Town, she moved to the rural Eastern Cape when she was twelve and spent most of her childhood there. Unlike many of her colleagues, she tends to be relatively liberal in her political and social views. But even she rejected the notion that corporal punishment was abusive and decried its illegality: "In our culture, we knew that if you did something wrong, your mother and your father are going to beat you. But children of today, they don't have that. Once you beat him or her, they'll go to the police station. So they are free to do anything. They think they are free to do anything." Ms. Zinhle expressed similar views: "If you don't punish a child, he will never take you seriously. Imagine at home if a child is not beaten. What kind of a home is that? What kind of children are you going to raise?" In this way, educators often tied students' success in later life to the teachers' use of systematic physical punishment during childhood. The idea that corporal punishment constituted a form of abuse elicited reactions ranging from laughter to outrage among most of the people with whom I spoke, whether parent, teacher, or even child. Imitha, a secondary school student, believed firmly that success in life was dependent on proper discipline early on: "If you go to Parliament, all those men, for them to be there, were beaten." The practice is not only justified but also seen as a necessary and critical element of social reproduction in rural life.

A rational extension of this logic for many people is that the current social ills plaguing rural South Africa, such as teenage pregnancy and alcohol and drug abuse, were formerly prevented by the practice of physical punishment. Mr. Hackula had much to say on the topic of corporal punishment and its intersections with culture: "Before 1994, everything went well. That white government was so strict, especially with students. A student was there to learn and nothing else. But now this government of ours says, 'Never touch any person.' But that is our culture. If my child doesn't want to learn, I used to use switches. But nowadays, our government doesn't want to use them. . . . They are trying to change our culture."

Ms. Tyrone reflected on her own childhood experiences to defend her position on corporal punishment: "[Beating] was good for us, because when I was a student I'd never get a 20 out of 200 [points]. Because of the discipline." She also told me that she has had many parents request that teachers continue beating their children, in order to keep them in line, despite knowledge of its illegality. This can put teachers in the difficult position of having to balance parents' desires with national laws.

Teachers often expressed fear of using the switch and thereby breaking the law, despite the fact that this did not usually change their behavior in the end. Ms. Andiswa is a young teacher at a local primary school. She teaches Arts and Culture, English, and Xhosa to Grades 4, 5, and 6. She also facilitated Sonke programs when the organization was in the community. Nonetheless, she displayed views on corporal punishment that directly contradicted Sonke's teachings on child abuse (Sonke is firmly and openly opposed to corporal punishment as antidemocratic, both in school and in the home). "These days, you're afraid when you punish a learner, because they go outside to the police station," Ms. Andiswa said. Interestingly, when I questioned her directly on her views on corporal punishment she shifted her position, emphasizing her opposition: "It is not good for solving problems. To solve problems you must speak." It seemed that people understood they were supposed to distance themselves from corporal punishment, yet found it difficult or impossible to put this into practice.

Even those teachers who did in fact seem committed to avoiding corporal punishment found it difficult to find a replacement. Ms. Cele, an elementary school teacher, traces her anti–corporal punishment stance both to her own experiences and to the fact that she is the youngest teacher at her school. "Some people might not understand me, because I'm a child of democracy," she explained. "Even before I heard about the law that corporal punishment is banned, with me it was a no-no. Because when I was a child, when I was beaten, I wouldn't even hear what you were saying. It never worked, so I swore I'd never use that myself." Although she has found ways around using the switch in her classrooms, she does see a pervasive problem with lack of discipline in rural schools. In the same conversation, she told me that "discipline is a very big problem here, because with our government you can't use a switch."

Mrs. Mbodi, the municipality's psychologist, works with teachers in the area's schools to train them to deal with children who have behavioral or emotional problems. A big part of her job is explaining to teachers and parents that there are other methods of discipline besides corporal punishment—a topic on which she encounters substantial resistance. "People say that the democratic government is making it so there won't be discipline. They base it on culture." In many cases, educators' identification with corporal punishment can act as a form of symbolic capital, in that it ties into feelings of prestige and social value in their communities

(Bourdieu 1977). Teachers wield the switch not just as a way to control the classroom, but also as a method that carries social weight amongst their peers. The teacher punishing his students through "African Love" has helped significantly increase graduation rates at the school since joining the staff, a statistic many of his colleagues attribute to his notorious beatings. Thus, part of being considered an effective teacher in rural areas (and one likely to retain a job), in many instances, relies on corporal punishment regardless of what official legislation dictates.

It is also not just adults who see corporal punishment as an essential element of Xhosa social reproduction. Imitha supported the practice and didn't think the state had any business outlawing it. "Teachers should beat us but not violently. Yes, it is illegal for teachers to beat us, but this causes a high rate of students disrespecting their teachers. They disrespect teachers, because they know they are not going to be beaten." Imitha, though, was unusual among students I spoke with in that she actually *knew* corporal punishment was illegal. When I interviewed young people about their knowledge of and feelings about the South African Bill of Rights, I found that most had no idea that corporal punishment was against the law. This is further evidence of the ways that teachers filter lessons according to cultural worldviews. While Life Orientation mandates teaching students about their constitutional rights, only some end up making it into the classroom. Practices that violate those rights but are deemed culturally significant are often upheld, regardless of what the official curriculum advocates.

Zinzi, who was in her junior year of high school when I first met her in 2012, told me that she is beaten often at school. I asked if she had learned about children's rights in class, and she said yes, she had learned a number of them: "The child has a right to education, the right to a roof over her head, she has the right to have what she needs." Nowhere did she mention the right to freedom from physical violence such as beatings. Indeed, many students were extremely surprised to learn in our conversations that corporal punishment is illegal. These ethnographic examples call into question the fundamental idea that the nation's liberal democratic policies actually represent the majority of South Africans. Students were often ardent proponents of corporal punishment, recognizing it as a critically important method of social control, cohesion, and learning. Even those students who found corporal punishment a flawed practice maintained that it must be upheld as a last resort in extreme cases. Zinzi continued: "First you have to talk to the child. Explain that this is wrong, this is right. If the child continues to do what she is doing, then you may scold her by beating." Ciko, an eighteen-year-old classmate of Zinzi, concurred: "Beating helps me; it encourages me not to do it [the bad behavior] again. It's necessary." Ciko's attitude is echoed in scholarship on corporal punishment that has shown it is not only adults who sanction the practice. What many might consider violence against children is not only sanctioned by "adults who perform and perpetuate the rights, but also children who are subjected to them [and] view these rites, however painful and terrifying, as having a positive long-term value" (Korbin 2003).

Speaking with Lonwabo on the lawn outside his high school one day, I found out that he had no idea that corporal punishment in schools was illegal. In fact, he was shocked to learn this from me as we went over the Bill of Rights together. With incredulity, he said, "If the children don't get beaten, the school will just be chaotic." And Noluvo, the student mentioned earlier who railed against the evils of abortion and homosexuality, reflected positively on her childhood home and the role corporal punishment played within it: "I think it was right for me, being beaten. I don't do a lot of stuff—for example, I don't drink, I'm not wild. . . . I'm very disciplined." Even those who are most likely to be subjected to corporal punishment often valorize it as a positive and necessary practice that democracy is infringing on. These examples challenge liberal perspectives on children's rights and subvert top-down understandings of democratic education in classes like Life Orientation.

LESSONS TRANSFORMED

Programs like Life Orientation are integral to state efforts to inculcate youth with an understanding of democracy and its attendant human rights. Through a series of curricular redesigns, the Department of Basic Education has created a topic that sits outside the rest of the academic day, offering students a chance to encounter lessons that differ radically from those taught during the days of apartheid under Bantu Education. Exposing youth to democratic ideas can indeed offer them a perspective that contrasts with the one they might be receiving at home or elsewhere (Ngwane 2001). Much like other places on the African continent, young people are at the crux of projects to rebuild the nation (Cheney

2007; Seiler 2018). School life and the national curriculum provide new, often competing ideologies to the next generation of citizens that challenge youth to renegotiate and transform existing social structures and cultural practices deemed threatening to democracy. School classrooms, as this chapter has demonstrated, are prime arenas in which democracy is reproduced.

And yet the ethnographic material in this chapter also evidences the fact that lessons on democracy and rights are recast through distinct cultural worldviews in local settings like the rural Eastern Cape. Rather than simply translate the curriculum, teachers, administrators, and students all play a role in renegotiating its ideas in significant ways. Many of today's Life Orientation teachers were educated under apartheid and find not just the class material itself but also the very pedagogical strategies of active, discussion-based learning either difficult or impossible to implement. While some of this is clearly due to insufficient resources and lack of teacher training, much can be attributed to such practices' uneasy tension with what people call "traditional" teaching and ways of positioning youth in the social order. The content of the curriculum may emphasize the importance of cultural diversity, but its pedagogical strategies fall short of embracing alternative ideologies on teaching and the roles of youth.

Because teachers are filtering democratic education through local perspectives, rural Eastern Cape students are receiving versions of lessons that have been transformed into something deemed culturally appropriate by elders seeking to maintain some semblance of tradition in the face of perceived loss. In some cases this is unconscious, as when the teacher assigned an essay on the evils of homosexuality as an interpretation of discussing social challenges in class. In other cases it is blatant and explicit, as seen among teachers who decry the state's mandate to stop beating children and articulate it as an attack on Xhosa culture. Delving into these classroom practices offers a unique understanding of both how democracy is produced and how it is resisted and reformed on the local level.

What are the consequences of the cultural and historical filtering of educational content for young South Africans? As my conversations with Kamva youth demonstrated, many students who go through the Life Orientation program are still unaware of some human rights granted by the state, despite the fact that teaching them is a major stated goal of the curriculum. Such realities suggest that local teaching strategies have the potential to affect young people's political knowledge and worldviews far into the future. In the face of a democratic curriculum that feels alien and intrusive, many teachers end up turning back toward the days of apartheid. In the next chapter I explore how this nostalgia for the past surfaces in the classroom and to what ends.

CHAPTER FIVE

Teaching Nostalgia

Awash in a sea of faces, we look back nostalgically to the shore in a sudden memory of a ground already lost. . . . Nostalgia becomes the very lighthouse waving us back to shore—the one point on the landscape that gives hope of direction.

—Kathleen Stewart, "Nostalgia: A Polemic"

REMEMBERING APARTHEID

South Africa's long-awaited transition to democratic rule was a cause for international celebration on its arrival in 1994. Today, however, an inescapable sense of disappointment and anger can be found in rural communities in the Eastern Cape. In light of the widespread feeling that the ANC has failed to deliver the freedom and equality that people widely associate with democracy, many people recall apartheid as a time of stability and control—even if it meant codified oppression and racial inequality. Teachers of democracy and human rights are no exception in this regard.

The previous chapters showed the many difficulties of transmitting liberal democratic ideas to rural communities like Kamva. In this chapter, I turn to nostalgic narratives of the apartheid past that arise in such settings.

I ask how intergenerational and collective memories influence people's views of and reactions to democracy. How might we make sense of longings for aspects of an internationally reviled and oppressive police state, especially when they are expressed by the very individuals and communities that system discriminated against? How can ethnographic encounters shed light on the unlikely epistemological connections people make between the transition to democracy and a variety of social ills, such as the HIV/AIDS epidemic, high rates of teenage pregnancy, and widespread unemployment? Should we understand nostalgia as political resistance, rhetorical performance, or affective experience? Making use of theoretical frameworks from the anthropology of memory and nostalgia, I argue that rural Black South Africans long for elements of life under apartheid because of the perceived failures of democracy as well as the way in which apartheid's homeland architecture allowed for spaces of apparent cultural autonomy, which now appear under threat. While people resist democracy on the grounds that it has failed them, a deeper examination reveals that pervasive economic and racial inequality combined with culturally specific translations of freedom are at the core of these sentiments.

These acts of translation are both literal and figurative. In the pages that follow, I demonstrate how language choices provide evidence for particular political perspectives. For example, Xhosa people frequently use the word *inkululeko* as a gloss for "democracy." And yet, if you ask native speakers, this word is most closely translated as "freedom." I contend that this colloquial translation among Xhosa speakers should be understood not as arbitrary or idiosyncratic. Instead, it reveals larger conceptual and hidden problems with how individuals envision a democratic government and what they expect one to deliver (Englund 2006). Embedded in my argument is a broader discussion on the reality of competing epistemologies within the cultural diversity of a pluralistic state such as South Africa. My examination includes not only how people react to the perceived failures of democracy but also what they expected from it in the first place. People's hopes for South African democracy incited by the antiapartheid movement structure their reactions to political and economic realities in the nation today in critically important ways that have bearing on the education of young people.

As the South African theorist Sipokazi Sambumbu (2010, 7) tells us, "Remembering, forgetting, and telling [are] all culturally mediated." To the outside observer, rural Black South Africans' nostalgia for elements of the apartheid regime may seem counterintuitive and illogical, and for good reason. This was certainly my initial reaction when Black South Africans would steer our conversations about youth political education toward fond memories of life during apartheid. The apartheid regime was objectively horrendous, and nonwhite people suffered physically, psychologically, and economically over many decades. However, the more I understood people's ideas about Xhosa culture and the role of youth, the more these narratives began to make sense. In this chapter, I show how the perception of cultural autonomy under apartheid combined with the perceived failures of democracy allow us to more comprehensively understand today's widespread political resistance. This local examination of political subjectivity is especially useful for grasping the role of memory in democratic education, as these nostalgic narratives seep into the classroom in various subtle and not so subtle ways.

TOWARD AN ANTHROPOLOGY OF NOSTALGIA

Ironically, studies of nostalgia may be the future of anthropology. Though the term started with a much narrower definition, today it is employed to describe a range of affective experiences and identity practices that are ubiquitous across the globe. As Svetlana Boym articulates in her seminal work, *The Future of Nostalgia* (2001), the term was originally used in seventeenth-century Europe to describe the allegedly curable medical condition of acute homesickness. This began with soldiers deployed overseas who displayed physical symptoms of their emotional suffering (3). Nostalgia, in this context, was about a paralyzing desire for one's homeland in the geographic sense and was thought of as something located in the physical body and ameliorated by scientific understanding and medical treatment (Davis 1979). In contrast, today the term more often refers to temporal rather than physical distance and focuses on affective rather than physiological experience (Rosaldo 1989). Nostalgia has moved from the body to the mind.

Though anthropologists have written extensively on historical and collective memory as well as its varied uses in political and cultural projects (e.g., Abu El-Haj 2001; Cole 1998; Hale 2013), to date there has been relatively little theoretical engagement within the discipline on nostalgia as a topic distinct from other forms of remembering and one that is fruitful for sociocultural analysis (with some notable exceptions: Bissell 2005; Davis 1979; Dlamini 2009; Klumbyte 2009; Piot 2010; Stewart 1988). A spate of recent publications suggests that the subfield is in its infancy and that the anthropology of nostalgia is just beginning to gain recognition as an important topic in its own right (Angé and Berliner 2014; Reed 2016).

So how exactly do we understand nostalgia not just as an individual psychological state but also as part of larger collective cultural and historical processes? Importantly, nostalgia is a concept and linguistic marker for something quite distinct from other avenues of remembering: it suggests a desire to hold onto an idealized past, one that differs markedly from factual events. In this sense, my primary interest here is not to uncover apartheid-era history as it actually occurred but instead to show particular culturally mediated perceptions of the past and how they reflect on the present moment. Rather than just recall something, nostalgia actually longs for it, idealizes it, and desperately seeks to preserve it in the face of change. As the anthropologist Kathleen Stewart (1988, 227) has suggested, we should think of nostalgia as a cultural practice that shifts depending on the context and the social actor. Or, as Fred Davis (1979) contends, nostalgia works to help construct favored identities through relationships with former selves.

Anthropological analyses of post-Soviet states provide a fruitful ground for comparison to South Africa in perhaps surprising ways. These studies have in recent years engaged with the concept of nostalgia, showing how many residents of the region long for various aspects of the Soviet regime and its socioeconomic policies despite the ubiquitous portrayal of suffering under Soviet rule (Angé and Berliner 2014). As a case in point, Neringa Klumbyte's examination of post-Soviet Lithuania challenges mainstream portrayals of the Soviet era, analyzing the visceral sensations that evoke nostalgia and recall specific visions of a glorified past—one that included access to heat, an absence of hunger, and the freedom to use alcohol. Her work is instructive in that it shows how nostalgia does not just manifest discursively, but also in bodily sensations (Klumbyte 2009, 96). In these narratives, a fondly remembered past, even one under a totalitarian regime, can provide a sense of place for the individual in a rapidly changing society that threatens cherished cultural practices and creates a sense of social and economic alienation. In both the literature and my own ethnographic experience, nostalgia is a way to carve out an identity through opposition to the present. It is an identity practice that is formulated through a distinct rejection of more hegemonic narratives of the past (Bucholtz 1999; Hebdige 1979). Importantly, then, scholars show how nostalgia for the Soviet era tells us much more about *post*-Soviet life than it does about anything else. I employ this framework here, reading nostalgia for apartheid in the case of South Africa as a rejection of the state's turn to liberal democracy rather than an actual desire to turn back the clock.

The Soviet case is also instructive in showing that nostalgic discourses are on the rise in places dealing with rapid economic neoliberalization. This has included structural adjustment policies, increased privatization of social services, and financial deregulation spurred by institutions such as the World Bank and the International Monetary Fund (Goldman 2005). In South Africa and elsewhere, these transnational economic shifts have led to skyrocketing rates of un- and underemployment, with enormous social consequences (Hickel 2015; Ngwane 2001). These global patterns have forged perhaps unlikely connections between disparate parts of the globe as their residents struggle to make sense of a new world order. In the face of ever-increasing wealth inequalities and corporatization of essential services, more individuals are turning to nostalgic discourses that uphold a fondly remembered version of the past and maintain preferred identification practices with which they are more familiar. The past becomes a place in which the culturally and economically alienated can take refuge, in which they can uphold essentialized ideas of tradition and culture in the face of change. While I look specifically at the case of nostalgia for apartheid, I also wish to suggest that nostalgia is an increasingly common discourse among residents of newly democratic states everywhere, places where people are trying to make sense of neoliberal economic reforms and the perceived tyranny of liberalism that often accompanies them. Where there is widespread nostalgia born out of feelings of cultural loss and disappointment with the present, we can likely expect to find the signs of capitalist accumulation and heightened wealth inequality that seem to go hand in hand with liberal democracy these days.

In South Africa, anthropologists have discussed the increased presence of nativism and traditionalism as sites of nostalgic discourse and practice that connect directly to the neoliberal state and late capitalist conditions (Comaroff and Comaroff 2009). South Africans label cultural practices traditional in order to hold onto and glorify the past in a country identified as the most socioeconomically unequal in the world (Beaubien

2018). Reifying tradition as something immutable and inherently knowable affords one the ability to organize culture hierarchically and mark it worthy of preservation and intergenerational transmission. Noluvo, the young woman who railed against liberal democracy, made this clear when she told me in a later conversation, "When I was born, tradition was already there. When my great-grandparents were born, tradition was already there. It has been there a long time, and it is important we keep it the same." For her, a sacred notion of tradition is placed in opposition to liberal, "anti-Xhosa" values. Or as Stewart (1988, 228) puts it, "Nostalgia is a pained, watchful desire to frame the cultural present in relation to an 'other' world—to make of the present a cultural object that can be seen, appropriated, refused, disrupted or 'made something of.'" This cultural object can have distinctly spatial elements, as people read the landscape as a series of images that serve as visible and tangible reminders of the past and rejections of the present, like a field once used for agriculture that now lays fallow (Basso 1996). In this sense, tradition is upheld as a static concept and culture is reified rather than recognized as a dynamic, relational process (Hobsbawm and Ranger 1983).

Along these lines, nostalgia relies on perceptions of the past rather than factual accounts. This is part of what makes it unique from other forms of remembering; it uses perceptions that may be fabricated and are highly subjective, not for their own sake, but rather as a lens through which to view the present. As William Cunningham Bissell (2005, 225) states, "Nostalgic discourses imaginatively rework time and space, conjuring up the plenitude of the past as a means of measuring the present." Here the imagination plays an active role in constructing specific idealizations of the past that are used as a yardstick by which to assess the failures of the present moment. Nostalgia for *then* does not and cannot exist unless in dialogue with a deeply unsatisfactory *now*. Therefore, cultural practices are often preserved, albeit in altered forms, as a manifestation of nostalgia that individuals can hold on to, especially when faced with threats of loss from outside. Many people in the Eastern Cape, like Noluvo, conveyed fear and dismay that Xhosa traditions were disappearing in the face of contact with neoliberal development and the tenets of liberal democracy. That Noluvo was born after the fall of apartheid demonstrates how nostalgia is passed down from one generation to the next.

While this discussion of generations and tradition makes clear that nostalgia has obvious political consequences, it is also worth asking whether we ought to examine the topic through the lens of affect. Affect suggests something ephemeral and presocial, an interior, bodily sensation. In this perspective, nostalgia is not performed, taught, or spoken but rather *embodied* (Guffin, Davie-Kessler, and McGrail 2010; Mazzarella 2009). Discussions of affect in anthropology have focused on its relationship to the individual and the unconscious, seeing it as dynamic and shifting. Considering nostalgia through the lens of affect offers us a different path for interpretation. If affect is felt rather than socially produced, can it be studied analytically in the same way as forms of sociality? Much like Renato Rosaldo's (1989) musings on the power of grief, perhaps nostalgia is best captured through empathy and force rather than the thick description of cultural analysis. While I still see nostalgia as inherently tied to the social, there is certainly an affective element in Kamva narratives that interacts with the social but is distinctly interior and subjective (Skoggard and Waterston 2015). This is particularly clear when we see how nostalgia is not isolated from other forms of affect. It is intimately linked to feelings of anger and fear in the rural Eastern Cape, as people recall a fond past in ways that stir up intense emotions and pour out into everyday social interactions. Many of my conversations in the area were not just about recalling the past but also about using nostalgia to locate and ground deeply personal and intense feelings of loss and frustration.

To claim that Black South Africans are nostalgic for *any* aspect of life during apartheid is to wade into contentious political waters. It requires a nuanced reading of history that shows how the racist state relied on a policy of indirect rule, one that allowed for circumscribed spaces of cultural autonomy within a larger system of suffocating oppression. Jacob Dlamini, in his powerful book *Native Nostalgia* (2009), uses his own childhood in a township outside Johannesburg to expose these complexities of Black life under apartheid. He vehemently rejects mainstream portrayals of Black-only areas like the township as merely "sites of struggle" (153). Through an exploration of the senses, he shows how longings for things like the subversive radio station Radio Zulu reflect the fact that apartheid necessitated spaces of resistance. These spaces have largely dissolved along with official desegregation and democracy, leaving a notable absence in their wake. It should also be emphasized that nostalgia does not require wholesale acceptance of the past. As Dlamini informs us, "To be nostalgic is not to wear rose-tinted glasses but to appreciate township life in its complexity" (109). In Kamva, residents constantly recycle and renegotiate narratives of nostalgia for a bygone era, painting a picture of life during apartheid that highlights specific elements while obscuring others. For instance, many of these nostalgic stories stress the economic and social stability enjoyed during apartheid as compared to the present, all while erasing or downplaying the era's racialization, violence, and oppression. As these narratives are transferred to future generations, they become real for participants as a way of structuring experiences and behaviors; the actual events of history take a backseat to the nostalgic imaginings that form identities and construct worldviews. As I show later in this chapter, there is an emerging wave of young people in rural South Africa who are nostalgic for a time during which they did not live. While this book is a case study of one particular rural area, recent scholarship has made evident that apartheid-era nostalgia among Black South Africans is far more widespread (Paret 2018).

CULTURE NOSTALGIA

The previous chapter showed that liberal democracy is perceived as threatening Xhosa culture; by comparison, the stories in this chapter suggest that apartheid did not seek to impose on ideas of Xhosa identity in the same way. Of course, the apartheid state certainly did disempower Black South Africans politically, economically, and socially. But the insidious strategy of racial segregation and ethnic homelands allowed for an illusion of cultural autonomy for which many people now wistfully reminisce (Phillips 2018). Building on the architecture installed by a racist settler colonial state, apartheid further entrenched divisive ethnic categories and helped, at least in part, create the very resurgence of traditionalism and reification of culture that now proliferates in places like Kamva. In the nostalgic narratives I encountered, culture is described as bounded, isolated, and timeless; people erase or elide the many ways in which Xhosa identity has shifted over time and in the face of external forces like Christianity and the introduction of a market economy (Wolf 1982). Apartheid codified and reinforced notions of culture, ethnicity, and race, tying them to each other and to geographic boundaries in ways that continue to penetrate the South African imagination and structure people's lives. This reification of culture is evident in people's nostalgic stories of how Xhosa culture is timeless and stands in direct opposition to the "West." In reality, these are carefully curated views of the past; as anthropologists elsewhere have discussed, modernity itself has been heavily implicated in the invention, construction, and reimagination of what many people call tradition (Ngwane 2001). In some cases, the ability to uphold so-called traditions in fact depends on modern outlets for their expression and maintenance (Turner 1992). In this sense, what I term "culture nostalgia" ties into larger conversations on how to understand culture within the discipline of anthropology writ large (e.g., Geertz 1973; Rosaldo 1989; Wolf 1982). A chief concern in this chapter is how culture intersects with power and how culture is inherently a political project—even when it may appear neutral.

In Kamva, nostalgia for apartheid is frequently tied to anxieties of cultural loss, particularly in relation to youth. Democracy and the new values it introduces are alleged to rupture previous intergenerational systems of cultural transmission. Children and youth, as people told me time and again, were no longer upholding traditional beliefs and practices deemed essential to one's identification as Xhosa. As one man phrased it, "As Xhosas, we are moving away from our culture." This ubiquitous fear of cultural loss and dilution is of course particularly problematic in a nation so committed, at least in official rhetoric, to multiculturalism and diversity. How can a state that prides itself on being the "Rainbow Nation" be perceived as intolerant of Xhosa culture?

For Mr. Gabela, the longtime principal of Cedarwood Secondary School, this loss of culture is everywhere. No matter what we discussed, he steered our conversations back to his fear, anxiety, and resentment over the disappearance of cultural practices. For example, he lamented the lack of agricultural skills among today's youth, identifying the ability to farm and raise livestock as an essential part of what it means to be Xhosa for him: "You'll find our people have moved away from their cultural backgrounds. We used to make use of land. If you can see around now, there's not much farming. We used to make a lot out of grain. Now we've moved to things that are used by these whites. And you will find that they are not nutritious. We are detached then from our original way of learning." Here white people are the locus of cultural destruction; in other parts of the same conversation, however, he describes whites as superior in their ability to effectively run the government. Mr. Gabela credits apartheid's policy of racial segregation with helping preserve Xhosa culture despite his awareness that it relied on the logic of racism and white supremacy.

Fundani also spoke of growing up in the Transkei in perhaps surprisingly similar terms: "There were no white people in this area when I was a child. We didn't experience the oppression. As a matter of fact, we were not aware we were in this area because of certain acts by white people. We enjoyed the place, and there was nothing wrong with it." In both narratives, the apartheid government is described as preferable because it kept its distance from rural areas and their cultural practices while effectively running the country. By contrast, the contemporary ANC-led government champions a version of liberal democracy that insists people change cultural practices while failing to provide economic stability.

Mr. Gabela continued this topic of conversation, remembering fondly a time when he felt Xhosa culture was safe from outside influences.

> During our time, we used to work hard; we used to be self-driven, because we wanted to improve our families. There were no grants. Life was very hard. And once we relaxed, we were going to feel that hardship, so we were pushed then to be responsible. The country has changed a lot, and young people are more exposed. Especially these people from neighboring countries: they are mixing, whereas during apartheid, the flow of people was strictly controlled. You couldn't interact with people from countries that were liberated before us. So there is also the inflow of the wrong things.

Here South Africa's recent episodes of xenophobia are given justification under the ideology of cultural preservation, as foreigners introduce foreign ideas that inevitably have an impact on local practices and expose young people to new perspectives (Hickel 2014). Part of this, for Mr. Gabela, is the democratic state's social welfare programs that give monetary grants. He sees these support systems as subverting local efforts to instill in youth a sense of autonomy and responsibility, instead giving young people free handouts that create a dangerous dependency on the state. This was a common sentiment among both elders and youth in Kamva: the social welfare programs of democracy, such as government grants for unemployed parents, scholarships for higher education, and pensions for the elderly, have eroded people's ambition and independence. Apartheid, by contrast, provided Blacks with no such handouts, instead allowing local customary leaders and elders to do the work of social and economic reproduction based on cultural values.

Similarly, Ms. Cele, a junior secondary school teacher who has taught a variety of subjects since her career began in 2006, explained:

> Democracy has not helped! Because you find that people don't want to do anything! They want to just wake up and sit, do nothing, wait for things to come because they know that the government is going to bring in grant money. They've got kids, they get pregnant, their children are fed by the government. . . . They go and build shacks, they sit, they do nothing, they wait for the government to build houses for them. Even respect has gone down. Nobody respects anybody else. . . . They are abusing this democracy. They think it means since we've got freedom of speech, you can say whatever you want. We've got values as a people, and they tend to forget their values.

Ms. Cele is staunchly opposed to some "traditional" practices, such as corporal punishment, which would suggest she aligns herself with liberal democratic ideals. And yet she maintains that overall democracy is harming young people more than it is helping them.

Ms. Mbodi, the municipality's psychologist, worried about the same thing as her colleagues: "The problem of poverty is worse now, because people don't want to use the fields. They don't want to work. They are expecting the government to do *everything* for them! They're just folding their arms." For many of the people I spoke with in Kamva, democracy is not only challenging Xhosa cultural values on skill development and labor practices but also creating what they view as an unhealthy state dependency that stands in direct contrast to the images of economic liberation and independence promised in the antiapartheid struggle. Rather than see young people as liberated and self-sufficient, they see them as dependent on a state that is corrupt and does not support them enough to lift them out of poverty.

Mrs. Dingana is an older woman who has taught at a junior secondary school in Kamva for over twenty years. She is tired, and when I spoke to her in 2012, she was close to retirement. Her daughter participated in a local Sonke program that advocated active democratic participation and liberal human rights, which makes Mrs. Dingana's nostalgia for intergenerational relations under apartheid especially surprising (she was very supportive of her daughter's participation in the program). She described her own childhood in a rural village on the outskirts of Kamva: "During our time, we were not exposed to these [new] things. With kids of today, they are free to do everything. . . . When I was a child, we really had no rights in this place. You listened to whatever was said by a parent, and you had no right to ask why. We didn't use that word [rights]. It was not allowed." "Asking why" is a signifier of Western cultural influences and their corrupting consequences for youth. Mrs. Dingana cited her retirement as largely the result of her exhaustion from dealing with these kids who are emboldened by rights and constantly ask why. She has had enough.

Many teachers elaborated on similar antidemocratic perspectives during our conversations. Ms. Mbodi continued, "People have taken this word *democracy* in the wrong manner. They have taken it as if a person is just allowed to do anything, anyhow. . . . If you go to the children, they have taken this democracy without the responsibility. They're only concerned with what? The rights. We still have a lot to do." Before the era of children's rights, Xhosa customs, which reinforced a rigid age and gender hierarchy, ensured that youth learned important cultural values. Mr. Gabela was nostalgic for traditions that governed youth and taught them respect before democracy: "We are now afraid to exercise our customs, like intonjane [the female puberty ritual], in which you are taught how to behave, how to keep yourself correctly. Now you'll find these values are being undermined, you'll find even some of these young pregnancies and so on. . . . We are trying to fit in with the standards of the world. But these standards are depriving society of its values."

Historical sources provide supporting evidence of this long-standing emphasis on young people's obedience to authority in Xhosa society. The South African anthropologist Monica Hunter Wilson explained this in her ethnographic notes on the Eastern Cape Xhosa from the early nineteenth century: "There is no age at which [a child] is regarded as being free of parental control" (Hunter 1936, 25). In light of this historical portrait of Xhosa cultural norms, it makes sense that adults feel threatened by democratic freedoms, particularly the granting of rights to children who are thought to be undeserving of them. By contrast, colonialism's reliance on indirect rule as a form of rural governance and the apartheid state's creation of separate homelands with "independent" chiefly rule allowed for Xhosa generational relationships to flourish in ways that today's elders feel have been eroded. Ironically, the largely maligned separate but equal policies of this reviled former government in some ways allowed for cultural freedoms that now appear threatened.

Many teachers were nostalgic for elements of the apartheid-era educational system in particular—the very same system that was at the epicenter of so many antiapartheid protests and riots. Much to my surprise at the time, Mr. Hackula told me, "Under the white regime . . . although we had great problems then, education was up to standard. The education system was better under apartheid." He claimed that students no longer had an interest in learning from their teachers and that the frequent changes in the national curriculum have not been accompanied by adequate teacher training to make them useful: "These [teacher] workshops only take two or three days, and they are not effective for us. Before 1994 it was good—it didn't change all the time." Fundani, having worked as a high school math teacher for several years in the area, echoed this perspective: "The education standards [since apartheid] have dropped *drastically*. They are low now. Yes, after apartheid the government wanted to attend to issues of inequality, but in other issues they have failed! You used to pass with a 50 percent, now you can pass with only 30 percent." The rote learning practices detailed in the previous chapter were frequently given credit for the higher academic performance of students during apartheid. People reiterated that this system delivered course content more effectively and used necessary discipline in order to create hardworking students. By contrast, democracy's support for children's rights and a student-driven pedagogy is deemed ineffective in actually producing well-educated youth.

ECONOMIC NOSTALGIA

As I sat in the sun stripping dried corn kernels from their cobs with an elderly Xhosa woman, I listened with rapt attention as she moved back and forth from the past to the future in internally consistent and yet outwardly confusing ways. Had I not already spent months witnessing this kind of temporal ambivalence, I might have struggled to keep up. At one moment, she lamented the spread of a market economy that has produced massive wealth inequality, yearning for the days when she says she never had to think about money. A minute later, she told me about the brochures she has stashed away in her house advertising the expensive urban retirement community in which she hopes to eventually reside, fantasizing about a life of solitude that is devoid of the responsibilities of a large extended family and the hardships of rural life. "I like the city," she said.

"I prefer it to this location. I just like to watch the people going back and forth. Even the sea—I would like to look at the sea. I like to watch the people going in the water." Torn between the perceived simplicity of life before democracy and the ever-increasing consumer desires of the capitalist state, she exists in a state of anxious tension, both looking at the past with longing and imagining the future with excitement and relief. The only time that seems intolerable is now.

A common perspective among nostalgic Kamva residents, not to mention South Africans more broadly, is a distinct and profound feeling that democracy has not delivered on its promises of economic equality (Besteman 2008; Chance 2018; Comaroff and Comaroff 2004b; Makhulu 2015). Instead, many people see the increased dependency on social welfare programs, coupled with the lack of viable employment opportunities, as irrefutable evidence that democracy has failed. This is a critical perspective with regard to the rejection of democracy among rural residents, as it evidences how people conflate democracy and capitalism in ways that lead to nostalgia for the antidemocratic past. As I alluded earlier, this conflation is not unique to South Africa but rather is something we see elsewhere, such as in the former Soviet states. It is also necessary to remember that most contemporary South Africans have no direct experience with the system of democracy other than its current incarnation, so their views are largely informed by the ways in which it has been paired with the ANC's neoliberal economics and resulting increase in wealth inequality. The consequences of these economic shifts are particularly devastating in rural areas of the Eastern Cape that continue to suffer from extremely high rates of poverty; here, wealth inequality still persists largely along color lines, mimicking apartheid's insidious racial hierarchies and perpetuating de facto segregation decades after the official version was laid to rest.[1] These ongoing problems have led most Kamva residents—if not most South Africans as a whole—to conclude that democracy has yet to deliver on its pre-1994 promises of a nonracial, classless society. Of course, it should be emphasized that apartheid also operated on a capitalist economic system; the homelands were a way to ensure a disenfranchised population of Black laborers to support white wealth. But the nature of this system made much of this inequality invisible to homeland residents, who were largely in the same socioeconomic position and rarely if ever witnessed white wealth firsthand. This history, combined with the particular forms of neoliberalism that have allowed for a minority of people to get spectacularly wealthy while further impoverishing the poor, has led to a nostalgia for elements of life during apartheid (e.g., Comaroff and Comaroff 2001; Edelman and Haugerud 2005; Ferguson 2006; Ferguson and Gupta 2002).

The neoliberal economic policies of the postapartheid state have increased privatization of many basic services, emphasized individual accumulation over communal identity practices, and prioritized the deregulation of international trade over public ownership of the modes of production (Von Schnitzler 2016). While I write this, these trends are perhaps nowhere more evident than in the violent conflict over mining rights in Pondoland on the Wild Coast of the Eastern Cape Province. The rural hills are rich in the ore that contains titanium, and an Australian company has applied for mining rights there. The issue has divided the community, as some contend it will destroy their rural homeland and others support efforts that will lead to new job creation. The conflict is dire enough that a local activist has been murdered (Pearce 2017). These news stories highlighting the impact of global finance on rural South African communities serve as reminders that the upper tiers of society— by and large, white people—from the apartheid era have retained their socioeconomic standing at the expense of the majority citizens, despite expectations of wealth redistribution during antiapartheid organizing. As Catherine Besteman writes in her 2008 study of poor townships on the outskirts of Cape Town, "Today, South Africans are deeply involved in the struggle to bring the promise of South Africa's miracle to fruition. It is an uphill battle" (2). While South Africa may not fit neatly into the category "neoliberal"—the postapartheid state has a relatively substantial state-sponsored welfare system—the ANC government nonetheless has jumped on the international bandwagon of neoliberal economics that has deepened the divide between rich and poor (Ferguson 2015).

In Kamva, the specter of material wealth hangs over the many residents who struggle to make ends meet on a daily basis. Luxury cars speed past poor hilltop villages on the National Highway. A few people who have become wealthy from jobs in urban areas have come back to build modern mansions, complete with indoor plumbing and two-car garages, in their ancestral homelands. These houses stand in stark contrast to their impoverished surroundings, dotted with small concrete dwellings and temporary shacks. The high walls surrounding these homes, along with packs of ferocious guard dogs, discourage the kinds of everyday social encounters that are otherwise commonplace in the area and seem to mimic the security-focused architecture of wealthy South African suburbs. As Fundani surmised, "I think they are trying to do like those rich people do, to keep everything inside that yard and everything else out. So that you can't see what is happening behind the wall." Though class mobility has become a possibility for Black South Africans in a way it certainly never was under apartheid, it remains tantalizingly out of reach—and yet visible—for most people.

Tando's abiding love of luxury cars is a vivid example of these economic shifts. The teenager constantly obsessed about expensive sports cars, regardless of the fact that he did not even possess a driver's license. Through the constant performance of knowledge about different models and brands of cars, Tando negotiated an identity that projected a preferred sense of self as capitalist subject and citizen. He prided himself on his ability to recognize the norms of economic capital in the newest Mercedes-Benz or Range Rover as it zoomed past on the National Highway, even though he had never been inside one. He may not have personally consumed these products, but he did so vicariously, in the form of advertisements, magazines, and television programs. Once in a while, on my way back from town or a nearby city, I would buy a car enthusiast magazine for Tando as a gift. One day, in an act that almost seemed a parody of capitalism itself, he took one of these magazines and cut out images of expensive vehicles. He then carefully pasted the images to cardboard he found around the house and took them to school. When he came home, I found out that he then sold them to his classmates for pocket change so that he could buy more car magazines.

Much of people's dissatisfaction with the current incarnation of South African democratic politics can be better understood when examining the pre-1994 ANC election platform that promised a socialist-based redistribution of wealth along nonracial lines as well as direct participation in government that was not possible for the majority under apartheid. As the anthropologist Steven Robins writes:

> During the anti-apartheid struggle, scholars on the left had described apartheid as a system of racial capitalism whose overthrow would require more than simply taking racially based legislation off the statute books. Addressing the raw facts of deeply entrenched race and class inequality, it was argued, would require nothing less than a socialist revolution. However, with the collapse of the Berlin Wall and the break-up of the former Soviet Union, socialism was no longer on the cards for a

liberated South Africa. These constraints became increasingly visible as the ANC took over the mantle of political power. (2008, 3)

Thus much of the ANC struggle to dismantle apartheid relied on a Marxist analysis of capitalism, which advocated seizing the modes of production and overthrowing an economic system that used racism as a justification for massive wealth inequality and structural poverty. Because of this logic, ANC activists in earlier days had close ties to Communist organizations and labor unions, championing redistribution of wealth and worker unionizing in South Africa as the only answer to widespread racial and class oppression. With the end of the Cold War, these partnerships have been rendered fragile or nonexistent. While it was widely believed that the revolution had to include more than just eliminating race-based legislation, that indeed seems to be primarily what has occurred.

Since apartheid relied on the values of capitalism and exploitation for its policies of economic and racial exclusion, the ANC saw the overthrow of this system as the only viable path forward. To those who were part of the fight, the party's more recent capitulation to global economic trends is especially disappointing and worrisome. Historical events in Europe and the fall of the Soviet Union during the late twentieth century shifted the formerly growing tides of socialism and communism such that today's ANC has largely abandoned its platform of economic revolution in all but rhetoric.[2] Since 1994, the ANC has adopted a "pro-business" approach to economics that has continued the privatization of state corporations begun during the last administration of apartheid (Clark and Worger 2004). Global shifts in political and economic ideology have altered the landscape in which the ANC exercises power and has led to the further entrenching of class inequality and systemic poverty across the South African state (Posel 2013, 60). In this sense, South African democracy has become intertwined with the norms of global capital, creating quotidian practices that can be recognized as embodiments of materialist norms coupled with the reality of widespread poverty that is unlikely to change any time soon. Taken together with the conflation of democracy and capitalism, it is understandable that many Kamva residents would perceive the liberal democratic state as failing them.

Take the example of Lulama, a young woman who has been a close friend in Kamva for many years. She had her only child as a teenager and was compelled to forgo her plans for a university education to stay at home and take care of him. She now lives in a single room with no kitchen, behind the doctor's office where her mother works. She shares this small space with her mother and young son. Lulama is bright-eyed and funny but hardened by the obstacles that life has presented her. She entertains herself with pictures on Facebook and new hairstyles as she constantly looks for work and tries to make ends meet. She has done a variety of odd jobs, such as government contract work fixing nearby roads, but nothing seems to last for more than a few months. At one point in 2012, she traveled alone to Limpopo and Gauteng Province looking for work in the mines, leaving her son behind with his grandmother for several weeks. She returned home more defeated and hopeless than ever. Particularly in the last months of 2012, she complained often of depression and crippling boredom. When I visited her again in 2014, she had found part-time work at a local grocery store as a cashier, and although she was grateful for the income, she hated the work and longed to do something that made use of her secondary schooling.

Unfortunately, Lulama's story is one that is relived constantly in rural South Africa. People often refer to the staggeringly high rates of unemployment when they talk about the frustrations of contemporary South Africa: in 2016, official statistics stated 26.7 percent of all South Africans were unemployed (Statistics South Africa 2016b). Unemployment is a massive problem among rural Eastern Cape residents, and it is cited as one of the most prominent and dire challenges facing today's young people in particular. Ms. Cele captured this succinctly: "When I was young, the jobs were there, but there were no qualified people to fill the posts. Now people have education, but there are no jobs." Many if not most young people I know in the Kamva area are worried, if not downright hopeless, about their future employment opportunities. Even college graduates in high-demand fields such as accounting and engineering cannot count on gainful employment. These high rates of unemployment are often discursively linked to democracy. One teacher complained, "[During apartheid] there were firms. My father was working in Joburg, in a firm. But because of democracy . . . they closed everything."

The acute rise in unemployment over the past couple decades has led to a multitude of new social norms in rural South Africa. People I spoke with frequently linked unemployment to other problems plaguing local youth, such as teenage pregnancy, drug and alcohol addiction, and involvement in crime. Adults in Kamva often saw the boredom and idleness caused by the lack of jobs as the reason that young people were turning so readily to destructive and unhealthy behaviors. This has led many people to connect democracy to a perception of societal decline, in which youth play the role of both the victims and the perpetrators of social ills (Bucholtz 2002; Cheney 2007). Ms. Mbodi, the psychologist, explained, "Prior to 1994, there were many government systems in place. But now, a person with a degree is not working. They are just moving up and down. That's why they use a lot of drugs." Similarly, people blamed democracy for the decline in public infrastructure and safety. According to Ms. Cele, "Today the problems of young people are worse than before. Teenage pregnancy is worse since 1994." And another teacher said, "Since democracy, everything is worse. If you go to town, you see there is no public toilet. There were toilets under apartheid! Things were safe!"

Many people also implicitly and explicitly linked the increased crime rate since apartheid with unemployment, arguing that idle youth in many cases become criminals. Ms. Andiswa said, "During apartheid, everyone was working, studying, . . . everything was quiet. There was no one who was just walking in the street, doing nothing. No *tsotsis*.[3] Things were safe." Educators constantly reminded me of this safety issue in Kamva, saying that they were afraid to leave their homes after 6 p.m. or that they already had experience with muggings and robberies. Indeed, the area's high crime rate is not just hyperbole. In 2012, when most of this research was conducted, the Kamva precinct reported 24 murders, 18 attempted murders, 74 sexual offenses, and 90 aggravated robberies, in a total population of approximately five thousand.[4] Many children echoed these sentiments, telling me they felt unsafe in their community.

Residents often discursively contrasted this with what they described as the relative peace and safety of rural life under the apartheid government, as the police state strictly controlled activities, movement, and the social roles of youth.[5] Kamva residents characterized today's police as slow to act and unhelpful in combating crime, which they cited as yet another example of their disappointment with democracy. Residents explained to me that they would take community problems, such as criminal activity, to their local chief before going to the police station. When questioned about such decisions, one young person responded, "Our police here are not doing enough work. You call them, and they maybe come next week."

In light of the contemporary dissatisfaction with the ANC and municipal government services, many Eastern Cape residents continue to rely on tribal chiefs for governance where the official state seems to have

FIGURE 5.1   In an after-school program, a child conveys her daily fear of crime in a drawing. Photo by author, 2012

failed them. For many, chiefs are preferable because they maintain intimate historical knowledge of families under their jurisdiction, making them better equipped to resolve disputes and mediate between opposing parties. As one young woman articulated, "Chiefs are the people you approach when you've got problems. The chief knows what is happening in the community. They are playing a big role."

Bernard Dubbeld, in his writing on a rural town in KwaZulu-Natal Province, interrogates a related element of South Africans' expectations of democracy under apartheid, showing how many people tied good governance to the visibility of elected leaders and their projects. Neoliberal norms of privatization and decentralization, however, have obscured processes of governance and made many feel alienated from the leaders meant to represent their interests and make them feel heard (Dubbeld 2013, 495). Nostalgia for apartheid, then, spills over into tales of democracy's failure to provide desperately needed economic equality. Both in South Africa and elsewhere, longing and desire have been so drastically restructured that freedom under neoliberal capitalism is about the theoretical ability to consume more than it is about true political liberation (Comaroff and Comaroff 2001).

A brief aside about a television commercial that ran in South Africa in 2012 illustrates my point. Kentucky Fried Chicken (KFC), which is immensely popular in South Africa, ran an ad that was geared to Xhosa and Zulu speakers. In fact, a lot of the ad was in Zulu with no subtitles (though words were not necessary to understand the meaning). The advertisement featured a little boy constantly being called on to offer his bald head as a napkin to an elderly male and his peers after they ate chicken. Each time he is summoned, the little boy looks both disturbed and resigned, slinking toward the adults with head bowed as they lavish him with blessings for the future ("You'll have many cows!") while wiping off their greasy hands. This practice is considered traditional and equated with an older generation, as it rests on Zulu and Xhosa conceptions of children as ranked firmly below adults in the hierarchy of the home. Children are meant to do anything adults ask, no matter their feelings, and they are meant to do so wordlessly and obediently. But here comes salvation in the form of consumerism: at the end of the ad, the child decides to buy his elder a box of KFC's "finger lickin' good" fried chicken. Because of its apparent deliciousness, the man ends up licking his fingers instead of calling on the boy to offer up his head. The ad ends with a happy adult and an even happier child sitting side by side, eating chicken together. The joke works for an African audience, of course, because it plays on a stereotype of traditional childhood and creates humor from the very antidemocratic sentiments the practice is now seen to represent.[6]

Nostalgia for the past therefore exists simultaneously alongside future-oriented consumer desires in perhaps unexpected ways. Although this longing for both the past and the future at once may seem paradoxical on the surface, heightened consumerism provides evidence of exactly how postapartheid life is rife with economic marginalization and therefore produces the precarious conditions in which nostalgia arises. The desire for capitalist accumulation coupled with its relative unattainability leads to both a longing for an imagined better future and an idealization of a "simpler" past, one free from the burdens of unrealized wealth, jealousy, and the precarity of the global economy. Rural residents in Kamva are torn between the alluring pull of consumer desire and the intense push back for seemingly simpler, noncommoditized existences.

Language is instructive in understanding how rural Black South Africans expected democracy to deliver a freedom that has yet to materialize. As noted earlier, many people use the isiXhosa word *inkululeko*, or freedom, as a gloss for the concept of democracy in everyday conversation—a concept that had no word in the precolonial language. In this seemingly small semantic fact lies a larger ideological concept: in the worldview of many Xhosa people, a democratic government is supposed to carry with it the promise of freedom. Often, this expectation of freedom is articulated in economic terms, as many South Africans expected a redistribution of wealth to accompany the transition from apartheid to democracy. Here we see yet another epistemological divergence between Western political understandings of democracy and local explanations of the idea.

Many anthropologists have extensively discussed the problematic nature of the concept of freedom more broadly, showing that what this term means is dependent on local cultural, social, and historical contexts and cannot be ascribed a single, fixed meaning (Abu-Lughod 2002; Laidlaw 2002). Feminist scholarship has provided a critical framework through which to decenter and reevaluate the ideological concept of freedom that I find especially useful here. Saba Mahmood, in *Politics of Piety* (2005), reminds us of the Western influence on the concept of freedom and its coupling with the progressive liberal politics of individual personhood. She warns scholars that to equate freedom with such specific ideals of liberalism runs the risk of reorientalizing Muslim women in ways seen under colonialism. She writes, "The terms people use to order their lives are not simply a gloss for universally shared assumptions about the world and one's place in it, but are actually constitutive of different forms of personhood, knowledge and experience" (2005, 16). On the African continent, Harri Englund's (2006) work in Malawi demonstrates how hegemonic ideals of democracy create a specific definition of freedom that instead feels imprisoning for ordinary Malawians. Once we consider this conflation of democracy and freedom, it becomes clear why Xhosa people often describe South Africa's postapartheid government as a failure. Buzwe, a young man and ANC Youth League activist who works with students in Kamva, discussed this perception of failure: "The ANC was a liberation movement.... We thought when the ANC won the election, in 1994, things were going to change. But the change is still far, too far, away." This dissatisfaction is especially notable coming from someone inside the party and working for it.

People who refer to democracy using the language of freedom clearly expected economic liberation, and their narratives of nostalgia reflect this. Mr. Gabela told me one day from behind his principal's desk, "This country is a rich country. Why then do the indigenous groups of this country suffer so much? Poor, illiterate, living in shacks ... that alone is questionable. It's a shameful thing." He also connected the dependency on mass-produced goods to the failure of democracy to free Black South Africans: "Though we say in fact that South Africa is liberated, they introduced various things so that people must be dependent. For example, even food.... We buy these Long Lifes,[7] and I don't know how they are prepared. I don't feel liberated at all, because there's a lot of suffering now. Things are worse than before." Mr. Gabela rightly questions how widespread poverty can continue to exist primarily along racial lines in a country with vast and abundant wealth in various forms, especially after the revolution that overturned apartheid. If anything, he feels *less* free because of his dependency on goods he does not produce himself.

Indeed, the huge profits from the natural resources and material wealth of South Africa, such as diamonds, gold, and platinum, remain largely inaccessible for the majority of Black South Africans, especially in rural areas like Kamva. Multinational corporations, such as Anglo American,[8] have retained ownership of the vast majority of the means of production while continuing to employ primarily Black South Africans as laborers in dangerous and poorly paid positions that perpetuate long-standing racialized dependency relationships that can be traced back to the colonial era.[9] Many Kamva residents view ANC party politics as serving a select few in power at the expense of their majority supporters. Many people are disenchanted with their choices in political representation because none of the elected leaders deliver on their promises of true liberation. Regardless of which party an individual votes for, virtually all are seen as the handmaidens of capitalism, unwilling or unable to uproot the structures of entrenched economic inequality across the country.

In the view of the elderly woman who longed to retire in the city, political leaders were disconnected from the obstacles she confronted on a daily basis. She also connected her disappointment to the shifting nature of intergenerational relationships in contemporary South Africa, frequently complaining that her adult son should be installing indoor plumbing in her house with a portion of his teacher's salary instead of concentrating his efforts on his wife and child and hoping to travel to exotic destinations. Her son, however, clearly saw himself as part of a new generation that focuses on nuclear family relations and individual accumulation instead of extended family obligations. While the woman had gone through life with the expectation that her son would support her in old age as generations before her had done, drastic societal changes had produced a man interested in living outside the confines of "traditional" Xhosa norms and in line with new forms of political economy. This presents yet another locus of nostalgia for his mother.

In seeming contrast to her fantasies of retirement, this woman waxed nostalgically for her childhood, which was in an area even more remote than her current home on the outskirts of Kamva. When she lived there, her family had no electricity, running water, or nearby grocery stores. "In the past, we never worried about money," she said. "Our mothers never carried around this money. Now I worry because I need to buy more milk. The walls in the house need to be painted, and the boys no longer know how to do it. In the past, our fathers would go to the kraal and milk the cows and we would use that milk for everything. We never went to stores to buy food. The only thing we bought was sugar." Particularly for the older generation of Kamva residents, then, the turn to capitalism has meant a simultaneous yearning for previous economic norms perceived as "simpler" and for the material pleasures of the neoliberal age. Such discrepancies expose the ways in which media and politics have naturalized capital accumulation while largely keeping it out of reach for most individuals. People either *want* or they want a time when *want* was not their primary frame of reference.

While chatting one day with Fundani, he reminisced about his childhood outside of Kamva. He said his childhood home "has changed a lot." "This used to be a nice place," he elaborated. "We used to grow everything.

People have stopped plowing and have become dependent on buying." Here he highlights the crucial difference between economic freedom and political freedom. Further, he articulates his disappointment that democracy has not meant economic and cultural liberation for Blacks.

> Many of the things that we claim to be our culture have changed to be something else, not what Blacks used to enjoy. Even the clothes that we wear, these come from Europe and elsewhere. These jeans, the blankets, the bed I sleep in, all those things are not of Black origin. The TVs, everything! And it worries me! Because at some point I find that maybe there's nothing to celebrate. I look around, and I don't see a single thing here that is us. We have changed. We have found the West. There is no way of resisting the West. The laws themselves that govern the country are of European origin.

Fundani's frustration at the lack of locally produced goods and ideas demonstrates a sense of failure in the movement to produce real Black liberation. Importantly, a collective racial identity is conjured up, as he chooses to use the word *Black* instead of "African" or "Xhosa" in his description. Although we obviously need to resist sweeping generalizations of any population, country, or continent, Fundani's words point to the historical and continued importance of a larger Black diasporic identity for feelings of pride and solidarity in the face of global structural inequality. In fact, Blackness was leveraged as a shared political identity during the antiapartheid movement, allowing people to band together and resist apartheid's insidious ethnic categorization (Beinart 1994). This is, of course, not specific to South Africa; pan-Africanist movements across the continent and larger diaspora have been characterized by a similar phenomenon in the past several decades, as people find strength in a shared sense of Black identity (Fanon 1968; Nyerere 1968).

Importantly, the nostalgia for apartheid and the rejection of democracy I have described so far in this chapter are not the exclusive purview of the lower socioeconomic classes in Kamva. While there certainly seems to be greater alignment with democracy among those people who have benefited from it financially, many wealthy Black South Africans still see problems with the way liberal democratic ideals have infringed on social and cultural norms they felt were protected under apartheid. Ndiliswa, the doctor mentioned at the beginning of this book, is a prime example.

She is in her thirties and grew up in a rural village in the Kamva area as an only child with a single mother. Though she attended the same rural public schools as her neighbors, she described herself as having been motivated academically from an early age and recounted how she excelled in school in ways her peers often did not. She is now a respected specialist at a nearby urban hospital. Doctors are generally paid well in South Africa today, and Ndiliswa's house is a visible marker of her success. The home's decor is a testament to conspicuous consumption: an area rug with flecks of purple sparkles, an oscillating fan with several digital settings, a display cabinet of seemingly unused glass dishware, and several indoor bathrooms with gleaming white tiles. A white Audi sits in the multicar garage, which is surrounded by carefully tended flowerbeds. In many ways, Ndiliswa epitomizes the consumerist fantasies of rural South Africa. She enjoys traveling abroad with friends, talks fondly of a trip to Paris a few years earlier, and is thinking of vacationing soon on the beaches of Mauritius—things unthinkable for almost every other area resident. She takes great pride in her ability to take good care of her elderly mother, who always encouraged her to focus on her studies and to whom she attributes her success today.

Clearly, one would assume that democracy and the abolition of apartheid have served Ndiliswa well. She is a member of South Africa's growing Black middle and upper classes and has been able to access career and educational opportunities that previous generations of Xhosa people never could (Manase 2016). And yet when we spoke in 2012, she surprised me by expressing many of the same frustrations with the state of her country as her less wealthy neighbors.

> I'm of the opinion that democracy brought freedom to the country; it has opened so many doors for us, and yeah, it has done a lot of good things for us. But on the other extreme, it has made things worse. I'm working at a public institution. Because people have "rights," they'll just come and demand this and demand that, forgetting that you are here to do your job. You are not here to be bossed around by them. They forget that you also have rights. You'll find that people are very selfish. They think of themselves alone; they don't think of other people. They tend to abuse those rights and to forget the fact that the rights come with responsibilities. Democracy has been misinterpreted

in some cases. I can't put blame on democracy itself, but it's the way it has been received by people.

Ndiliswa enjoys many of the equal rights democracy has enshrined in the South African Constitution, yet she feels people are abusing these rights. She assured me that it was not only the medical profession that was plagued by abuses of rights but that everywhere you look people are demanding whatever they want because they have "freedom." Her perspective that people in the nascent democracy are selfish suggests nostalgia for previous communal identification practices that stressed prioritizing the good of the community or family over self-promotion. She also brought up and defended corporal punishment to me in much the same way local teachers did, saying that it has helped her get where she is today by instilling in her a critical sense of discipline. As her comments above illustrate, she shared my own assessment that it is not so much a rejection of democracy as a political system but rather specific laws and local interpretations of the concept of democracy that are seen to conflict with Xhosa culture.

This reading of nostalgia in the rural Eastern Cape can be taken one step further. Nostalgia can also be a desire not just for the past but also for desire itself. Nostalgia for apartheid in South Africa not only provides evidence of capitalist inequalities and political resistance; it is structured by these very obstacles. Nostalgia itself has become a market, as people in South Africa offer up memory for mass consumption in the form of ANC T-shirts featuring a young Mandela or framed apartheid-era covers of *Drum* magazine, famed for its empowering images of township life, stories on African independence, and iconic celebrations of Blackness (Curnow 2013). In a sense, South Africans, not to mention international tourists, are consuming memory itself through the commodification and recasting of apartheid history. Memories, not for the evils of apartheid's racist state but instead for the unity of resistance to it, are for sale everywhere you look.

PARROTING NOSTALGIA

The nostalgic discourses about life under apartheid vis-à-vis the failures of democracy are not confined to elders in the Kamva community. In fact, young people sometimes echo their elders' fears that democracy is to blame for the erosion of culture and that life under apartheid was actually better. Nostalgia is transmitted from one generation to the next, suggesting an ability to have nostalgia for a time during which one never actually lived.

Noluvo became visibly emotional when she told me about the ways she thought Xhosa culture flourished under apartheid as opposed to the present day.

> I just think that [the apartheid] government was better. Because everything was under control! Let me put it that way. In apartheid, everything was under control. But now, not everything is under control! In apartheid, they controlled crime. You know? In apartheid, they controlled violence, you know, they controlled everything! And you wouldn't do a thing that you know is wrong. But now, they can't control crime. They can't control pregnancy. Instead of controlling those things, they just introduced gay marriage. They just introduced abortion. Instead of fighting what is there, they add more. That's what I think, that's how I think this apartheid was good and democracy is bad. Now we are moving from better to worse. Despite the fact that they say Black people were not wanted by whites. Yes, they were not wanted, but when it comes to living life, they made us live better. If you look at that time, nobody was living in shacks. Everybody was working. Now, not everybody is working. At that time at the age of twenty, you'd be getting a job. Now, people even have degrees and they are not employed! Also, now with democracy people don't have respect for each other. If I get married to an Indian, I don't know the traditions of an Indian. I do not respect them, you know? I just think that [apartheid] government was better.

Noluvo's portrayal of the apartheid era is one of control, structure, and stability. She also evidences support for some elements of apartheid's policy of racial segregation, explaining that she sees the freedom to marry across racial lines as diluting culture. Other young people spoke similarly about cultural loss in the face of Western liberal values, even if they were not quite as extreme. For example, Imitha explained with exasperation in one of our conversations, "Today's children don't want to listen. They are Westernized. They are learning from TV."

In some cases, it became evident that internalized racism was inter-twined with young people's views on democracy and apartheid. Man-galiso, who was also a Sonke participant, was in college the year I spoke to him about this issue. He is an ambitious young man who studied electri-cal engineering and was looking forward to earning money to support his elderly mother and grandmother, despite his immense difficulty finding steady employment. He prides himself on his work ethic and moral com-mitment to family, not to mention his views on gender equality after par-ticipating in Sonke's Digital Stories project. Mangaliso has been deeply frustrated by the proliferation of state welfare programs under democracy, which he sees as a destructive force in his community. He had a similar assessment of government dependency on the part of other people in the area, but in this case he cast it specifically along racial lines.

> It's not always about the government! That's what I hate about Black people. Like, they sit at home, and are like, "Oh, government is not building anything for us! Any houses." But you are sitting there and you are not doing anything! It's not always about the government. That means the government has to go to each and every house, each and every town, looking—it's not always about that! What I hate about Black people—they don't want to work. They want income, but they don't want to work.

Instead of blaming colonialism and apartheid for creating socioeconomic and racial inequality, Mangaliso uses the apartheid-era language of racial hierarchy and essentialism in deeply troubling ways. He even suggested that his perspective on this issue could be traced to white influence in his family history: "I think my mom is different because of the way she grew up. Her father grew up with Afrikaners and went to a farm school. . . . I think that's why he was different in his views."

Amahle, now a college student who once participated in Sonke's Digital Stories project with Mangaliso, expressed a similar attitude: "That's the thing with us. We don't wanna get educated, so we are always going to have this mentality that white people will always have money. We don't study a lot. We choose being corrupt. If Black people get in power, they just abuse their power." And in a moment of nostalgia for the alleged stability of the predemocracy era, she said, "In our culture it has always been that you can make something work out of nothing. That's what I love about my culture. . . . But democracy has made our people very lazy. They don't want to do stuff. The mentality of our people has changed. I don't like how this democracy is turning out." Such sentiments reveal the ideological remnants of the apartheid system that structure people's actions and self-assessments and perpetuate the racialization of African communities (Pierre 2013). Rather than recognize the oppressive structural conditions that lead to widespread corruption and poverty, people blame individuals for making poor choices and lacking a moral compass. Both here and elsewhere across the globe, such "culture of poverty" mentalities ensure that marginalized groups remain oppressed (e.g., Bourgois 1995; Goode and Maskovsky 2001).

I present these narratives to also insist that nostalgia is a significant and competing pedagogical discourse in classrooms, NGO programs, and at home. Young people learn about the past through the perspectives of the adults around them. And, as we saw in the previous chapter, when educators and elders are ambivalent about the democratic lessons they are meant to transmit to youth, those lessons are both consciously and unconsciously filtered and recast.

This chapter examined the daily narrative practices and intergenerational relationships of Eastern Cape residents, showing how they work to construct subjective visions of the past that align with desired cultural values and social norms. Nostalgia allows us to understand how individuals express longing for elements of the apartheid regime in the face of widespread dissatisfaction with South African democracy as introduced by the ANC after apartheid. Previous scholars have shown that nostalgia critically frames the present more than it actually reflects the past, which is an important theoretical lens through which to view the narratives in this chapter (Angé and Berliner 2014; Klumbyte 2009; Stewart 1988). I have joined these discussions on nostalgia by showing how apartheid's homeland system created the very conditions for recollections of cultural autonomy and stability. I have revealed how different epistemological understandings of democracy and freedom lead to rejections of liberal policies like children's rights as well as the perception that liberalism is an oppressive force that threatens Xhosa culture. Add to this the widespread conflation of democracy and neoliberal capitalism, and the logic behind Black South Africans' rejection of the present and nostalgia for the past becomes clear.

Although this reading of apartheid-era nostalgia allows for a more nuanced understanding of its existence within the democratic state and the ways in which people construct political subjectivity, it does little to resolve the tensions of a democratic education taught by the people most dissatisfied with it. What impact might these mixed messages on democracy and human rights have on the next generation of South African voters? What, if anything, can we learn about global resistance to democracy from the case of rural South Africa?

CHAPTER SIX

Freedom from Democracy?

When I can vote in the next election, I'll vote for another party besides the ANC. I think it's time to change, to see what other parties can do for South Africa.

—Tando

In May 2019, South Africa once again went to the polls to vote on the National Assembly, which is the representative body that chooses the country's president. This was five years after President Jacob Zuma won his second term in office and one year after he was forced to resign after a slew of corruption scandals and was replaced by his deputy president, Cyril Ramaphosa. Although the African National Congress has handily won every national election since apartheid, its numbers are certainly not as strong as they once were.[1] In recent years, media coverage has highlighted the way many people, especially "born frees" (young people born after 1994), have voiced widespread dissatisfaction with the pro-business, pro-capitalist policies of the ruling party and the allegations of corruption at the local and national levels (Herskovitz 2013). Even Archbishop Desmond Tutu, famous for his role as a social rights activist and close friend of Mandela during the antiapartheid movement and longtime ANC supporter, officially declared he would not vote for the ruling party in 2014 (Makinana 2014).

In the Eastern Cape, the relationship to the ANC is somewhat more complex because of the province's particular historical position. When I was in Kamva in 2012 and again in 2014, many people expressed their strong condemnation of Zuma as corrupt and yet simultaneously cited their lasting loyalty and allegiance to the ANC (see also Onishi 2014). Fundani, for example, said, "[I've] long been ANC. The ANC remains a good organization that has good policies and principles that can take the Black people to freedom. The ANC is built on a very strong foundation. It's just that *tsotsis* joined the ANC and are taking the intentions of the organization in the other direction." The number of ANC supporters is always high in the Eastern Cape, Mandela's home province and the birthplace of many apartheid-era activists. In 2014, the ruling party captured 70 percent of the vote in the province; by 2019, it was down to 69.26 percent ("Electoral Commission" 2019). Despite the numbers, however, Tando's comments cited in the epigraph suggest that a potential shift in future political alliances is emerging in the newest generation of voters, even in the heart of the ANC's ancestral homeland. Frequent narratives of disappointment with the status quo evidence the fact that loyalty to Mandela should not be confused with ideological agreement with the larger tenets of Western liberalism, and his relatively recent death in 2013 might be enough to let people's current frustrations overtake their historical allegiances (if they have not already). What I find especially intriguing here is how people negotiate and balance multiple systems of knowledge and competing interests in crafting identities as citizens, political subjects, and members of local cultural groups in complex ways that electoral statistics often obscure.

Tando's older cousin, a young woman who in 2014 was working in a nearby town, is another good example of the loyalty so many Xhosa people feel for the ANC. She told me she would still vote for the party in the next election, despite all the national portrayals of corruption and inefficiency. "If I vote differently," she said, "it would be like I'm a sellout or something. Because Mandela, wherever he is, would want the ANC to lead for the rest of South Africa's life or until Jesus comes back. I'm sure people might not see the ANC being the same, because of corruption. . . . People love the ANC just because of Nelson Mandela and nothing else. And they will keep on voting for the ANC just to keep what Mandela fought for. If it doesn't function, Nelson Mandela's name would just fade." This is a kind of party loyalty seen elsewhere on the African continent, reminding us of the importance of decentering hegemonic views of what democracy ought to look like and how democratic citizens are likely to behave (Comaroff and Comaroff 1997).

And yet, despite the words of those like this loyal young woman, there is no doubt that people are increasingly unhappy with the ruling party. In the early months of 2014, before the elections, a fresh round of service delivery protests spread across the country like wildfire, and competing political parties, such as the Democratic Alliance and the Economic Freedom Fighters, capitalized on these events and waged a media campaign that emphasized the dire need for resource redistribution and crackdowns on corruption (South African Broadcasting Corporation 2014). The protests drew attention not only to political dissatisfaction but also to the perceived economic failures of the ANC to make good on its pre-1994 promises of equality for all people on the basis of nonracial wealth redistribution. The EFF, with the controversial firebrand Julius Malema at the helm, is one example of the widespread youth dissatisfaction and rejection of Western liberal values seen throughout this book. Despite the fact that Malema remains a highly polarizing figure, he has managed to capture the imaginations of young people across South Africa, especially in his home province of Limpopo. For many the EFF seems to be what the ANC once was to a different generation of young people: radical, socialist, and ready to fight to overturn the status quo. Added to this picture of political disenchantment are the recent bouts of xenophobic violence directed at African immigrants, largely a result of very high rates of unemployment and accusations that foreigners are stealing the few jobs available to South African citizens. These increasing dissatisfactions with the ANC help explain why so many Kamva residents increasingly feel a sense of disappointment with democracy and a nostalgia for spaces of seeming autonomy under apartheid. In this book, I have revealed how these interrelated realities trickle into rural classrooms and extracurricular education: while on the national level, liberalism and human rights structure democratic socialization and ideals, on the local level culture and traditionalism play an equally or even more prominent role in ways unintended in the official curriculum.

ETHNOGRAPHY OF POLITICAL EDUCATION

A fundamental and primary contention of this book is that democracy is created first in the classroom. If this is the case, any serious attempt to understand the production of a democratic state needs to start with sustained ethnographic engagement in these educational spaces. In places like South Africa, with a strong emphasis on liberalism and human rights and a cohesive national curriculum, the creation of political identity and civic participation is meant to happen first in the early years of life. Shouldn't scholars of democracy and political socialization start there as well?

In South Africa, national discourses of liberalism and individual human rights often give the appearance of drowning out contrasting points of view. I have used ethnographic methods in a rural community to reveal the much more complex negotiations that are involved in teaching democracy to youth, particularly among historically oppressed populations that continue to suffer from high levels of poverty and discrimination. Situating my research in the former Transkei provides a vantage point for analyzing these issues that is historically specific and yet illustrative of larger trends in the postapartheid state. This area remains critically underserved on multiple levels, yet is part of national and international discourses through institutions such as schools, municipal government programs, and NGOs. My work provides both a local case study and a window into larger national and transnational sociopolitical trends. Here the well-intentioned rhetoric of liberal human rights and democracy can seem hollow in the face of persistent structural inequality and a perception that meaningful change has yet to arrive.

A critical examination of the ways in which the apartheid era both structured and continues to inform the present is clearly of central importance to this work. South Africa's notorious and prolonged struggle with codified racism and inequality continues to permeate all areas of life throughout the rural Eastern Cape, not to mention the rest of the country. Economic relations provided much of the foundation for the racist policies of the National Party government from 1948 to 1994; strict controls and regulations around the movement of nonwhite bodies allowed a white minority to remain in power while securing a large, disempowered labor force that benefited the few (Clark and Worger 2004; Posel 1991). Indeed, the antiapartheid struggle focused at least in part on this understanding of economic relations in order to dismantle the National Party government. Much of the movement hinged on youth activities, reaffirming the importance of anthropology's continued focus on the ways in which young people craft political subjectivities while simultaneously inheriting and reproducing social norms from previous generations (Cheney 2007; Cole and Durham 2008).

Delving into local classroom practices and narrative accounts in rural Kamva has allowed me to argue for the ways in which individuals filter democracy through Xhosa worldviews and ideologies. Life Orientation, a class pioneered by the democratic government's Department of Basic Education, focuses on constructing engaged and informed citizens and follows a state-mandated curriculum. In reality, however, lessons are negotiated on the local level through conscious and unconscious practices that reflect the habitus of individual teachers and their larger communities (Bourdieu 1977). While the course's curriculum emphasizes a commitment to diversity and multiculturalism, it prioritizes Western liberal norms of children's rights that are in sharp contrast to local perspectives on the proper roles of youth within society. Although the curriculum advocates acceptance and cultural pluralism, it nonetheless adheres to a bottom line based on constitutional principles derived from Western liberal frameworks of justice and individual personhood. Ethnography is particularly useful for investigating these discrepancies; while state language communicates one official message, daily narratives and behaviors offer a nuanced and diverse interpretation of these ideas beyond the bounds of national rhetoric.

Rote educational practices were one striking example of the dissonance between the official curriculum and local teaching. As I highlighted in chapter 4, in Kamva, classroom lessons written in the curriculum as discussion based and meant to foster debate and respect diverse opinions often became lectures that projected an objective concept of right and wrong to students. In this sense, the curriculum is being adapted to fit within cultural and historical practices already firmly embedded in the community rather than the other way around. I connected these observations on education in the classroom with the fact that research participants constantly reiterated the importance of young people's understanding that democratic rights must be paired with an awareness of a citizen's *responsibilities*. I see this framing as reflective of Xhosa generational and gendered hierarchies, communalism, and notions of youth positioning in society. In other words, this was an arena in which teachers could further their own agendas (whether conscious or not) as they taught the national lessons. Rather than see such emphases as antidemocratic, importantly, I believe we should read them as suggesting a more expansive concept of what constitutes democracy in different contexts (Owusu 1997). For example, teaching that stresses the individual person as the fundamental unit of democracy is inappropriate in many rural African communities, as stated elsewhere (Englund 2006; Nyamnjoh 2002; Rice 2017).

At times, complaints about the lack of emphasis on responsibilities in the national curriculum, among other perceived societal ills, led individuals to wax nostalgic for elements of apartheid-era education. This is despite the fact that legislative acts like the Bantu Education Act of 1953 subjected Blacks to vastly inferior schools that prepared them only for low-wage jobs and outlawed native languages such as Xhosa and Zulu. I have theorized that seemingly counterintuitive alignment with discriminatory educational policies under apartheid makes sense when examining the importance of rigid age and gender hierarchies as a method of social control in Xhosa communities. The liberal curriculum of the democratic state is alien to many rural South Africans and stands in contrast to the illusion of cultural autonomy that the apartheid government carefully cultivated in the "independent" homelands like the Transkei. In other words, some teachers preferred the apartheid-era curriculum because it allowed them to exercise control over classrooms that more closely mapped onto local cultural ideologies of intergenerational relationships and social reproduction, and the apartheid state had little interest in interfering with such practices. Adding to this sense of nostalgia is the fact that the contemporary state curriculum offers what feels like little in the way of alternative practices of social control and discipline for teachers. It is unsurprising, then, that these preferences for specific educational practices became clear not just in rhetoric but also in the embodied practices of individual teachers, such as in forms of bodily policing through the use of corporal punishment despite its official illegality. These connections with an oppressive past emerge on the conscious level in conversations but also unconsciously in the classroom in ways not easily altered by brief teacher training or new curricular materials that offer glowing endorsements of democracy and children's rights. These deeply embedded norms are extremely tenacious, even in the face of changes in educational rhetoric, political shifts, and new legal measures. For example, many teachers told me that even if they did refuse to beat their students, some parents would specifically ask them to do it.

Aligned with these sentiments on the role of young people in society was the presence of persistent fears of cultural loss. Community members frequently expressed, through both personal narratives and classroom teaching, the importance of keeping Xhosa traditions alive into the next generation, especially in the face of outside threats. As the example of the girl embracing Satanism after an internet search on her mobile phone illuminated, the "outside" world is often perceived as a serious threat to the elements of life deemed essential to Xhosa identity. For these reasons, as I show, many people view notions of "freedom" under democracy as actually constraining and oppressive.

Relatedly, many people were concerned with appropriate labeling of practices as "authentic." I have contended that these fears of loss reveal the way many people see democracy as an infringement on rights to cultural traditionalism. Drawing on long-standing debates within anthropology on the nature of tradition and notions of cultural authenticity (Hobsbawm and Ranger 1983; Myers 2002), I have discussed how seemingly continuous and unbroken Xhosa practices, such as male circumcision rites and marriage rituals, have actually taken on new underlying meanings and forms in the modern era, even if they appear the same on the surface (Vincent 2008). This is crucial to keep in mind in order that we not continue the long history of Western cultural essentialism of African communities.

I have brought nongovernmental organizations into this discussion of youth political socialization because of their enormous role in the construction of civil society not just in contemporary South Africa, but around the world. The chapters on the Sonke Gender Justice Network demonstrate the ways in which neoliberal norms of privatization and decentralization of government have affected local social and cultural relations as well as processes of political education. Organizations like Sonke would not exist if it were not for the failure of the government to provide needed services in rural areas (Goldman 2005). Complaints about the failures of the ANC to reform class relations and redistribute wealth along nonracial lines are inextricably linked with the proliferation of NGOs such as Sonke in rural South Africa (Robins 2005, 2008). These organizations strive to provide social services, ideological training, and political advocacy seen as missing or incomplete in current state efforts (Fisher 1997; Markowitz 2001). And yet such organizations are often closely aligned with the state's ideology based on Western human rights discourse from international agencies such as the United Nations.

Ethnographic research within Sonke's walls demonstrated the contrasting perspectives that exist on democracy and the politics of culture among different segments of society in the postapartheid state. The office climate at Sonke in Cape Town can be viewed as a microcosm of larger discourses on democratic liberalism and is also illuminating when trying to understand the cultural negotiations with which Sonke engages on the ground in their countrywide programming. Sonke staff members constantly stress recognition of cultural diversity and mutual respect as key values in their liberal ideology, for instance. And yet they also insist that their work revolves around "changing culture" where it is considered harmful and antidemocratic. Importantly, I have illustrated how highly subjective liberal discourses that circulate on the international level inform ideas of what constitutes harmful practices and where interventions should be made.

One of the primary challenges Sonke faces is competing identity practices among rural Black South Africans. The NGO's programs require that participants adopt specific notions of democratic citizenship and nationalism that many people in rural Xhosa communities view as incompatible with local identity practices. Staff narratives of their original exposure to Sonke, often through community workshops, bear a striking resemblance to earlier missionary conversion stories and narratives of colonial encounters on the African continent. These stories frame individuals' transitions to Sonke's view of gender equality as a radical shift from local to national and international modes of belonging. In these narratives, employees frequently cited instances in which they realized elements of their cultures were "harmful" when situated within the ideals of democracy, justice, and equality and should be changed.

Relatedly, Sonke staff members work hard to illuminate the origins of specific cultural practices, aiming to debunk what they see as myths of the authenticity of many beliefs and behaviors in order to call for their abolishment. When contrasted with local emphases in places like Kamva on protecting "authentic" culture, it is easy to see why Sonke would zero in on this strategy. Much of the time, this process involves unpacking the colonial influence on Xhosa cultural and social practices, such as the Christian origins of homophobic attitudes in the rural Eastern Cape, to name but one example. This work has interesting and significant ties to anthropological debates on the very concept of culture itself and how it ought to be defined and employed, as well as who has the power to define it (e.g., Geertz 1973; Hobsbawm and Ranger 1983; Rosaldo 1989). Here the NGO plays a critical role in conversations about what constitutes culture.

Beyond scholarship, ethnographic investigations into democratic teaching offer potential benefits to curricular design and educational policy. How might the state craft curricula that better attend to indigenous cultural hierarchies, for example? What would it look like to infuse multiculturalism not just into lesson contents, but into pedagogical strategies themselves? While answering these questions has not been the focus of this book, I hope a greater understanding of the ways in which the national curriculum alienates so many South Africans might lead to more meaningful forms of inclusivity on all levels of democratic education.

THE GLOBAL RISE OF NOSTALGIA POLITICS

Theoretical engagements with the concept of nostalgia have provided an essential framework for this book, helping frame my contention that longings for aspects of the apartheid government can be understood as a significant commentary on the disappointments of the present (Bissell 2005; Dlamini 2009; Piot 2010; Stewart 1988). Kamva residents fondly recall specific legislation and social norms under apartheid that they perceive as aligning closely with local cultural ideologies. Nostalgic narratives of apartheid in historically oppressed communities are the result of the often-unconscious conflations of freedom, democracy, and capitalism. For example, the assessment of the Xhosa word commonly used for democracy, *inkululeko*, provides evidence of this phenomenon in a seemingly quotidian language practice. To use the word as a gloss for democracy suggests particular conscious and unconscious conceptions of what this political system ought to entail and what it means to be truly "free." This nostalgia is evidenced in both discursive and embodied practices that reject and renegotiate elements of liberal democracy, as well as in narratives on apartheid that comment on the past while outlining the inadequacies of the present. Seen from this vantage point, South Africa's celebrated "peaceful" transition to democracy looks a lot messier on the ground. While the world has memorialized Mandela's life and the creation of a "free" state after one of history's most reviled political regimes, many South Africans insist that democracy is a failed project and that they were better off before the so-called liberation.

In addressing these perhaps surprising realities, I have shown that understanding the widespread disappointment and nostalgia among rural

Black South Africans requires a deeper attention to historical, cultural, spiritual, and economic trajectories of the postcolonial state. The backlash against contemporary South African politics, then, is due to both an ideological conflation of democracy and capitalism and a discrepancy between local cultural practices and statewide projects of citizenship construction and nationalism that are influenced by Western hegemonic narratives and colonial histories. When people speak of the failures of democracy, it should be read at least in part as a commentary on the continued wealth inequality and structural poverty exacerbated by international capitalist relations of production, the increased privatization of state institutions, and "free" market trade that keeps wealth flowing out of the majority's hands. In fact, contemporary South Africa might be considered an exemplary model of the late capitalist system at work: the majority of South Africans, primarily Black, today find themselves jobless, in debt, and excluded from much of the consumer culture available to wealthier—and usually white—segments, who have an unending supply of cheap labor, access to "first world" luxuries, and an increasingly powerful position in global economics. It is no wonder so many South Africans find democracy a massive disappointment. In fact, the political and economic disenchantment of so many South Africans, combined with the widespread longing for aspects of an oppressive and racist government, should force us to address the conflicting interpretations of democracy itself and lead us to question our assumptions about the universal goals of "freedom" as a shared human project (Englund 2006).

Intergenerational tensions are an outgrowth of these differing experiences of economic relations. As seen in the new architecture of many Eastern Cape homes, capitalist norms of consumerism and accumulation have become part of the identity of many people in the rural Eastern Cape. In this sense, the self becomes constructed through consumer culture and the symbolic capital provided by material possessions that are fetishized far beyond their use value (Taussig 1980). These changing forms of capital have the effect of creating increased ideological differences between generations, as seen in the varying attitudes toward government welfare support among individuals in Kamva. Therefore, discussing the impacts of neoliberal capitalism on rural South Africans along with ethnographic research on discourses of democracy and youth socialization reveals important connections between global economic trends and citizen production in local contexts.

This analysis has implications beyond the individual case of rural South African youth in Kamva or individual NGOs such as the Sonke Gender Justice Network. In the past few decades, the world has seen many countries shift to some version of "democracy"—though of course the specific incarnations and circumstances of these political changes vary wildly (Paley 2002). Indeed, it seems that democracy, at least in rhetoric, is increasingly naturalized as the only morally sound and effective way to govern (Abu-Lughod 2002). Concurrently, norms of privatization and decentralization of national governments are quickly supplanting or have supplanted older modes of production. These economic and political changes have been accompanied by a rise in NGOs like Sonke that work to provide social services and ideological training that is beyond current government provisions. Thus new forms of civil society are emerging in which organizations outside of explicit state control contribute to notions of citizenship and work to hold the government accountable. I have examined these institutions and their relationships to local communities on the ground in ways that statistical analyses and media outlets often ignore or are unable to capture. Such anthropological engagement has the ability to ask critical questions about the sustainability of NGOs, their (often tenuous) relationship to national governments, and their role in broader civil society movements, not to mention the reception of their ideas among historically marginalized populations such as Black South Africans.

We also must maintain a critical awareness of the continued presence of racialized discourses and behaviors in the "Rainbow Nation" and how they structure people's understanding of their own possibilities as well as government and NGO actions. Far from the nonracial society for which it might strive, apartheid's insidious racial logics remain embedded in South African life, not to mention in its highly racialized geography left over from the homeland system. Some rural Black residents, far removed from their elected representatives and white compatriots, equate Blackness with corruption, laziness, and inability to govern, echoing discourses of the past and obscuring broader structural factors. These racialized ideologies and histories influence rural teachers and their students in a multitude of ways.

Critically, my support for a sustained and expanded anthropology of nostalgia reaches far beyond the case of South Africa. As other scholars have demonstrated, nostalgic discourses often exist in areas that have experienced relatively recent political and economic upheaval, such as many of the former Soviet states (Boym 2001; Fournier 2012; Klumbyte 2009). I have argued that the increasing wealth inequality wrought by neoliberal capitalism and its frequent pairing with Western democratic ideologies act as predictive measures of nostalgia within national populations, particularly those with histories of marginalization and oppression. In this sense, it is critical that anthropologists pay close attention to nostalgia as a commentary on shifting social norms and economic realities and that they recognize these sentiments as distinct from other types of remembering. While the history of nostalgia as an analytic and linguistic category places it firmly in the realm of individual experience, I argue that its importance in contemporary democracies bleeds into collective identity practices and has become a social phenomenon reliant on the intergenerational transmission of culture. This nostalgia morphs into dissatisfaction that has an impact on individuals' voting practices, party allegiances, and political socialization and will likely continue to do so far into the future. In fact, nostalgia is quite literally transmitted to future generations, as I showed in the nostalgic renderings of life under apartheid from those young people in Kamva who never experienced it firsthand.

In 2015 and 2016, it seemed a potential sea change in South African politics was afoot. Images of angry Black students throwing rocks at police in riot gear and burning down university property were broadcast by South African and international news organizations, conjuring up the violence of the antiapartheid movement near the end of the twentieth century and the prominent role of youth in it. When I first started to draft this conclusion, rocks and excrement were being thrown through University of Cape Town windows in an effort to disrupt regular classes and advance a national fight to decolonize higher education and to lower tuition fees across the country. There were heated debates among scholars, media analysts, and community members about whether or not this kind of violent protesting was a necessary and productive political action on the part of those in desperate situations or a populist movement hampering education and stymieing real change by destroying the very systems it hoped to amend. Such recent events pose a problem for this book, as it suggests a surge in political activism and civic consciousness despite my contention that resistance to democracy and a desire for return to the past abound in places like Kamva, even among young people (Makhulu 2016). It perhaps signals a shift in which youth are rejecting the narratives of their elders and instead forming new types of political action that look to the 1980s and 1990s for inspiration. While the South African government has done little but offer Band-Aid solutions to the problem of inequality and the continued legacy of colonialism in higher education, many students remain committed to the cause and continue to protest (Motala et al. 2019).

And yet the #RhodesMustFall and #FeesMustFall movements serve to highlight the drastically different histories at play in rural former homelands and urban centers. While the former Transkei retains the legacy of indirect rule that allowed for illusions of cultural autonomy, universities in places like Cape Town and Johannesburg retain highly visible legacies of colonialism and racial segregation, not to mention the increasing privatization of higher education institutions as seen across so much of the world. Monuments and artwork celebrating colonial leaders as well as jarring racial divides in terms of financial need among student bodies serve as constant reminders that apartheid is far from over in all but name. Maybe this is why Tando recently told me, after just moving to a suburb of Johannesburg to attend a "better" school and live with his aunt and uncle, that he greatly misses living in Kamva. Perhaps it is easier to romanticize the past *and* the future there.

Young people all over the globe are being socialized into new permutations of democracy at this very moment. How might local cultural forms intersect with these national projects in ways that politicians and educators may not anticipate, yet to which they should pay close attention? What kinds of democratic citizens are being produced through these intersections of politics and culture? How can anthropology make sense of seemingly counterintuitive discourses of nostalgia for previous eras that were less "free"? For me, these questions are only the beginning: future ethnographic research will allow an increased and essential understanding of the ways in which youth learn about democracy and human rights under capitalist regimes of power and within local settings that have very different norms on political subjectivity and the roles young people ought to occupy in their communities.

While beyond the purview of this book, a longitudinal examination of the young people learning from their elders' ambivalence and nostalgia would offer a fascinating window into the consequences of locally specific forms of democratic education. In an era of world history that seems rife with backlash to democratic liberalism, this is of particular import. Recent political elections around the world that have hinged on anger toward liberal policy and the swelling tides of support for "traditionalism"—think of Bolsonaro's backlash against liberal LGBTQ tolerance in Brazil or Trump's nostalgia for some unspecified past through the "Make America Great Again" campaign in the United States—are symptoms of larger national sentiments among ordinary citizens. It would be naive to think these sentiments are not trickling down into a nation's classrooms and shaping lessons for even the youngest students.

These musings lead me to speculate about the potential of what I call a "postdemocratic" state in South Africa and beyond. As the tides of neoliberal economic reforms continue to wash over the African continent and as more people feel the rights of the few are protected at the expense of cultural diversity and the living conditions of the general populace, one has to wonder if the project of liberal Western democracy will hold in future generations. Will the backlash against capitalist inequality and cultural hegemony result in a push for increasingly socialist states that call for a redistribution of resources? Will people instead rally behind potentially autocratic leaders because of the promise of security, stability, and return to "tradition" they might offer, even if this means a sacrifice of basic, individual rights?[2] Will citizens of nations such as South Africa insist on more transparent and direct forms of democracy? Regardless of what the future of South African politics holds, it is evident that young people, as always, will play a critical role in its negotiation.

APPENDIX

This is a selection of the most relevant sections of the Bill of Rights for the discussion in this book. For the full version, see www.gov.za/documents /constitution-republic-south-africa-1996.

Bill of Rights from Chapter 2 of the Constitution of South Africa

Section 7. Rights

1. This Bill of Rights is a cornerstone of democracy in South Africa. It enshrines the rights of all people in our country and affirms the democratic values of human dignity, equality and freedom.

2. The state must respect, protect, promote and fulfil the rights in the Bill of Rights.

3. The rights in the Bill of Rights are subject to the limitations contained or referred to in section 36, or elsewhere in the Bill.

Section 9. Equality

1. Everyone is equal before the law and has the right to equal protection and benefit of the law.

2. Equality includes the full and equal enjoyment of all rights and freedoms. To promote the achievement of equality, legislative and other measures designed to protect or advance persons, or categories of persons, disadvantaged by unfair discrimination may be taken.

3. The state may not unfairly discriminate directly or indirectly against anyone on one or more grounds, including race, gender, sex, pregnancy, marital status, ethnic or social origin, colour, sexual orientation, age, disability, religion, conscience, belief, culture, language and birth.

4. No person may unfairly discriminate directly or indirectly against anyone on one or more grounds in terms of subsection (3). National legislation must be enacted to prevent or prohibit unfair discrimination.

5. Discrimination on one or more of the grounds listed in subsection (3) is unfair unless it is established that the discrimination is fair.

Section 10. Human dignity

Everyone has inherent dignity and the right to have their dignity respected and protected.

Section 11. Life

Everyone has the right to life.

Section 12. Freedom and security of the person

1. Everyone has the right to freedom and security of the person, which includes the right

    a. not to be deprived of freedom arbitrarily or without just cause;

    b. not to be detained without trial;

    c. to be free from all forms of violence from either public or private sources;

    d. not to be tortured in any way; and

    e. not to be treated or punished in a cruel, inhuman or degrading way.

2. Everyone has the right to bodily and psychological integrity, which includes the right

    a. to make decisions concerning reproduction;

    b. to security in and control over their body; and

    c. not to be subjected to medical or scientific experiments without their informed consent.

Section 13. Slavery, servitude and forced labour

No one may be subjected to slavery, servitude or forced labour.

Section 14. Privacy

Everyone has the right to privacy, which includes the right not to have

a. their person or home searched;

b. their property searched;

c. their possessions seized; or

d. the privacy of their communications infringed.

Section 15. Freedom of religion, belief and opinion

1. Everyone has the right to freedom of conscience, religion, thought, belief and opinion.

2. Religious observances may be conducted at state or state-aided institutions, provided that

a. those observances follow rules made by the appropriate public authorities;

b. they are conducted on an equitable basis; and

c. attendance at them is free and voluntary.

3.   a. This section does not prevent legislation recognising

i. marriages concluded under any tradition, or a system of religious, personal or family law; or

ii. systems of personal and family law under any tradition, or adhered to by persons professing a particular religion.

b. Recognition in terms of paragraph (a) must be consistent with this section and the other provisions of the Constitution.

Section 16. Freedom of expression

1. Everyone has the right to freedom of expression, which includes

a. freedom of the press and other media;

b. freedom to receive or impart information or ideas;

c. freedom of artistic creativity; and

d. academic freedom and freedom of scientific research.

2. The right in subsection (1) does not extend to

a. propaganda for war;

b. incitement of imminent violence; or

c. advocacy of hatred that is based on race, ethnicity, gender or religion, and that constitutes incitement to cause harm.

Section 17. Assembly, demonstration, picket and petition

Everyone has the right, peacefully and unarmed, to assemble, to demonstrate, to picket and to present petitions.

Section 18. Freedom of association

Everyone has the right to freedom of association.

Section 19. Political rights

1. Every citizen is free to make political choices, which includes the right

a. to form a political party;

b. to participate in the activities of, or recruit members for, a political party; and

c. to campaign for a political party or cause.

2. Every citizen has the right to free, fair and regular elections for any legislative body established in terms of the Constitution.

3. Every adult citizen has the right

a. to vote in elections for any legislative body established in terms of the Constitution, and to do so in secret; and

b. to stand for public office and, if elected, to hold office.

Section 20. Citizenship

No citizen may be deprived of citizenship.

Section 21. Freedom of movement and residence

1. Everyone has the right to freedom of movement.

2. Everyone has the right to leave the Republic.

3. Every citizen has the right to enter, to remain in and to reside anywhere in, the Republic.

4. Every citizen has the right to a passport.

Section 26. Housing

1. Everyone has the right to have access to adequate housing.

2. The state must take reasonable legislative and other measures, within its available resources, to achieve the progressive realisation of this right.

3. No one may be evicted from their home, or have their home demolished, without an order of court made after considering all the relevant circumstances. No legislation may permit arbitrary evictions.

Section 27. Health care, food, water and social security

1. Everyone has the right to have access to

a. health care services, including reproductive health care;

b. sufficient food and water; and

c. social security, including, if they are unable to support themselves and their dependants, appropriate social assistance.

2. The state must take reasonable legislative and other measures, within its available resources, to achieve the progressive realisation of each of these rights.

3. No one may be refused emergency medical treatment.

Section 28. Children

1. Every child has the right

a. to a name and a nationality from birth;

b. to family care or parental care, or to appropriate alternative care when removed from the family environment;

c. to basic nutrition, shelter, basic health care services and social services;

d. to be protected from maltreatment, neglect, abuse or degradation;

e. to be protected from exploitative labour practices;

f. not to be required or permitted to perform work or provide services that

i. are inappropriate for a person of that child's age; or

ii. place at risk the child's well-being, education, physical or mental health or spiritual, moral or social development;

g. not to be detained except as a measure of last resort, in which case, in addition to the rights a child enjoys under sections 12 and 35, the child may be detained only for the shortest appropriate period of time, and has the right to be

i. kept separately from detained persons over the age of 18 years; and

ii. treated in a manner, and kept in conditions, that take account of the child's age;

h. to have a legal practitioner assigned to the child by the state, and at state expense, in civil proceedings affecting the child, if substantial injustice would otherwise result; and

i. not to be used directly in armed conflict, and to be protected in times of armed conflict.

2. A child's best interests are of paramount importance in every matter concerning the child.

3. In this section "child" means a person under the age of 18 years.

Section 29. Education

1. Everyone has the right

a. to a basic education, including adult basic education; and

b. to further education, which the state, through reasonable measures, must make progressively available and accessible.

2. Everyone has the right to receive education in the official language or languages of their choice in public educational institutions where that education is reasonably practicable. In order to ensure the effective access to, and implementation of, this right, the state must consider all reasonable educational alternatives, including single medium institutions, taking into account

a. equity;

b. practicability; and

c. the need to redress the results of past racially discriminatory laws and practices.

3. Everyone has the right to establish and maintain, at their own expense, independent educational institutions that

a. do not discriminate on the basis of race;

b. are registered with the state; and

c. maintain standards that are not inferior to standards at comparable public educational institutions.

4. Subsection (3) does not preclude state subsidies for independent educational institutions.

Section 30. Language and culture

Everyone has the right to use the language and to participate in the cultural life of their choice, but no one exercising these rights may do so in a manner inconsistent with any provision of the Bill of Rights.

Section 31. Cultural, religious and linguistic communities

1. Persons belonging to a cultural, religious or linguistic community may not be denied the right, with other members of that community

a. to enjoy their culture, practise their religion and use their language; and

b. to form, join and maintain cultural, religious and linguistic associations and other organs of civil society.

2. The rights in subsection (1) may not be exercised in a manner inconsistent with any provision of the Bill of Rights.

Section 36. Limitation of rights

1. The rights in the Bill of Rights may be limited only in terms of law of general application to the extent that the limitation is reasonable and justifiable in an open and democratic society based on human dignity, equality and freedom, taking into account all relevant factors, including

a. the nature of the right;

b. the importance of the purpose of the limitation;

c. the nature and extent of the limitation;

d. the relation between the limitation and its purpose; and

e. less restrictive means to achieve the purpose.

2. Except as provided in subsection (1) or in any other provision of the Constitution, no law may limit any right entrenched in the Bill of Rights.

Section 39. Interpretation of Bill of Rights

1. When interpreting the Bill of Rights, a court, tribunal or forum

a. must promote the values that underlie an open and democratic society based on human dignity, equality and freedom;

b. must consider international law; and

c. may consider foreign law.

2. When interpreting any legislation, and when developing the common law or customary law, every court, tribunal or forum must promote the spirit, purport and objects of the Bill of Rights.

3. The Bill of Rights does not deny the existence of any other rights or freedoms that are recognised or conferred by common law, customary law or legislation, to the extent that they are consistent with the Bill.

NOTES

PREFACE

1. The name of the town has been changed.

INTRODUCTION

1. The name of the school has been changed.
2. South Africa 2018.
3. All names of individuals in this book have been changed.
4. *Sonke* means "all" or "together" in the Zulu and Xhosa languages.

CHAPTER 1   Being Xhosa, Being South African

1. Part of South Africa's national highway system.
2. These numbers are for the immediate town vicinity rather than the larger municipal area.
3. Interestingly, lobola can be viewed from a very different perspective: many families see the practice as a type of insurance against abusive or disappointing marriages. Because lobola is usually paid off over time, it acts as an incentive for the husband to maintain positive relations with both his wife and his in-laws.
4. A school in a nearby city that is well known for its high academic standards.
5. Porridge made with ground maize.
6. For weeks afterward, I was subjected to mocking yet friendly taunts of my plea, "Can I please take her to the hospital?," from the other teachers.
7. An examination of shifting racial categories over the decades of apartheid rule helps make visible the political constructions of race within particular histories and cultural contexts (Clarke and Thomas 2006; Pierre 2013).
8. The racism of early anthropologists certainly provided ammunition for this systemic oppression.

9. Transkei means literally "across the Kei [River]."

10. "Young people" is a controversial term to define (e.g., Bucholtz 2002; Lancy 2008), but in this book I focus on adolescents because of their participation in secondary school education. Note that this contrasts with South African legal definitions of young people as those up to the age of thirty-five.

11. See the appendix for a version of the Bill of Rights from the South African Constitution meant for distribution.

12. As stated earlier, as of 2011, 48.9 percent of the population was unemployed, compared to the national average of 25.2 percent.

13. In the period 2006–11, 50.2 years for males and 54.4 years for females (as compared to the national average of 52.1 years for males and 56.2 years for females).

14. According to the Centers for Disease Control (CDC) website, in 2012, HIV/AIDS-related deaths were responsible for 52 percent of all deaths in South Africa.

CHAPTER 2   The NGO as Moral Compass?

1. According to Sonke's website, the Judicial Inspectorate for Correctional Services has found that almost half of all inmates in South Africa have experienced some form of sexual abuse. One quarter of South African prison inmates are HIV-positive, and up to 95 percent of all deaths in prison are estimated to be HIV/AIDS related. Sonke uses a variety of tactics, such as first-person narratives, education programs, and legal advocacy to battle these epidemics (www.genderjustice.co.za).

2. See https://genderjustice.org.za/article/the-alliance-for-rural-democracy -sonke-and-partners-rally-against-the-traditional-courts-bill/.

3. Most Xhosa families subscribe to gender roles that see women as the bearers of physical labor in the household, contrary to many Western conceptions of masculinity vis-à-vis femininity. In Kamva, a woman carrying several bags in her arms and on her head while a man walks empty-handed by her side is a common sight.

4. In South Africa, colleges are essentially private versions of universities.

5. The anthropologist Jason Hickel (2015) writes similarly in his analysis of death rituals and traditionalism in rural Zululand.

6. Girls, on the other hand, have less tangible markers of age transition today; traditionally the intonjane ritual would signify a girl's entrance into womanhood. This ritual occurred at first menstruation and required seclusion, skin bleaching, animal sacrifice, a feast, and the drinking of homemade beer (*utywala*); it was meant to prepare the girl for marriage. Though the practice has largely died out, some diviners still attribute problems such as infertility

to omission of the ritual. Today marriage is less common than in previous eras and also delayed until a later age among Eastern Cape residents. Girls gradually become women as they take on more adult responsibilities, such as child-rearing, which often happens as a result of teenage (usually nonmonogamous) sexual encounters. As many villagers explained to me, the fact that girls are engaging in sexual relations at earlier ages today obviates both the need and the ability to conduct the intonjane ritual and provides further evidence of the changes in normative processes of social reproduction.

CHAPTER 3   "Thinking Outside the Box": Sonke in Kamva

1. The organization's name has been changed.

2. Funding was provided in part by a number of international organizations, such as UNICEF, the Open Society Foundation, SIDA, the Ford Foundation, the South Africa Development Fund, First National Bank, USAID/PEPFAR, and the UCLA Program in Global Health, among others (Genetski and Peacock 2006).

3. http://mg.co.za/article/2013-02-28-education-gets-the-bigger-budget-bite-with-a-reprimand.

4. Sonke often does provide food for participants during workshops.

5. Silence Speaks is part of the Center for Digital Storytelling, an organization whose headquarters are in Berkeley, California (Reed 2011; Reed and Hill 2010).

CHAPTER 4   Life Orientation as Democratic Project

1. The teachers highlighted in this chapter are a diverse group. The majority identify as Xhosa, but some are migrants from other African nations. In addition, they vary in terms of age, gender, and religious affiliation.

2. In 2011, 83 percent of seniors at Cedarwood passed the nationwide matriculation exam (South Africa Department of Basic Education 2015). Across the Eastern Cape, only 56.8 percent of students passed in 2015; this was the lowest rate of all provinces (Quintal 2016).

3. Teachers in South Africa must complete a four-year bachelor's of education degree or a three- or four-year bachelor's degree in another subject plus a one-year postgraduate certificate in education. They then must register with the South African Council for Educators (SACE) and choose an age range: Foundation (± 5- to 9-year-olds): Grades R–3; Intermediate Phase (± 10- to 12-year-olds): Grades 4–6; Senior Phase (± 13- to 15-year-olds): Grades 7–9; Further Education and Training (FET) Phase (± 16- to 18-year-olds): Grades 10–12 (www.education.gov.za).

4. This is the exam required for obtaining a high school diploma in South Africa (South Africa Department of Basic Education 2015).

5. Senior Certificate Examinations 2017, South Africa Department of Basic Education, www.education.gov.za/Home/2017NSCNovemberpast papers.aspx.

6. See www.genderjustice.org.za/news-item/victory-child-rights-violence -prevention-sa-defence-reasonable-chastisement-ruled-line-constitution/.

7. Dispatch Live, www.dispatchlive.co.za/news/2018-09-24-teacher-on -trial-for-striking-pupil/.

CHAPTER 5   Teaching Nostalgia

1. In the Eastern Cape in 2011, 60.8 percent of residents were living below the poverty line. Notably, the percentage of *all* people living in poverty in South Africa has decreased since 2006 (Lehohla 2011).

2. Julius Malema, former ANCYL president, has taken up this cause through his relatively new Economic Freedom Fighters political party.

3. South African slang for a gangster or criminal.

4. Crime Stats South Africa 2015. www.crimestatssa.com.

5. Of course, it is almost certain that in Black communities fewer crimes would have been reported and officially recorded under apartheid given that relations with the police were hostile and racially charged.

6. John and Jean Comaroff (1997, 124) recall the words of Malcolm Bradbury's novel *Doctor Criminale*: "'Democracy, the free market,' she muses, 'do you really think they can save us? Marxism [was] a great idea, democracy [is] just a small idea. It promises hope, and it gives you [Kentucky] Fried Chicken.'"

7. A company that produces ultra-high temperature (UHT) processed milk, an extremely popular product in rural South Africa because it is cheaper than fresh milk and does not require refrigeration.

8. A British multinational mining company with extensive operations in South Africa.

9. This is the rationale for many recent proposals to nationalize South Africa's mineral extraction industry; it would allow capital that leaves the country via private corporations to stay within national borders and theoretically reduce poverty through a shift in ownership. Of course, this is nothing new; the far more leftist, radical ANC of the apartheid years made nationalization a central issue and rallying point. This was abandoned as Mandela negotiated a new government and worked to keep capital from leaving the country in the 1990s (Marais 2011).

CHAPTER 6   Freedom from Democracy?

    1. In 2009, the ANC won approximately 66 percent of the vote. In 2014, it was down to 62 percent. The closest competitor, the Democratic Alliance, came in at 22 percent—up from 17 percent in 2009 (Grant 2014).

    2. Elsewhere, I have discussed this with respect to the election of Donald Trump in the United States (Reed 2017).

BIBLIOGRAPHY

Abdi, Ali A. 2002. *Culture, Education, and Development in South Africa: Historical and Contemporary Perspectives*. Westport, CT: Bergin & Garvey.

Abu El-Haj, Nadia. 2001. *Facts on the Ground: Archaeological Practice and Territorial Self-Fashioning in Israeli Society*. Chicago: University of Chicago Press.

Abu-Lughod, Lila. 2002. "Do Muslim Women Really Need Saving? Anthropological Reflections on Cultural Relativism and Its Others." *American Anthropologist* 104 (3): 783–90.

Alves, Isabbel, Margarida Coelho, Christopher Gignoux, Albertino Damasceno, Antonio Prista, and Jorge Rocha. 2011. "Genetic Homogeneity Across Bantu-Speaking Groups from Mozambique and Angola Challenges Early Split Scenarios between East and West Bantu Populations." *Human Biology* 83 (1): 13–38.

Angé, Olivia, and David Berliner, eds. 2014. *Anthropology and Nostalgia*. New York: Berghahn Books.

Apter, Andrew. 1999. "Nigerian Democracy and the Politics of Illusion." In *Civil Society and the Political Imagination: Critical Perspectives*, edited by John L. and Jean Comaroff, 267–308. Chicago: University of Chicago Press.

Ashforth, Adam. 2005. *Witchcraft, Violence, and Democracy in South Africa*. Chicago: University of Chicago Press.

Austin-Broos, Diane. 2003. "The Anthropology of Conversion: An Introduction." In *The Anthropology of Religious Conversion*, edited by Andrew Buckser and Stephen D. Glazier, 1–14. Lanham, MD: Rowman & Littlefield.

Bank, Leslie J. 2011. *Home Spaces, Street Styles: Contesting Power and Identity in a South African City*. London: Pluto Press.

———. 2016. "Engaging Mafeje's Ghost: Fort Hare and the Virtues of 'Homeland' Anthropology." *African Studies* 75 (2): 278–95.

Baquedano-Lopez, Patricia. 1997. "Creating Social Identities through 'Doctrina' Narratives." *Issues in Applied Linguistics* 8 (1): 27–45.

Basso, Keith H. 1996. *Wisdom Sits in Places: Landscape and Language among the Western Apache*. Albuquerque: University of New Mexico Press.

Bayart, Jean-François. 1989. *L'État en Afrique: La politique du ventre*. Paris: Fayard.

Beaubien, Jason. 2018. "The Country with the World's Worst Inequality Is . . ." *Goats and Soda: Stories of Life in a Changing World* (blog). April 2. www .npr.org/sections/goatsandsoda/2018/04/02/598864666/the-country -with-the-worlds-worst-inequality-is.

Beer, K. J. de. 1991. *A Pocket Guide to Black Political Groupings in South Africa*. Clubview, South Africa: K. J. de Beer.

Beinart, William. 1981. "Conflict in Qumbu: Rural Consciousness, Ethnicity and Violence in the Colonial Transkei, 1880–1913." *Journal of Southern African Studies* 8 (1): 94–122.

———. 1994. *Twentieth-Century South Africa*. Oxford: Oxford University Press.

Beinart, William, and Colin Bundy. 1987. *Hidden Struggles in Rural South Africa: Politics and Popular Movements in the Transkei and Eastern Cape, 1890–1930*. London: J. Currey.

Bell, Kirsten. 2015. "HIV Prevention: Making Male Circumcision the 'Right' Tool for the Job." *Global Public Health* 10 (5–6): 552–72.

Bennett, Tony. 2015. "Cultural Studies and the Culture Concept." *Cultural Studies* 29 (4): 546–68.

Besteman, Catherine Lowe. 2008. *Transforming Cape Town*. Berkeley: University of California Press.

Bhabha, Homi K. 1994. *The Location of Culture*. London: Routledge.

Bissell, William Cunningham. 2005. "Engaging Colonial Nostalgia." *Cultural Anthropology: Journal of the Society for Cultural Anthropology* 20 (2): 215–48.

Bond, Patrick. 2014. *Elite Transition: From Apartheid to Neoliberalism in South Africa*. London: Pluto Press.

Boonzaier, Emile, and John Sharp, eds. 1988. *South African Keywords: The Uses and Abuses of Political Concepts*. Cape Town: David Philip Publishers.

Bornstein, Erica. 2001. "Child Sponsorship, Evangelism, and Belonging in the Work of World Vision Zimbabwe." *American Ethnologist* 28 (3): 595–622.

Bornstein, Erica, and Peter Redfield, eds. 2011. *Forces of Compassion: Humanitarianism between Ethics and Politics*. Santa Fe, NM: School for Advanced Research Press.

Botha, R. J. (Nico). 2002. "Outcomes-Based Education and Educational Reform in South Africa." *International Journal of Leadership in Education* 5 (4): 361–71.

Bourdieu, Pierre. 1977. *Outline of a Theory of Practice*. Translated by Richard Nice. Cambridge: Cambridge University Press.

Bourgois, Philippe. 1995. *In Search of Respect: Selling Crack in El Barrio*. Cambridge: Cambridge University Press.

Boym, Svetlana. 2001. *The Future of Nostalgia*. New York: Basic Books.

Breakfast, Siviwe. 2018. "Education Sector Records Highest Number of Corruption Complaints." *South African*, August 7. www.thesouthafrican.com /most-corrupt-government-sectors-in-sa/.

Brown, Roderick. 2012. "Corrective Rape in South Africa: A Continuing Plight Despite an International Human Rights Response." *Annual Survey of International & Comparative Law* 18: 45–66.

Brown, Wendy. 1998. "Democracy's Lack." *Public Culture* 10 (2): 425–29.

Bucholtz, Mary. 1999. "'Why Be Normal?': Language and Identity Practices in a Community of Nerd Girls." *Language in Society* 28 (2): 203–24.

———. 2002. "Youth and Cultural Practice." *Annual Review of Anthropology* 31 (1): 525–52.

Buckser, Andrew, and Stephen D. Glazier, eds. 2003. *The Anthropology of Religious Conversion*. Lanham, MD: Rowman & Littlefield.

Chalfin, Brenda. 2010. *Neoliberal Frontiers: An Ethnography of Sovereignty in West Africa*. Chicago: University of Chicago Press.

Chance, Kerry Ryan. 2018. *Living Politics in South Africa's Urban Shacklands*. Chicago: University of Chicago Press.

Cheney, Kristen E. 2007. *Pillars of the Nation: Child Citizens and Ugandan National Development*. Chicago: University of Chicago Press.

Chipkin, Ivor. 2007. *Do South Africans Exist? Nationalism, Democracy, and the Identity of "The People."* Johannesburg: Wits University Press.

Chisholm, Linda. 2005. "The Making of South Africa's National Curriculum Statement." *Journal of Curriculum Studies* 37 (2): 193–208.

Christoffersen-Deb, Astrid. 2005. "Taming Tradition: Medicalized Female Genital Practices in Western Kenya." *Medical Anthropology Quarterly* 19 (4): 402–18.

Clark, Nancy L., and William H. Worger. 2004. *South Africa: The Rise and Fall of Apartheid*. Harlow, UK: Pearson Longman.

Clarke, Kamari M., and Deborah A. Thomas, eds. 2006. *Globalization and Race: Transformations in the Cultural Production of Blackness*. Durham, NC: Duke University Press.

Cobban, Donna. 2010. "Making Sense of Curriculum Changes." *Child Magazine*. www.childmag.co.za/content/making-sense-curriculum-changes.

Cole, Jennifer. 1998. "The Work of Memory in Madagascar." *American Ethnologist* 25 (4): 610–33.

Cole, Jennifer, and Deborah Lynn Durham. 2008. *Figuring the Future: Globalization and the Temporalities of Children and Youth.* Santa Fe, NM: School for Advanced Research Press.

Comaroff, Jean, and John L. Comaroff. 2000. "Millennial Capitalism: First Thoughts on a Second Coming." *Public Culture* 12 (2): 291–343.

Comaroff, John L., and Jean Comaroff. 1990. "Goodly Beasts, Beastly Goods: Cattle and Commodities in a South African Context." *American Ethnologist* 17 (2): 195–216.

———. 1997. "Postcolonial Politics and Discourses of Democracy in Southern Africa: An Anthropological Reflection on African Political Modernities." *Journal of Anthropological Research* 53 (4): 123–46.

———. 1999. *Civil Society and the Political Imagination in Africa: Critical Perspectives.* Chicago: University of Chicago Press.

———. 2001. *Millennial Capitalism and the Culture of Neoliberalism.* Durham, NC: Duke University Press.

———. 2004a. "Criminal Justice, Cultural Justice: The Limits of Liberalism and the Pragmatics of Difference in the New South Africa." *American Ethnologist* 31 (2): 188–204.

———. 2004b. "Policing Culture, Cultural Policing: Law and Social Order in Postcolonial South Africa." *Law & Social Inquiry: Journal of the American Bar Foundation* 29 (3): 513.

———. 2009. *Ethnicity, Inc.* Chicago: University of Chicago Press.

———, eds. 2018. *The Politics of Custom: Chiefship, Capital, and the State in Contemporary Africa.* Chicago: University of Chicago Press.

Cowell, Alan. 2018. "Seminude School Performance Sparks Debate about Tradition in South Africa." *New York Times,* June 2.

Crais, Clifton. 1998. "Of Men, Magic, and the Law: Popular Justice and the Political Imagination in South Africa." *Journal of Social History* 32 (1): 49–72.

Crais, Clifton, and Thomas V. McClendon, eds. 2014. *The South Africa Reader: History, Culture, Politics.* Durham, NC: Duke University Press.

Curnow, Robyn. 2013. "Selling Mandela: From T-Shirts to TV Shows, How Madiba Became a Brand." CNN. www.cnn.com/2013/08/01/business /selling-mandela-from-t-shirts-tv/.

Davis, D. M. 2003. "Constitutional Borrowing: The Influence of Legal Culture and Local History in the Reconstitution of Comparative Influence: The South African Experience." *International Journal of Constitutional Law* 1 (2): 181–95.

Davis, Fred. 1979. *Yearning for Yesterday: A Sociology of Nostalgia.* New York: Free Press.

Davis, Richard Hunt, Jr. 1969. "Nineteenth-Century African Education in the Cape Colony: A Historical Analysis." PhD diss., University of Wisconsin.

Diale, Boitumelo, Jace Pillay, and Elzette Fritz. 2014. "Dynamics in the Personal and Professional Development of Life-Orientation Teachers in South Africa, Gauteng Province." *Journal of Social Sciences* 38 (1): 83–93.

Dixon, Robyn, and Kylé Pienaar. 2010. "Boys Hoping to Gain Their Manhood Lose It—Forever." *Los Angeles Times*, August 23.

Dlamini, Jacob. 2009. *Native Nostalgia*. Auckland Park, South Africa: Jacana Media.

Dubbeld, Bernard. 2013. "Envisioning Governance: Expectations and Estrangements of Transformed Rule in Glendale, South Africa." *Africa* 83 (3): 492–512.

Dube, Saurabh, ed. 2009. *Enchantments of Modernity: Empire, Nation, Globalization*. Critical Asian Studies. London: Routledge.

Edelman, Marc, and Angelique Haugerud. 2005. *The Anthropology of Development and Globalization: From Classical Political Economy to Contemporary Neoliberalism*. Malden, MA: Blackwell.

"Electoral Commission: 2014 National and Provincial Elections: National Results." 2019. www.elections.org.za/content/elections/results/2014-national -and-provincial-elections-national-results/.

Englund, Harri. 2006. *Prisoners of Freedom: Human Rights and the African Poor*. Berkeley: University of California Press.

Erlank, Natasha. 2003. "Gendering Commonality: African Men and the 1883 Commission on Native Law and Custom." *Journal of Southern African Studies* 29 (4): 937–53.

Evans, Martha. 2014. *Broadcasting the End of Apartheid: Live Television and the Birth of the New South Africa*. New York: Palgrave Macmillan.

Evans, Sarah. 2014. "Nkandla Report: Zuma Unduly Benefitted from Upgrades." *Mail & Guardian*, March 19. https://mg.co.za/article/2014-03 -19-nkandla-report-zuma-unduly-benefitted-from-upgrades.

Fanon, Frantz. 1968. *The Wretched of the Earth*. New York: Grove Press.

Feinberg, Joel. 1980. "The Child's Right to an Open Future." In *Whose Child? Children's Rights, Parental Authority, and State Power*, edited by William Aiken and Hugh LaFollette, 76–97. Totowa, NJ: Rowman & Littlefield. Reprinted in Joel Feinberg, *Freedom and Fulfillment*. Princeton, NJ: Princeton University Press, 1992.

Ferguson, James. 2006. *Global Shadows: Africa in the Neoliberal World Order*. Durham, NC: Duke University Press.

———. 2010. "The Uses of Neoliberalism." *Antipode* 41 (Suppl.): 166–84.

———. 2015. *Give a Man a Fish: Reflections on the New Politics of Distribution.* Durham, NC: Duke University Press.

Ferguson, James, and Akhil Gupta. 2002. "Spatializing States: Toward an Ethnography of Neoliberal Governmentality." *American Ethnologist* 29 (4): 981–1002.

Fisher, William F. 1997. "Doing Good? The Politics and Antipolitics of NGO Practices." *Annual Review of Anthropology*, no. 26: 439–64.

Fournier, Anna. 2012. *Forging Rights in a New Democracy: Ukrainian Students between Freedom and Justice.* Philadelphia: University of Pennsylvania Press.

Freire, Paulo. 1970. *Pedagogy of the Oppressed.* New York: Herder and Herder.

Geertz, Clifford. 1973. *The Interpretation of Cultures: Selected Essays.* New York: Basic Books.

Genetski, Honor, and Dean Peacock. 2006. "Sonke Gender Justice Network's Fatherhood and Child Security Project: PhotoVoice to Empower Children and Educate Men about Gender and HIV and AIDS in Nkandla, Kwa-Zulu Natal, and Mhlontlo, Eastern Cape." https://genderjustice.org.za/publication/photovoice-to-empower-children-and-educate-men-in-two-rural-communities/.

Gennep, Arnold van. 1960. *The Rites of Passage.* Chicago: University of Chicago Press.

Geschiere, Peter, and Stephen Jackson. 2006. "Autochthony and the Crisis of Citizenship: Democratization, Decentralization, and the Politics of Belonging." *African Studies Review* 49 (2): 1–7.

Gibbs, Timothy. 2011. "Chris Hani's 'Country Bumpkins': Regional Networks in the African National Congress Underground, 1974–1994." *Journal of Southern African Studies* 37 (4): 677–91.

Gilroy, Paul. 2005. *Postcolonial Melancholia.* New York: Columbia University Press.

Goldman, Michael. 2005. "Tracing the Roots / Routes of World Bank Power." *International Journal of Sociology and Social Policy* 25 (1–2): 10–29.

Goode, Judith, and Jeff Maskovsky. 2001. *New Poverty Studies: The Ethnography of Power, Politics, and Impoverished People in the United States.* New York: New York University Press.

Government of South Africa. 2016, 2019. The South African Constitution. www.justice.gov.za/legislation/constitution/resources.html.

———. 2018. "Public Holidays in South Africa." www.gov.za/about-sa/public-holidays.

Grant, Laura. 2014. "Live Elections 2014 Results." *Mail & Guardian*, May 7.

Guffin, Bascom, Jesse Davie-Kessler, and Richard McGrail. 2010. "Affect, Embodiment and Sense Perception: Editorial Introduction." *Cultural*

Anthropology. https://journal.culanth.org/index.php/ca/catalog/category
/affect-embodiment-and-sense.

Gwata, Feri. 2009. *Traditional Male Circumcision: What Is Its Socio-Cultural Significance among Young Xhosa Men?* Rondebosch: Centre for Social Science Research.

Hale, Sondra. 2013. "The Memory Work of Anthropologists: Notes toward a Gendered Politics of Memory in Conflict Zones—Sudan and Eritrea." In *Anthropology of the Middle East and North Africa: Into the New Millennium*, edited by Sherine Hafez and Susan Slyomovics, 125–44. Bloomington: Indiana University Press.

Hall, Kathleen. 2002. *Lives in Translation: Sikh Youth as British Citizens*. Philadelphia: University of Pennsylvania Press.

Hammond-Tooke, W. D. 1985. "Descent Groups, Chiefdoms and South African Historiography." *Journal of Southern African Studies* 11 (2): 305–19.

Hanks, William F. 2010. *Converting Words: Maya in the Age of the Cross*. Berkeley: University of California Press.

Hansen, Holger Bernt, and Michael Twaddle, eds. 2002. *Christian Missionaries and the State in the Third World*. Oxford and Athens: James Currey and Ohio University Press.

Harber, Clive. 2001. *State of Transition: Post-Apartheid Educational Reform in South Africa*. Monographs in International Education. Oxford: Symposium Books.

Harding, Susan F. 1987. "Convicted by the Holy Spirit: The Rhetoric of Fundamental Baptist Conversion." *American Ethnologist* 14 (1): 167–81.

Harley, Ken, Fred Barasa, Carol Bertram, Elizabeth Mattson, and Shervani Pillay. 2000. "'The Real and the Ideal': Teacher Roles and Competences in South African Policy and Practice." *International Journal of Educational Development* 20: 287–304.

Healy-Clancy, Meghan. 2014. *A World of Their Own: A History of South African Women's Education*. Reconsiderations in Southern African History. Charlottesville: University of Virginia Press.

Hebdige, Dick. 1979. *Subculture, the Meaning of Style*. London: Methuen.

Herskovitz, Jon. 2013. "Deep Read: 'Born Free' Voters May Not Choose ANC." *Mail & Guardian*, January 29.

Hickel, Jason. 2014. "'Xenophobia' in South Africa: Order, Chaos and the Moral Economy of Witchcraft." *Cultural Anthropology* 29 (1): 103–27.

———. 2015. *Democracy as Death: The Moral Order of Anti-Liberal Politics in South Africa*. Oakland: University of California Press.

Hobsbawm, Eric, and Terence Ranger. 1983. *The Invention of Tradition*. Cambridge: Cambridge University Press.

Hues, Henning. 2011. "'Mandela, the Terrorist': Intended and Hidden History Curriculum in South Africa." *Journal of Educational Media, Memory & Society* 3 (2): 74–95.

Hunter, Monica. 1936. *Reaction to Conquest: Effects of Contact with Europeans on the Pondo of South Africa*. London: Oxford University Press.

Jeske, Christine. 2016. "Are Cars the New Cows? Changing Wealth Goods and Moral Economies in South Africa." *American Anthropologist* 118 (3): 483–94.

Jones, Michelle. 2013. "Education 101." *Child Magazine*. www.childmag.co.za /content/education.

Klumbyte, Neringa. 2009. "Post-Socialist Sensations: Nostalgia, the Self, and Alterity in Lithuania." *Lithuanian Ethnology* 9 (18): 93–116.

Knight, J. B., and G. Lenta. 1980. "Has Capitalism Underdeveloped the Labour Reserves of South Africa?" *Oxford Bulletin of Economics & Statistics* 42 (3): 157–201.

Korbin, Jill E. 2003. "Children, Childhoods, and Violence." *Annual Review of Anthropology* 32: 431.

Krabill, Ron. 2010. *Starring Mandela and Cosby: Media and the End(s) of Apartheid*. Chicago: University of Chicago Press.

Laidlaw, James. 2002. "For an Anthropology of Ethics and Freedom." *Journal of the Royal Anthropological Institute* 8 (2): 311–32.

Laing, Aislinn. 2010. "South African Adverts Threaten Men with Prison Rape If Caught Drink Driving." December 21, sec. World. www.telegraph.co .uk/news/worldnews/africaandindianocean/southafrica/8216970/South -African-adverts-threaten-men-with-prison-rape-if-caught-drink-driving .html.

———. 2012. "Jacob Zuma 'The Spear' Painting Defaced Ahead of Court Action." *Telegraph*, May 22.

Lancy, David F. 2008. *The Anthropology of Childhood: Cherubs, Chattel, Changelings*. Cambridge: Cambridge University Press.

Lehohla, Pali. 2011. *Census 2011*. Pretoria: Statistics South Africa.

Lester, Alan. 1997. "The Margins of Order: Strategies of Segregation on the Eastern Cape Frontier, 1806–c. 1850." *Journal of Southern African Studies* 23 (4): 635–53.

Locke, John. [1689] 1960. *The Second Treatise of Government*. In John Locke, *Two Treatises of Government*, edited by Peter Laslett, 283–446. Cambridge: Cambridge University Press.

MacDonald, Michael. 2004. "The Political Economy of Identity Politics." *South Atlantic Quarterly* 103 (4): 629–56.

Mahmood, Saba. 2005. *Politics of Piety: The Islamic Revival and the Feminist Subject*. Princeton, NJ: Princeton University Press.

Makhulu, Anne-Maria. 2015. *Making Freedom: Apartheid, Squatter Politics, and the Struggle for Home*. Durham, NC: Duke University Press.

———. 2016. "Reckoning with Apartheid: The Conundrum of Working through the Past." *Comparative Studies of South Asia, Africa and the Middle East* 36 (2): 256–62.

Makinana, Andisiwe. 2014. "Tutu Calls on South Africans to Vote with Their Heads." *Mail & Guardian*, April 23.

Mamdani, Mahmood. 1996. *Citizen and Subject: Contemporary Africa and the Legacy of Late Colonialism*. Princeton, NJ: Princeton University Press.

———. 2001. *When Victims Become Killers: Colonialism, Nativism, and the Genocide in Rwanda*. Princeton, NJ: Princeton University Press.

Manase, Irikidzayi. 2016. "Black Diamonds and Excess in the Fictional and Lived South African City of the Early 2000s." *English Academy Review* 33 (1): 87–96.

Mandela, Nelson. 2007. "An Ideal for Which I Am Prepared to Die." *The Guardian*, April 23. www.theguardian.com/world/2007/apr/23/nelson mandela.

Marais, Hein. 2011. *South Africa Pushed to the Limit: The Political Economy of Change*. London: Zed Books.

Markowitz, L. 2001. "Finding the Field: Notes on the Ethnography of NGOs." *Human Organization* 60: 40–46.

Mavundla, Thandisizwe, Fulufhelo Netswera, Ferenc Toth, Brian Bottoman, and Stembele Tenge. 2010. "How Boys Become Dogs: Stigmatization and Marginalization of Uninitiated Xhosa Males in East London, South Africa." *Qualitative Health Research* 20 (7): 931–41.

Mayer, Philip, and Iona Mayer. 1970. "Socialization by Peers: The Youth Organization of the Red Xhosa." In *Socialization*, edited by Philip Mayer, 159–89. London: Routledge.

Mazzarella, William. 2009. "Affect: What Is It Good For?" In *Enchantments of Modernity: Empire, Nation, Globalization*, edited by Saurabh Dube. London: Routledge.

Mbembé, J. A. 2001. *On the Postcolony*. Berkeley: University of California Press.

McAllister, P. A. 1989. "Resistance to 'Betterment' in the Transkei." *Journal of Southern African Studies* 15 (2): 346–68.

Meintjes, Graeme. 1998. *Manhood at a Price: Socio-Medical Perspectives on Xhosa Traditional Circumcision*. Grahamstown, South Africa: Institute of Social and Economic Research, Rhodes University.

Mills, Wallace G. 1992. "Missionaries, Xhosa Clergy, and the Suppression of Traditional Customs." Paper presented at the conference People, Power and Culture: The History of Christianity in South Africa 1792–1992, University of the Western Cape, August 12–15.

Motala, Enver, Mondli Hlatshwayo, Salim Vally, and Siphelo Ngcwangu. 2019. "South African Students Are Protesting—Again. Why It Needn't Be This Way." The Conversation. February 8. http://theconversation.com /south-african-students-are-protesting-again-why-it-neednt-be-this -way-109964.

Mtuze, P. T. 2004. *Introduction to Xhosa Culture.* Alice, South Africa: Lovedale Press.

Mudimbe, V.Y. 1988. *The Invention of Africa: Gnosis, Philosophy, and the Order of Knowledge.* Bloomington: Indiana University Press.

Mufson, Steven, and Sudarsan Raghavan. 2014. "After Mandela's Death, ANC Faces Growing Risk of Losing Power in South Africa." *Washington Post,* January 2. www.washingtonpost.com/business/economy/after -mandelas-death-anc-faces-growing-risk-of-losing-power-in-south -africa/2014/01/01.

Myers, Fred R. 2002. *Painting Culture: The Making of an Aboriginal High Art.* Durham, NC: Duke University Press.

Nel, Etienne, Tony Binns, and Nicole Motteux. 2001. "Community-Based Development, Non-Governmental Organizations and Social Capital in Post-Apartheid South Africa." *Geografiska Annaler, Series B: Human Geography* 83 (1): 3–13.

Ngwane, Zolani. 2001. "'Real Men Reawaken Their Fathers' Homesteads, the Educated Leave Them in Ruins': The Politics of Domestic Reproduction in Post-Apartheid Rural South Africa." *Journal of Religion in Africa* 31 (4): 402–26.

Niekerk, Philip van. 1987. "Winds of Change in Transkei as Matanzima Brothers Exit." *Globe & Mail,* November.

Nkomo, Mokubung, ed. 1990. *Pedagogy of Domination: Toward a Democratic Education in South Africa.* Trenton, NJ: Africa World Press.

Nyamnjoh, Francis B. 2002. "'A Child Is One Person's Only in the Womb': Domestication, Agency and Subjectivity in the Cameroonian Grassfields." In *Postcolonial Subjectivities in Africa,* edited by Richard Werbner, 111–38. New York: Zed Books.

Nyerere, Julius K. 1968. *Freedom and Socialism. Uhuru Na Ujamaa: A Selection from Writings and Speeches, 1965–1967.* London: Oxford University Press.

Onishi, Norimitsu. 2014. "In South Africa, A.N.C. Is Counting on the Past." *New York Times*, May 5.

Onishi, Norimitsu, and Selam Gebrekidan. 2018. "South Africa Vows to End Corruption. Are Its New Leaders Part of the Problem?" *New York Times*, August 4. www.nytimes.com/2018/08/04/world/africa/south-africa-anc -david-mabuza.html.

Ortner, Sherry B. 1984. "Theory in Anthropology since the Sixties." *Comparative Studies in Society and History* 26 (1): 126–66.

———. 2006. *Anthropology and Social Theory: Culture, Power, and the Acting Subject*. Durham, NC: Duke University Press.

Owusu, Maxwell. 1997. "Domesticating Democracy: Culture, Civil Society, and Constitutionalism in Africa." *Comparative Studies in Society and History* 39 (1): 120–52.

Paley, Julia. 2002. "Toward an Anthropology of Democracy." *Annual Review of Anthropology* 31 (January): 469–96.

———. 2008. *Democracy: Anthropological Approaches*. Santa Fe, NM: School for Advanced Research Press.

Paret, Marcel. 2018. "Critical Nostalgias in Democratic South Africa." *Sociological Quarterly* 59 (4): 678–96.

Pearce, Fred. 2017. "Murder in Pondoland: How a Proposed Mine Brought Conflict to South Africa." *The Guardian*, March 28, sec. Environment. www.theguardian.com/environment/2017/mar/27/murder-pondoland -how-proposed-mine-brought-conflict-south-africa-activist-sikhosiphi -rhadebe.

Peires, J. B. 1989. *The Dead Will Arise: Nongqawuse and the Great Xhosa Cattle-Killing Movement of 1856–7*. Johannesburg: Ravan Press.

———. 2003. *The House of Phalo: A History of the Xhosa People in the Days of Their Independence*. Johannesburg: Jonathan Ball.

Pells, E. G. 1938. *European, Coloured and Native Education in South Africa*. Cape Town: Juta & Co.

Phillips, Laura. 2018. "The Peculiar Nostalgia for the Former Bantustans in South Africa." March 27. https://africasacountry.com/2018/03/the -peculiar-nostalgia-for-the-former-bantustans-in-south-africa.

Pierre, Jemima. 2013. *The Predicament of Blackness: Postcolonial Ghana and the Politics of Race*. Chicago: University of Chicago Press.

Piot, Charles. 1999. *Remotely Global: Village Modernity in West Africa*. Chicago: University of Chicago Press.

———. 2010. *Nostalgia for the Future: West Africa after the Cold War*. Chicago: University of Chicago Press.

Posel, Deborah. 1991. *The Making of Apartheid, 1948–1961: Conflict and Compromise*. Oxford: Oxford University Press.

———. 2013. "The ANC Youth League and the Politicization of Race." *Thesis Eleven* 115 (1): 58–76.

Prinsloo, Erna. 2007. "Implementation of Life Orientation Programmes in the New Curriculum in South African Schools: Perceptions of Principals and Life Orientation Teachers." *South African Journal of Education* 27 (1): 155–70.

Quintal, Genevieve. 2016. "Matric Results 2015: Pass Rate Drops to 70.7%." *Mail & Guardian*, January 5. www.mg.co.za/article/2016-01-05-matric-pass-rate-drops-to-707.

Rawls, John. 1996. *Political Liberalism*. New York: Columbia University Press.

Reed, Amber R. 2011. "Creating New Leaders: Youth Involvement in Community Activism in South Africa." *Ufahamu: A Journal of African Studies* 36 (1). Online.

———. 2016. "Nostalgia in the Post-Apartheid State." *Anthropology Southern Africa* 39 (2): 97–109.

———. 2017. "Make Democracy Great Again?" *Anthropology News* (blog). January 17. www.anthropology-news.org/index.php/2017/01/17/make-democracy-great-again/.

Reed, Amber R., and Amy Hill. 2010. "'Don't Keep It to Yourself!': Digital Storytelling with South African Youth." *Seminar.net* 9 (1). https://journals.hioa.no/index.php/seminar/article/view/2447.

Rice, Kathleen. 2017. "Rights and Responsibilities in Rural South Africa: Implications for Gender, Generation, and Personhood." *Journal of the Royal Anthropological Institute* 23 (1): 28–41.

Robins, Steven L. 2005. *Limits to Liberation after Apartheid: Citizenship, Governance and Culture*. Oxford, Athens, and Cape Town: James Currey, Ohio University Press, and David Philip Publishers.

———. 2008. *From Revolution to Rights in South Africa: Social Movements, NGOs and Popular Politics after Apartheid*. Scottsville: University of Kwazulu-Natal Press.

Robins, Steven, and Bettina von Lieres. 2004. "Remaking Citizenship, Unmaking Marginalization: The Treatment Action Campaign in Post-Apartheid South Africa." *Canadian Journal of African Studies / Revue Canadienne des Études Africaines* 38 (3): 575–86.

Roitman, Janet L. 2005. *Fiscal Disobedience: An Anthropology of Economic Regulation in Central Africa*. Princeton, NJ: Princeton University Press.

Rosaldo, Renato. 1989. *Culture and Truth: The Remaking of Social Analysis*. Boston: Beacon Press.

Rousseau, Jean-Jacques [1762] 1973. *The Social Contract and Discourses*. Translated by G. D. H. Cole. New York: Dutton.

Said, Edward W. 1978. *Orientalism*. 1st ed. New York: Pantheon Books.

Sambumbu, Sipokazi. 2010. "Social History, Public History and the Politics of Memory in Re-Making Ndabeni's Pasts." Master's thesis, University of the Western Cape.

Scheper-Hughes, Nancy. 1995. "The Primacy of the Ethical: Propositions for a Militant Anthropology." *Current Anthropology* 36 (3): 409–40.

Seekings, Jeremy. 2008. "The Continuing Salience of Race: Discrimination and Diversity in South Africa." *Journal of Contemporary African Studies* 26 (1): 1–25.

Seiler, Gale. 2018. "New Norms and Forms of Participation in Rural South African Science Classrooms." *Anthropology & Education Quarterly* 49 (3): 262–78.

Se-Puma, Peter, Raymond Sargent, and Bobby Heany. 1996. "Suburban Bliss." South African Broadcasting Corporation.

Skoggard, Ian, and Alisse Waterston. 2015. "Introduction: Toward an Anthropology of Affect and Evocative Ethnography." *Anthropology of Consciousness* 26 (2): 109–20.

Soga, John Henderson. 1930. *The South-Eastern Bantu (Abe-Naguni, Aba-Mbo, Ama-Lala)*. Johannesburg: Witwatersrand University Press.

———. 1931. *The Ama-Xosa: Life and Customs*. Lovedale: Lovedale Press.

Sonke Gender Justice Network. 2009. "Engaging Men to Reduce Violence against Women and Children, Prevent the Spread of HIV/AIDS and Promote Health, Care and Support to Orphans and Vulnerable Children in Nkandla, KwaZulu-Natal and Mhlontlo, Eastern Cape: Phase II." https://genderjustice.org.za/publication/engaging-men-reduce-violence-women-children-prevent-spread-hivaids-promote-health-care-support-orphans-vulnerable-children-nkandla-kwazulu-natal-mhlontl/.

———. 2011. "Sonke Welcomes Malema's Apology but . . ." July 5. https://genderjustice.org.za/article/sonke-welcomes-julius-malemas-apology-but/.

South Africa Department of Basic Education. 2011a. "Curriculum and Assessment Policy Statement, Grades 10–12, Life Orientation." www.education.gov.za/Curriculum/CurriculumAssessmentPolicyStatements(CAPS)/CAPSIntermediate.aspx.

———. 2011b. "National Curriculum Statement." www.education.gov.za/Curriculum/NationalCurriculumStatementsGradesR-12.aspx.

———. 2015. "Education Statistics in South Africa." March. www.education
.gov.za.

———. 2017. "Senior Certificate Examinations: History P1 2017 Memoran-
dum." www.education.gov.za/Portals/0/CD/Computer/2017%20May
-June%20past%20exam%20papers/Non-Languages%20May-June
%202017/History%20P1%20May-June%202017%20Eng.pdf?ver=2017
-07-07-142728-000.

South African Broadcasting Corporation. 2014. "South Africa: 'Protest Capital of the World.'" January 27. www.sabc.co.za/news.

Southall, Roger, ed. 2001. *Opposition and Democracy in South Africa*. London:
Frank Cass.

Statistics South Africa. 2016a. "Community Survey." www.statssa.gov.za
/?page_id=1854&PPN=Report%2003-01-08&SCH=7350.

———. 2016b. "Quarterly Labour Force Survey." July 28. www.statssa.gov.za
/publications/P02111stQuarter2016.pdf.

Stewart, Kathleen. 1988. "Nostalgia: A Polemic." *Cultural Anthropology:
Journal of the Society for Cultural Anthropology* 3: 227–41.

Strickland, Ronald. 2002. *Growing up Postmodern: Neoliberalism and the War on
the Young*. Lanham, MD: Rowman & Littlefield.

Stromberg, Peter G. 1990. "Ideological Language in the Transformation of
Identity." *American Anthropologist* 92 (1): 42–56.

Szeftel, Morris. 2004. "Two Cheers? South African Democracy's First Decade." *Review of African Political Economy*, 31 (100): 193–202.

Taussig, Michael T. 1980. *The Devil and Commodity Fetishism in South America*.
Chapel Hill: University of North Carolina Press.

Thompson, Leonard Monteath. 1990. *A History of South Africa*. New Haven,
CT: Yale University Press.

Timmer, Andria D. 2010. "Constructing the 'Needy Subject': NGO Discourses of Roma Need." *PoLAR: Political & Legal Anthropology Review*
33 (2): 261–81.

Tsing, Anna Lowenhaupt. 2005. *Friction: An Ethnography of Global Connection*.
Princeton, NJ: Princeton University Press.

Turner, Terence. 1992. "Defiant Images: The Kayapo Appropriation of Video."
Anthropology Today 8 (6): 5.

Turner, Victor W. 1967. *The Forest of Symbols: Aspects of Ndembu Ritual*. Ithaca,
NY: Cornell University Press.

UNAIDS. "South Africa." 2019. www.unaids.org/en/regionscountries/countries
/southafrica.

van Allen, Judith. 1972. "'Sitting on a Man': Colonialism and the Lost Political Institutions of Igbo Women." *Canadian Journal of African Studies /*

Revue Canadienne des Études Africaines 6 (2): 165. https://doi.org/10 .2307/484197.

Van Driel, Francien, and Jacqueline Van Haren. 2003. "Whose Interests Are at Stake? Civil Society and NGOs in South Africa." *Development Southern Africa* 20 (4): 529–43.

Venter, Rienie. 2011. "Xhosa Male Initiation: An Evaluation of Children's Human Rights." *Child Abuse Research in South Africa* 12 (2): 87–97.

Vincent, Louise. 2008. "'Boys Will Be Boys': Traditional Xhosa Male Circumcision, HIV and Sexual Socialisation in Contemporary South Africa." *Culture, Health & Sexuality* 10 (5): 431–46.

Von Schnitzler, Antina. 2016. *Democracy's Infrastructure: Techno-Politics and Citizenship after Apartheid*. Princeton, NJ: Princeton University Press.

Weiss, Brad, ed. 2004. *Producing African Futures: Ritual and Reproduction in a Neoliberal Age*. Leiden: Brill.

West, Harry G. 2005. *Kupilikula: Governance and the Invisible Realm in Mozambique*. Chicago: University of Chicago Press.

White, Hylton. 2004. "Ritual Haunts: The Timing of Estrangement in a Post-Apartheid Countryside." In *Producing African Futures: Ritual and Reproduction in a Neoliberal Age*, edited by Brad Weiss, 141–66. Leiden: Brill.

Wilson, Monica. 1982. "Monica and Godfrey Wilson Papers, 1881–1982." University of Cape Town Libraries.

Wolf, Eric R. 1982. *Europe and the People without History*. Berkeley: University of California Press.

INDEX

Amber R. Reed is an assistant professor of anthropology
at Southern Oregon University.